EGG WOM*** DAUGHTER

a Tanka memoir

EGG WOMAN'S DAUGHTER

a Tanka memoir

Mary Chan Ma-lai

Asia 2000 Limited
Hong Kong

ISBN 962–7160–53–9

An Orchid Pavilion Book
Published by Asia 2000 Ltd.
Fifth Floor, 31A Wyndham Street
Central, Hong Kong

http://www.asia2000.com.hk

Typeset in Adobe Garamond by Asia 2000 Ltd.
Printed in Hong Kong by Editions Quaille

First Printing March 2001

Some names have been changed to protect the identity
of the persons described.

This book is dedicated to Father Edward, S.J.,
my mother Leung Sai, my sister Irene,
and to the many "kind hearts"
who have helped me along the way.

ACKNOWLEDGEMENTS

I would like to thank most warmly those who helped me tell my story. Without their assistance, which they offered freely, this book would not have been possible.

In the first instance I am indebted to Carolyn Thompson who, as long ago as 1988, corrected my first essays about my experiences, and to Frances Rasmussen who retyped them.

I am particularly grateful to my friend Heung Jiu, who about a year later began a more serious effort to record my story simply as an interesting way of improving my English. She began by encouraging me to continue writing about experiences, but in more detail. She clarified and expanded these essays, together with my earlier ones, by dragging more information out of me, mostly over the telephone. She edited them and improved the English to a more readable state before she read them back to me. At the same time she taught me the new words and expressions she had inserted, hoping I would remember them when she tested me later. She also researched for me where necessary and made suggestions. The most difficult task was arranging the events in chronological order. But during the six years of this painstaking exercise Heung Jiu succeeded in putting the giant jigsaw of my life together, and in doing so, to our surprise, a manuscript suitable for publication had been created.

Finally, I owe special thanks to the late Sally Rodwell for her valuable advice in the beginning; Anthony Lawrence for his advice and encouragement; Kay Grynyer for proof reading; Barbara Simpson for helping me correspond with Heung Jiu, who moved abroad before my story was completed; Hilary Prior for enthusiastically helping to seek publication; Gael Black for liaising with the publisher on my behalf and Alan Sargent for editing the 600-page original manuscript into a workable size.

FOREWORD

Mary's path first crossed mine in August 1995 despite my being a long-term resident of Hong Kong and involved at times with the Duchess of Kent Hospital. Mary and I actually met when I was asked to deliver some English teaching books to her in Wah Kwai. Shortly after that, Barbara Simpson, custodian of Mary's manuscript, left Hong Kong and it was given to me for safekeeping.

It was very easy to become friends with Mary and soon all my overseas visitors were taken on the "Wah Kwai tour" to meet Mary and to see the Wah Kwai Public Housing estate near Aberdeen. All the visiting women left with the gift of one of Mary's crocheted shawls, an insight into public housing in Hong Kong and an absolute admiration for my amazing, spirited, voluble friend. Her rogues' gallery — photos of friends and family on the living room wall — was a testament to her large circle of friends worldwide. Her handicaps were definitely secondary to the conversations.

My friendship with Mary was fun and full of laughter. Our discussions ranged from hilarious explanations of blue language to cats and religion. She scolded me for my appalling Cantonese and I tried to tell her scold was a very old-fashioned word. When I was cajoling and persuading Oxford University Press (China) Ltd., Macmillan Publishers (China) Ltd. and Addison Wesley Longman China Ltd. to give Mary free sets of English teaching books, Mary demanded and enjoyed explanations of the difference between cajole and persuade. She would then sign and have me post thank you cards when we received the books. Mary's English became peppered with antipodean words. My abysmal Cantonese stayed as such, but my appreciation and understanding of life in Hong Kong improved enormously.

Mary's sense of humour was always foremost. One day we went to Queen Mary Hospital to see her mother, who was there for tests. Mrs Chan, deaf as a post, was shouting in Cantonese very loudly. I asked Mary for a translation and was wryly told: "She's having trouble with her hearing aid. She's demanding soft rice and saying she is not going to die until the book is published." Mary sighed and commented, "We are a comedy act — the cripple and the *gweilo* — and the amahs are giggling." Mary spent a day in Queen Mary in 1997 to receive medical clearance to fly to New Zealand, and an amah recognised us from that time. The amah must have remembered that I had not understood the Cantonese instructions to leave the ward at nurse changeover time. I had slumped down in my chair, buried myself in my book and ignored everyone, much to the amusement of the amah, who calmly cleaned round me and the sleeping Mary.

The writing of this book and subsequent preparation for publishing is testament that Mary truly has been surrounded by "kind hearts," as foretold in the prophecy made in Macau in 1978. The events related in this book end in 1994 and the intervening years were spent organising publication. Six hundred pages had to be edited — a sighted person would have had the manuscript returned, been given a red pencil and told to cut out or rewrite large chunks of it. Alan Sargent, a former editor at Asia 2000, managed to get the book to a ready state for final fact checking.

Mary had been in good health for the last five years. But in February 2000 she went into hospital and pressure sores developed. With the onset of diabetes she did not get better. In August she was fading fast. I went to see her on Tuesday, September 12, at 2 p.m. with a draft of the manuscript. Mary knew I was there so I read her my favourite bit about the cat diet, said farewell and left. She died the next morning. On the day of Mary's funeral two weeks later, Carolyn Thompson and Heung Jiu were in England consulting by telephone on the finer points of the draft. Mary would have approved — the two women most responsible for her book were in action again on her behalf.

Mary Chan was my best Chinese friend. Once, another Chinese friend said to me very fiercely and emphatically that Mary's story was not uncommon. This may be so — but what is special about this book is that Mary wrote her story down and it went from there. It is a story about a family going through the usual highs and lows of family life. You can recognize, sympathise and identify with tricky family relationships; we all have them in our own families. *Egg Woman's Daughter* is also a social history of the Tanka people living in Hong Kong, and as it is from a handicapped person's viewpoint, all the more poignant.

This book is a fitting memorial to my friend Mary Chan. Read it, enjoy it and know Mary will know you have read it.

Gael Black

"Ma-lai's destiny was preordained in her previous life," the spirit replied. "Nothing can change it. But do not despair; there will be many kind hearts along the way to help her."

1

Taste Of Brine

For generations my family had been fisherfolk, leading a nomadic existence on the waters of the South China Sea. We are Tanka people, from the Chinese words *Daan Ga*, meaning "Egg Family." The origin of this name is obscure, but I know of two theories: one that it derived from the fact that the canopies of our boats are thought to be egg-shaped, the other is that the *Daan Ga* used to pay their taxes with eggs. We, ourselves, had the practice of strengthening our fishing nets by soaking them in egg whites. We also believe that we have been ridiculed by this name and prefer to be called *Sui Seung Yan*, meaning "people who live on the water," or the Boat People.

The Tanka have lived on the waters of South China for thousands of years. For centuries, we were despised by land dwellers because it was believed we were the descendants of a ruler of Guangzhou who revolted against the emperor in the second century B.C. Another story widely believed was that we were descended from a band of traitors who were considered not worthy of living on the land — hence, we were banished to the sea.

Until the Communist government came to power in China, we were not permitted to marry into land-dwelling families or settle on land, except in a few coastal fishing villages. Even today, we are considered to be inferior by some Chinese land people and still face discrimination.

Before I was born, my parents and my two brothers, Chan Sum and Chan Lai Yan, lived with my paternal grandparents on a very large fishing junk, a flat-bottomed wooden vessel with a high poop deck — an overhanging stern — and large butterfly-wing shaped sails. At one time, there were about twenty fisherfolk, including five or six deck hands, living on this boat and wresting a living from the waters of south China, Macau and Hong Kong.

My paternal grandfather Chan Ying Ho had two wives. The first bore him three sons and four daughters and the second, a widow with a young daughter who he married during the Second World War supposedly to help his sick wife, eventually bore him three daughters.

As was the custom in China, my mother Leung Sai joined the Chan family fishing junk when she married my father Chan Yung in the mid 1930s. She was in her early twenties at the time. It was an arranged marriage and when she saw Chan Yung for the first time at her wedding ceremony she fell for him immediately. She thought him handsome, his eyes being round like a Westerner's, and with his demeanour appearing to be that of a prosperous, educated man, she could not believe her luck!

It was not long before she became disillusioned with her handsome husband and the rest of the Chan family, too.

It happened that my grandparents were conservative, stubborn old people and hard taskmasters. My mother being the wife of the eldest son was expected to carry out the most strenuous and servile tasks for the family without question. She dared not show the slightest reluctance to carry out their bidding, no matter how unreasonable it was. Adhering to convention, my father did not say a good word for her or ever take her side.

During the years with her in-laws, my mother witnessed many aspects of life on board that disturbed her. My mother felt, for instance, that my third uncle and aunt were a greedy and selfish couple. They kept any money they could get hold of from the family fishing business for themselves. They were also determined to reduce the family expenditure by cutting down the amount of food consumed on board. Consequently, because of my mother's lowly status, this parsimonious exercise resulted in her becoming the most undernourished member of the family.

Not only did my mother have to contend with being nothing more than a slave to her in-laws, but she also had to suffer the endless bickering, gossip and rumours among them. My third uncle and my grandfather continually fought, and my aunts were cross and proud women who did not hide the fact that they despised my mother.

It was in 1941, as far as my mother remembers, during the Japanese occupation of China that she and my father adopted my eldest brother Chan Sum. They came across him when the family junk was moored next to his parents' junk in a fishing harbour in Guangdong Province.

At the time, Chan Sum's parents were going through a hard time trying to feed their eight children. So they were very grateful when my parents, being moved by the family's plight, gave them a large bag of rice. Incredibly, the couple insisted on repaying my parents by giving them their six-year-old son Chan Sum, and also one of their daughters. They had such a large family and realising my mother was childless at the time, they thought the children would be a welcome gift in return for the rice.

My parents did not expect any repayment and adamantly refused to take the children, but their parents would not take no for an answer and insisted that my parents take at least one child. In the end, it was just little Chan Sum who was forced into my parents' care.

Touchingly, from the very first moment with my mother, the little boy stuck to her like glue and followed her everywhere. He was quite content to stay on a strange boat with a strange family, although his family boat was still moored right alongside ours. In fact, when my mother tried to make him go back to his own boat, he ran from her in tears and hid in my parents' cabin. During the next few days, he proved to be a quiet, helpful child, and was always willing to give my mother a hand with her wearisome daily chores. Even so, my mother had no intention of keeping him forever.

My parents were surprised on waking up one morning to find that Chan Sum's parents' boat had left its mooring. Frantically, my parents searched the harbour and further along the coast, but it was nowhere to be found. My parents now had no other choice but to consider Chan Sum their adopted son.

It was not long before they firmly believed the little waif had brought them good fortune because my mother had become pregnant with her first child. From then on, one pregnancy followed another — eight in all. Sadly, only three children survived.

During the Japanese occupation my grandfather's junk operated out of Man Kin Sha Harbour in Guangdong Province. When the Japanese passed through, my father tried hard to keep out of their way by joining those fisherfolk who hid in the fields by day and only fished at night. My mother did not fear the enemy. She often ferried them across the harbour in her sampan, a small boat with a long oar in the stern worked by a standing rower. They treated her well, but did not pay her.

My mother cannot remember exactly in which year she gave birth to my second brother Chan Lai Yan. As far as she remembers, it was during the Japanese occupation and he was two or three years old when the Second World War ended. After a hard day's work on the family boat, she delivered him herself on her birthday. My grandmother was on board at the time, but she was busy helping my third aunt cope with her new baby and could not spare any time to attend to my mother. After all, my mother was only a servant as far as the family was concerned.

My father, on the other hand, was a slave to no one. He indulged in wandering aimlessly around the south China coastal areas, drinking and gambling with his useless friends. He did nothing in particular to earn his living, just the odd deal when he needed money. He amounted to nothing more than a rascal.

He smoked opium daily, an expensive vice that kept his family in poverty. He covertly pawned blankets and clothes and even some of our most valued possessions to finance his addiction. All my mother's precious jewellery, which she had been given at her wedding ceremony, was pawned and never seen again.

Skulduggery

Eventually, my parents left the family boat and started their own business. At the time, my grandfather's armed junk was in the business of escorting cargo ships from province to province along the coast of southern China, protecting them from pirates. My father decided to branch off on his own and do likewise. He acquired his own fifty-foot junk that proudly displayed two very large guns. My mother took charge of overseeing the employment and welfare of the crew, as well as controlling both the business and household expenditure. My father did not concern himself with such matters and continued to live a carefree life.

My mother treated the deck hands well and provided the best living conditions she could afford; each received the same share of food as a family member. She even gave food and lodging on board to a widow and her two children in exchange for the woman cooking for all on board and looking after my young second brother.

All were content and generally life was peaceful until one day when the boat was attacked by pirates who suspected it was laden with gunpowder and ammunition. Though shots were fired, my mother summoned the courage to confront the robbers boldly and a skirmish ensued.

The deck hands were amazed at her daring as she led them to repel the attackers. Bravely, the crew and my mother stood their ground and after a fierce struggle the pirates fled.

While my mother stood on the fore-deck presenting a bold front to the armed assailants, my father cowered in a cabin below, clutching my second brother in his arms. When the incident was over, much to the astonishment of all on board, he boasted heartily of his brave behaviour!

Another frightening occasion, which almost cost my parents their livelihood, was when they were mistaken for smugglers. Customs officials tried to board their vessel to investigate the cargo. In the confusion, my parents and their crew mistook the officials for more pirates and successfully fought them off.

All on board considered themselves very fortunate to have had such a lucky escape, but a few hours later the customs boat reappeared with a contingent of soldiers. This time, no one dared attempt to fight off the boarding party. The fishing junk was impounded and all on board were detained and taken ashore.

My poor mother was in a state of shock. She begged the officials to let them go, pleading that the boat was the only home she and her husband had for their small children and their only means of earning a living. After several harrowing hours talking with officials, they were all released.

During these precarious years plying a trade with their own vessel, my mother did her utmost to create a harmonious atmosphere on board but my father made life difficult. He would often bicker with the hands and he threatened on one occasion during a disagreement to throw one of them overboard. Fortunately, my mother intervened with her advice and suggested a compromise; soon the misunderstanding was cleared up. Without her intervention, she told me, the men would have certainly attacked my father and there is no telling what the outcome would have been.

Despite the troubles my father brought her, my mother had no choice but to tolerate his shortcomings; a wife should not disobey or criticise her husband, according to the Chinese custom. Where family matters were concerned, she remained silent and endured.

Castaways

In 1950, my parents abandoned their cargo-escorting business because of decreasing trade. They rejoined the family junk with their two sons, allowing another brother and his wife to take over their boat to try their luck.

My mother had lost a few babies since the birth of my second brother, so as another pregnancy progressed she dared not risk being far out at sea when the time came for her confinement. She left my second brother in the care of his grandparents and left the family junk. She took Chan Sum, her fifteen-year-old adopted son, with her to stay in a room at a private maternity clinic in the Portuguese colony of Macau, a small peninsula west of Hong Kong. Unfortunately, she had no money and received no support from my father either while she waited, so she earned a meagre living making fishing nets.

Once, when food was scarce, my mother sent Chan Sum scurrying around the harbour to find the Chan family junk to beg for some rice, but the family refused to give him even a handful! After this bitter rejection, my mother realised she could not rely on any help or sympathy from her in-laws, whatever her predicament.

No one knows the exact date of my birth, but as far as my mother remembers it was during December 1950. Immediately after I was born, my mother desperately needed to find somewhere to live and also a more lucrative job now that she had an extra mouth to feed. Fortunately, she did not have to wait long for good fortune to come her way.

During her confinement she had made friends with an *amah*, a domestic helper at the maternity clinic. Her name was Ah Ding and she agreed to lend my mother the money to buy a small sampan to ferry passengers to and from the large vessels anchored in the harbour.

The three of us lived and slept aboard the small craft, under the shelter of its arch-shaped collapsible canvas canopy. There was room for a small wood-fired stove and to store water, but for nothing else except a few wooden benches, enough to seat six passengers.

Going to the toilet afloat was a very precarious performance. Mother used to hold me over the side, but she and Chan Sum had to protrude their rear ends over the bobbing bows and hang on for all they were worth.

Mostly, mother's passengers treated her kindly and some gave her food as well as money, pitying her as she had a very small baby and a young son to support. This aroused jealousy among the other sampan owners. The most envious among them was my great aunt.

In an attempt to thwart my mother's popularity with her customers, this spiteful old woman spread the story that my mother's small boat was not seaworthy. Fortunately, the passengers ignored the rumours and continued to give my mother their custom.

One day there was a big commotion in the harbour. Our sampan had collided with a large Japanese freighter. Our sampan sank and left Chan Sum and my mother, with me still strapped to her back, struggling for our lives in the water. My mother could not swim, but fortune was on our side; the three of us were plucked from the murky water in no time by the freighter's crew.

One of the rescuers was a very kind, young sailor. He soon calmed us and after making us as comfortable as possible on board the freighter, he organised a meal for us. Despite these attentions, my mother remained extremely agitated. Believing our only possessions and money had been lost in the ocean forever, despair had overcome her.

Luckily, the Japanese crew managed to retrieve a few of our belongings, which were floating on the surface. Much to mother's relief, a pillow wrapped in a plastic bag containing her hard-earned savings was among them.

Shaken and bedraggled, we eventually left the ship with enough food to last a few days and a generous amount of money for lodging. Within a short time, mother was able to resume her business with a new sampan, bought with the compensation from the shipping company.

This occupation was certainly a precarious and onerous way for my mother to earn a living. She was on call day and night and I was strapped to her back while she manoeuvred the boat. Chan Sum, as willing as ever, ran errands and helped as much as he could on the trips around the harbour. Although he was now fifteen years old, he had not yet been able to attend school because my mother had neither the money to send him, nor could she spare his willing hands.

Turbulent Tides

During these years struggling to earn a living from the sea, my mother had the additional stress of trying to cope with me — a very sickly child. I was not yet a year old when an ugly abscess developed on my upper right thigh and I had to be taken to a hospital in Macau for an incision to drain the wound.

I cried bitterly, so she stayed with me in the hospital. During the night she was awakened by the nurses moving around the ward. Poor mother had only known a life of ignorance and superstition, and she became alarmed when she saw white uniforms moving to and fro in the dimness. She thought they were ghosts!

Night after night she quaked so with fear that she hardly slept at all, but she did not desert me; bravely, she endured her harrowing nights among the "ghosts" till I was discharged.

Apparently, not only was I a sickly child, but I was also stupid. I hardly uttered a sound and when food was placed in front of me I made no attempt to pick it up with my hands and put it into my mouth. Our neighbours laughed and gossiped about my abnormal behaviour. Some exclaimed: "What a stupid child! She is so quiet and at twelve months old she fails to react to anything!" These remarks upset my mother, of course, but she put on a brave face and clung to the hope that in time I would not be so dull and stupid and would progress like any other child.

I must have been about two years old when my eyes became inflamed and the corneas appeared to be cloudy and dotted with black specks. My mother was so alarmed that she sought advice from my paternal grandmother. The old lady bathed each of my eyes with a concoction she believed to be a holy ointment blessed by a powerful god — incense ash mixed with mud!

Unfortunately, after a long spate of bathing my eyes with this special "ointment from the gods," my eyes became even more opaque. Finally, my right eye became totally sightless and my left eye was left with only blurred, partial vision. At the time, my mother had no money to spare to seek medical treatment for me and it was not until years later she learned the reason for my loss of vision.

Eventually, the relatives on my mother's side discovered that I had become blind. True to Chinese convention at that time, they were horrified and ashamed at having a *mang gwai*, a derogatory term meaning "blind ghost," in the family. My mother was advised by one of my aunts to abandon me on the street. It was common to treat handicapped children in this way throughout China in those days. Though my mother was beginning to lose hope for me, she was determined to take care of her little blind child and she strongly opposed my aunt's suggestion.

Despite this, my aunt would not give up and again she tried to persuade my mother to get rid of me. "If you relinquish your blind child, I'll give you one of my own," she bargained. "I have too many to look after."

After hearing this proposition, my mother became incensed and replied adamantly: "How dare you suggest such a thing! I want to keep and nurture my little blind daughter, no matter what difficulties prevail. I have to love her, for she is my child and my responsibility. Nothing will induce me to get rid of her!"

This time, on realising that my mother was determined not to abandon me, my aunt dared not say another word.

It seemed that during the first few years of my existence, encounters with bad luck had come one after another. My father added to our misery. He squandered any money our family earned through his extravagant and irresponsible lifestyle, forsaking us to spend idle time with his friends who could still afford to indulge themselves.

Meanwhile, my mother struggled to earn a living and the three of us continued our cramped existence on our little sampan in Macau Harbour. For three years we endured this uncomfortable lifestyle. Nevertheless, my mother ignored the tribulations I brought her and my apparent lack of potential and continued to love and cherish me.

Winds of Change

In 1952, communal life on the family junk came to an end. By now, all my grandparents' sons and daughters had married and disputes among all on board were becoming unbearable. So it was deemed the right time to divide the assets among the family and for everybody to go their separate ways.

By the time this decision to "abandon ship" had been made, my second grandmother had left the junk because of the family's hostility towards her. She had taken her two daughters and settled in Macau.

According to my mother, my father received the least share of the family estate because my grandparents maintained he had squandered his share already.

Grandfather's large fishing vessel was in such a dilapidated condition when the family left that he decided to sell it. He still continued to fish with my father, who had bought a smaller junk. They took my second brother with them.

About this time, my mother found she could no longer make an adequate living with her ferry business. The Macau government had closed the harbour to large ships and removed the passenger pier. Consequently, the steady supply of passengers dried up.

After a vain attempt to support us by making fishing nets again, she had no alternative but to join my father's boat. Father sold her sampan to my sixth uncle and aunt, who had settled in Cheung Sha Wan Harbour in Hong Kong together with my third uncle and his family. They had taken my first grandmother with them to help out with their families.

Most of the time, the two families earned their living by diving into the sea to retrieve nails. These were dropped by workmen who were building and repairing ships in the dockyard near the fishing harbour.

There was an occasion when my father sailed our junk into this dockyard at Cheung Sha Wan for repair. This meant we had to spend a few weeks ashore before we could venture out to sea again.

My two brothers thought they would bring in some money by helping my uncles dive for nails. These were sold by weight so they concentrated on picking up the big nails rather than the small ones.

For their age, my brothers were working hard and doing a dangerous job, so they expected a decent wage, especially from their uncles. After a while, they realised they were not being paid fairly, so rather than be cheated, they gave up their work. This incident brought to light our kinfolk's uncaring attitude towards our family. We were all disappointed in them and prepared to leave the harbour very disgruntled over the whole affair. With our junk now repaired and loaded with the usual provisions, we ventured out to sea again.

Ill Winds

Nowadays, most junks have engines and gone are the beautiful butterfly-wing shaped sails that graced our vessel. At the mercy of the prevailing winds, many long hours were spent reaching and returning from the fishing grounds. We often spent two or three days at sea.

My grandfather and my father, being Tanka had generations of seafaring in their blood and could study the evening sky and foresee a looming typhoon. They would immediately abandon fishing and stow away everything on board, then depending on the wind direction, run or beat as fast as our tattered sails would carry us for the nearest typhoon shelter. This was usually at the harbour at Cheung Chau, an island northwest of Hong Kong.

Because we always left the fishing grounds in ample time ahead of a typhoon, the sea would be relatively calm until a few miles from the island. Then our vessel would join the armada of fishing junks nosing their way through the troughs and swells as they raced towards the typhoon shelter where they could ride out the storm.

By then, banks of heavy, black clouds would have gathered and gusts of wind would come more often and send swells crashing against the hull. Very soon, they would thrash above our bows, spewing spray across our decks as our vessel swung towards the shore. They would not relent until we were through the breakwaters into safe anchorage. The worst we would have to suffer now would be the rolling of our junk and the strong gusts of wind buffeting our groaning and grinding timbers and then a day or two of torrential rain.

Our way of life and primitive fishing methods were inherited from our ancestors. We trawled, or sometimes pair-trawled with another junk and also seined, which is floating and weighting a net in a circle to trap the fish. Unfortunately, none of these methods yielded an abundance of fish.

Paying homage to deities who relate to the sea usually plays an important part in the life of fisherfolk. The most popular deity is the Taoist sea goddess Tin Hau, the Queen of Heaven. Tin Hau lived in the 10th century and was reputed to have had supernatural powers. She was the daughter of a fisherman and spent her life rescuing seafarers and protecting them from storms. It is believed that a good fishing season will be assured only when homage and offerings are made to such sea deities as Tin Hau. My family members were never fervent worshippers of any deity, not even of Tin Hau. Maybe that is one of the reasons father's catch was never very large and our livelihood at sea a very poor one.

Another reason was our dilapidated fishing gear. There were only two old fishing nets which mother repaired time and time again. They were periodically dipped into hundreds of egg whites to strengthen them. To lessen the cost of this operation, my mother used to sell all but two of the yolks back to the egg seller.

We always looked forward to the meal at the end of a net-dipping day because my mother used to mix the two egg yolks she had reserved with rice — a special treat for us all.

Mother used to sell the catch in the markets of Tsuen Wan and Castle Peak in the New Territories. With the proceeds she would buy rice, pickled salted vegetables and dried salted black dates. If there were no fish to sell, we would eat only rice soup till the next catch. While ashore, she collected water from a standpipe, wood for our stove and provisions for our next fishing expedition.

It was in June 1955 that my sister was born while we were living on my father's boat. We happened to be moored in Aberdeen Harbour at the time and while I was playing on the deck of our boat I heard what sounded like a kitten meowing. Being curious, I traced the sound to my parents' cabin. I dared not go inside because entry was strictly forbidden, so I tried to listen through the cracks in the timber walls. I still could not make out what was making the strange sound; puzzled, I went back up to the deck and continued playing.

One of my aunts arrived a while later and I was surprised to learn from her that my mother had just delivered her own baby. The meowing I had heard had been the first cries of my new baby sister. My mother named her Choi Ha.

During the two years that followed, my baby sister and I were mostly kept below while my brothers helped with the fishing. We had nothing to play with except shells, but when we were moored in the harbours I was given more freedom to move around. It was while I was scampering around our boat one day that I injured my back. I could not see that a hatch had been left open and I fell into the hold.

No medical attention was sought for me, though for a long time the only way I could move around was on all fours like a crab. Eventually, the pain subsided and I was able to walk upright again. Gradually, however, my spine grew very curved. No one knew until years later that a serious disease had taken hold.

My mother worried about my health and did her best to feed and clothe me, but she was ignorant of the medical treatment she could have sought for me ashore, especially in Hong Kong. She just put her trust in the Taoist gods and sought the help and advice of our ancestors.

Unfortunately, at this time, life was not so good. Our livelihood was so poor that my parents and my grandfather had to admit that their life at sea had not proved to be very profitable. They could not afford to replace their poor fishing equipment to improve their catch, so they decided to abandon fishing altogether and try their luck ashore.

Moorings

In 1956 my father stopped fishing and we abandoned our nomadic way of life completely. We settled in Aberdeen Harbour on Hong Kong Island where our fifty-foot fishing junk gradually was converted into a houseboat. When the work was completed, our home could provide refuge for more than twenty souls and our houseboat was the biggest of all in the harbour.

The stern was higher than the bow and the new wooden superstructure ran from the bow end of the well-deck to the stern. It was divided into three large compartments inside and the whole length was covered with a continuous roof that was waterproofed with black roofing felt. The structure was stained and varnished to match the teak hull.

Access was by gangplanks at the bow. The forward deck was open except for a large awning attached to the roof of the first compartment in the well-deck. This open-plan compartment housed my grandfather's sleeping quarters and the galley, which had a small area attached where we used to squat to eat our meals. We had a large enough sleeping area to accommodate my father's friends who stayed on board from time to time. It was divided from the galley by only a few open shelves.

The spacious living room took up the middle part of the well-deck. It was divided from the galley area by a wooden partition and a door, and was furnished with a few wooden benches against the walls. It was rather dark inside, illuminated only by the oil lamp of our ancestral altar and the thin shafts of light filtering through the small, unglazed windows. These windows were equipped with removable wooden shutters, normally used during inclement weather only.

When friends and relatives used to visit, the men ate in the living room, squatting in a circle around the dishes on the floor and the women and children ate in our usual family eating area next to the galley.

The children of our family slept on the sitting room floor while my parents slept in a compartment that occupied the whole of the poop. They had to crawl up into it from the sitting room through small hatches in a wooden partition. There was sitting head-room only inside.

There was no access around the outside of my parents' poop sleeping compartment to the stern of the boat, but walkways ran from the bow along both starboard and port side and stopped short of the poop deck. They gave access to my grandfather's sleeping quarters, the galley and the sitting room, which were all adjoining compartments.

The two holds we had previously used for storing fish and water were now used for normal household storage. The toilet was a very small wooden cubicle outside on the starboard verandah aft. The only place we could wash privately was in the confined space of this cubicle, using a pail of water. Sewage went directly into the harbour through a hole in the deck.

A large kerosene lamp was rigged up on the awning support in the bow. It was lit only on special occasions because fuel was expensive. Otherwise, at night we carried small portable kerosene lamps both inside the cabins and outside on the deck.

Fresh water was bought from the "water boat" which plied its trade through the crowded sea-lanes in the evenings. It was stored in large tin cans near the galley.

At first, we were moored a long way out in the harbour, so we used small sampans to go ashore. Later, when we found a mooring closer to the shore, we walked on gangplanks from boat to boat until we reached the quayside. Thus, we abandoned the mode of life of our forefathers. Now, our life would revolve around the busy fishing port of Aberdeen, with its backdrop of low-rise buildings and lush green mountains.

The Cantonese name of Aberdeen is Heung Keung Tsai, which means "Little Fragrant Harbour." When we arrived, the harbour and typhoon anchorage provided refuge for up to one third of the colony's boat dwellers, both Tanka and Hoklo.

Our boat had joined a floating village of three thousand or more junks, houseboats, barges and sampans — a bobbing mass strewn with masts, bamboo washing poles, fishing nets, ropes and gangplanks. Water taxis criss-crossed the bustling harbour and vendors precariously paddled their sampans around the floating community along a maze of narrow channels. The resounding calls of the vendors were now the sounds that filled our waking hours. They offered to sell anything from provisions to fortune telling.

Amid this chaos stood two grand floating restaurants. At night they sparkled with myriad neon lights and reflections danced on the water.

Changing Tides

Gradually, traditional fisherfolk were finding they could not compete with large fleets of modern fishing boats fitted with diesel engines and the latest equipment. Some turned to smuggling to earn a living, others stayed moored in the harbours and looked for work on land. Land-life offered them a chance to find steady work and to have easy access to medical services and education for their children. They also knew that eventually they would be able to leave their unsanitary living conditions and move into government housing in one of the new high-rise resettlement estates that were springing up all over Hong Kong, Kowloon and the New Territories.

No doubt my parents had these benefits in mind when they decided to moor their home in the crowded, polluted waters of Aberdeen Harbour. In my family's case, the benefits took a very long time to materialise.

My father's first business venture ashore in Aberdeen was as an agent for the owners of a fleet of shrimp boats. He had been sponsored by a wealthy member of the Chan clan, who, for some reason, had great confidence in him. True to form, though, with the money for investment in the venture, my father led an extravagant lifestyle and most of his friends took advantage of him when he boasted of his newfound wealth. This resulted in the business failing and Mr Chan losing all his investment. Of course, my father did not admit his extravagance. Instead, he claimed that the shrimp boat owners had disappeared to Macau and owed the business money.

After this fiasco, my father managed to find a few casual jobs but the family seldom saw any of his earnings. My mother had to take on the heavy burden of looking after and providing for us all.

By now, most of my grandfather's family had settled in the harbour. My first grandmother, Leung Chueng Ho, and her two sons and their families had arrived and were living on boats nearby. So now grandfather did not always lodge with us; there were spells when he lived with his other two sons.

I remember wishing my grandmother had not come to live in the harbour. I dreaded her visits to our boat. When I recognised her voice I would whimper and shrink away in fear. Recurring bouts of skin infections plagued me and she would take great pleasure in exercising her knowledge of folk medicine on my tender skin. She used to light the end of a stem of a special plant, having dipped it in oil, and then dab it on my rash or abscess. The stem would make a popping sound as it began to burn and as soon as I heard this, I would shriek and struggle for all I was worth in anticipation of the pain. How I feared that popping sound!

Having changed their location, my uncles were in need of employment. Not long after they had become our neighbours, my father did them a favour. He found them jobs in another business set up by Mr Chan. They became fishermen in a fleet of new fishing boats fitted with the latest equipment for deep-sea fishing; the were going out to sea about twice a week.

Father also found work for some of my cousins in a restaurant that Mr Chan owned.

The relatives he had helped took umbrage when my father demanded a percentage of their earnings as his commission. He claimed that he needed the money to send my second brother to school. So eventually, begrudgingly, they paid up.

Now that we were permanently moored, my second brother Chan Lai Yan, about fourteen years old, had begun attending classes at the government primary school nearby. My adopted brother Chan Sum did not take up the chance to attend school even though up to that time he had had no schooling at all. Understandably, he felt that he was too old to begin going to school. Instead, he found a job as an apprentice on a fishing boat. He more or less supported himself and from time to time was able to give my mother a small amount of his earnings.

My mother helped my father with various jobs connected with Mr Chan's businesses while we lived in the harbour. She cooked meals for the hands and cleaned the boats. As usual, my father neglected to pay her and kept their earnings for himself.

The Creek

After about a year in the harbour, my father moved our houseboat further east along the coast to the anchorage at the mouth of Staunton Creek, called Tai Hang Hau in Cantonese. Now that we were moored alongside the quay, we could use just our own gangplank to step ashore.

It was here that my mother had her first encounter with the Hong Kong authorities. One morning, while she was busy on our boat, she noticed a uniformed man coming across our gangplank. As he approached, to her dismay, she realised that he was a policeman.

At first, she stayed calm by reassuring herself that he must have come to the wrong boat.

"Good morning," he said. "We have apprehended a young man who we suspect has stolen from this area. We believe that some items may have been stolen from you."

My mother was puzzled. She had not noticed that anything was missing. "What goods are these?" she inquired.

"A package of dried fish and a boat woman's straw hat," he replied.

Mother's heart sank. She had suddenly remembered that she had left these things on the quayside near our gangplank, not thinking anyone would ever want to steal them. She really did not want to get involved but she was too scared to lie to the law. So she croaked: "Yes, they could be mine, but they are of no consequence."

"Nevertheless," replied the policeman, "please accompany me to the police station to identify the items."

My mother paled at the idea of having anything to do with the authorities, especially the police. But after a few "wahs" and "aiyahhs," she reluctantly agreed to go. She grabbed my little sister Choi Ha, but was so flustered it was all she could do to strap the child on her back.

"Aiyahh! What a calamity! The neighbours will think I'm being arrested," she muttered to herself as they negotiated the gangplank. Hoping no one had noticed their departure, she waddled alongside the policeman as they made their way to the police station, her heart beating faster with every step.

Sure enough, the goods belonged to her and the police advised her that she should attend the court when the culprit came to trial. How she dreaded that day! On the day of the trial, a policeman came to escort her to the court in Sai Ying Pun. Once again, she left our boat under a cloud of apprehension but when she arrived at the court she began to relax. She was fascinated by all the goings on around her and she found the court case very interesting. After the very brief trial, the culprit was given a jail sentence of just a few months. My mother considered this rather a brutal punishment for such a small crime.

Having spent her life on the sea, poor mother had been ignorant of the ways of the land people. It had been an ordeal for her to face the unknown and the affair had left her mystified. "Wah! Fancy making such a big fuss over such a small thing and putting me through all that anxiety, too!" she complained. "Those land people are very strange. I'll make sure that I leave nothing on the quayside in the future. I don't want to go through that performance ever again."

Nevertheless, she was very pleased that her goods had been returned. She was very attached to her old straw hat; she had worn it since her days on her sampan in Macau Harbour when I was a baby.

At this time, my mother earned her dollars in a variety of ways. She made fishing nets with my grandmother and collected clams that she sold for three or four cents a *catty*, which is a measure of weight equivalent to a little under one and a quarter pounds. She also sewed together gloves that were distributed by a local trader to the boat women who needed work.

We ate only the cheapest of food, usually unsavoury scraps of vegetables only fit for pigs. But taste does not bother hungry mouths; we were just thankful we could fill our stomachs.

On occasion, we begged for rice from our neighbours on the surrounding boats who were better off than us. Some were very generous and were glad to give, such as an old man who used to give us some of his catch and some rice, but others always found an excuse to refuse us.

When my father returned home very late at night with his friends, sometimes one of them used to bring some rice. "Please cook this rice for your little blind girl, for she will not be able to bear her hunger throughout the night," he used to say to my mother.

Though she was tired and complained that she did not like to cook so late at night, she always roused herself to cook a simple rice meal for me.

If there happened to be no food for my breakfast, I was left with hunger pangs in my tummy. Mother worked, and in my misery I would sob loudly, hoping someone would take pity on me but no one ever paid any attention to my wailing.

Some lonely days, if I felt hungry and knew there was no prospect of having anything much to eat at home, I used to wander up to the banks of the nullah, a man-made water channel, where the ropemaker lived. If I was lucky, I would find his daughter sitting under an awning outside their wooden hut eating a meal. I would then linger beside her until she gave me the skin of her fish, something she did not care to eat. I am sure she did not realise how much her acts of kindness brightened my days.

I remember feeling very hurt and disgruntled at the times when my father and his friend took my little sister to a restaurant. My father did not even consider taking me.

I realise now that my father had found it hard to accept a handicapped child and could not help but shun me. I wish he had not been so ashamed of me; the hurt is still imprinted on my heart.

I remember vividly the times during our houseboat days when he scolded people in my presence and called them a *mang gwai*. My heart would lurch at his thoughtlessness. I would fill with indignation, too, but dared not say a word. I was too young to have the courage to rebuke him.

Practically everyday was dull for me. I had no toys and because I was handicapped, I had few playmates. My second brother and my sister were not close to me. We never played together because of our age differences and the fact that I was disabled. Most days, I just hung around the creek playing with shells or stones.

On the odd occasion, my spirits were raised when my cousins living on nearby boats came to play. They would never play for long, as they soon found me a nuisance and would tease me because of my strange and ugly appearance. Though I felt so hurt I tried hard to forgive them for I desperately needed their friendship.

When I felt adventurous, I scrambled up the mountainside near the creek to the pools formed by the waterfalls. Here, the local children used to splash around and try to swim. Sometimes, the pools were deep after the typhoons and I would fumble around in this deep water trying to imitate the other children. Aiyahh — looking back, there were times when I almost drowned!

Typhoon

Unfortunately, the quayside at Staunton Creek was not a very safe haven for our floating home. On several occasions, when typhoons struck, water cascaded down the mountain and along a gully that emptied into the creek. If our boat should break its moorings and then float around in the gale-force winds and turbulent sea, it would be in danger of capsizing or of being driven away.

One summer day, during a strong typhoon, the wind was howling and waves were exploding high above the sides of our houseboat. Water poured onto the decks and panic gripped us as it began to pour into our cabins. Above the cries of alarm I could hear the creaking and groaning of the timbers growing louder as our vessel battled against the storm. It was tossing violently and strained against its moorings. If it broke loose and was taken by the swift current, we feared that it would collide with the other vessels in the creek and break up.

Only Mr Wong, a rather portly fellow, volunteered to do anything about our dilemma. The water in the creek was by now very deep and swift and it was raining heavily, but he showed no hesitation in taking action. He took off his clothes and jumped into the surging sea, carrying with him our heavy iron anchor. Using all his strength, he successfully embedded it into the seabed and our home was secured.

As a result of Mr Wong's timely effort, our humble home was saved. My mother could not thank him enough for his selfless, courageous feat. The others on board were extremely grateful to him, too, except for my drunken father. He happened to be in a bad mood and made it clear that he did not appreciate Mr Wong's brave effort.

Still, Mr Wong did not take offence and no animosity remained between us. Not long afterwards, though, he left us to find a job in another area. It was about this time that my father's friend Leung Kong came to live on our boat. He shared the same surname as my mother but was not related to her. As he was a member of her clan he called her *Ga Tse* meaning "Older Sister." In the Chinese tradition, he was welcomed to live with us as family. He shared my grandfather's cabin.

Ah Kong was in his middle thirties and married. All his relatives, including his wife, were still living in China. He was a compulsive gambler, so we gave him the nickname, *Dai Se*, meaning "Big Snake." This would change to either *Loong,* meaning "Dragon," if he was in the money, or *Chung,* meaning "Insect," if he lost his bets.

A tall, thin, gaunt-looking man, his bespectacled face was long and sallow with sunken cheeks. His voice was very hoarse and he often suffered from bronchitis. As his health was poor he would often not take cold food or drink, conforming to a Chinese belief that cold food weakens the health. His pace was slow and his disposition so calm that he rarely became frustrated or lost his temper. He had no regular job but he earned a few dollars by doing piecework that traders distributed to the unemployed among the Boat People.

Not long after he had moved into our houseboat, Ah Kong bought some ducklings which he let loose into the creek. I was fascinated by the way they would swim back to our boat in the evening to be fed. None of them ever got lost. It was a shame that they were cooked for celebrations when they grew bigger.

Another enterprising idea of his was to scatter rice on the ground to attract sparrows that he caught with a net. They ended up in the cooking pot, too!

Fair Winds

It was during the year before we moved into Staunton Creek that I had my first encounter with the medical profession. My father had at last sought help for my blindness and badly curved spine without much success, unfortunately. We were told nothing could be done about my eyes but treatment for my back was available. I would have to attend a clinic in the Western District everyday, and lie for hours on a plaster bed.

On my first visit to the clinic my mother talked to a young lady in the long queue of people waiting to use the plaster beds. She said she had been using them everyday for the past three years. "Aiyahh!" my parents cried. It would be impossible for me to attend so regularly, so they abandoned the idea altogether.

Not long after we had moved into Staunton Creek, a young Chinese gentleman brought a *gweilo*, which literally translates as "foreign devil," to our houseboat and introduced him to us as a Western Roman Catholic priest, a member of the Society of Jesus. The Chinese gentleman was a seminarian who had seen me during his social work among the Boat People. He was so concerned about my handicaps and my living conditions that he brought the foreign priest to see me.

The priest, a softly spoken bespectacled Irishman, was slightly built and of medium height. We guessed that he was in his middle thirties. His name was Father Edward and he was one of the Jesuit priests teaching at the Regional Seminary for south China, a fort-like building on the summit of a nearby hill. The Seminary, known as the Holy Spirit Seminary since 1964 when it became a Diocesan Seminary, still dominates the small peninsula, which in those days formed one side of Staunton Creek.

At first, our family was rather nervous at the approach of a *gweilo*, as foreigners rarely mixed with folk like us. But when he began to talk to us in fluent Cantonese, we soon felt at ease and began to call him a Chinese name, Kwok San Fu; *San Fu* means "priest."

After this brief acquaintance, Father Edward came to see us regularly. There was no direct road to the peninsula on which he lived, so he used to hire a small sampan to cross the creek.

Seeing that we were very poor and that my parents did not have much of an idea of how to seek medical treatment for me, he wanted to help improve my sorry state. So each time he came, he tried to find out more about the nature of my disabilities and the details of my family background. He also tried to converse with me, but I was shy. "Why don't you talk to me? Come on — don't be timid. We can become good friends," he used to say.

Actually, I was too scared to talk to a Westerner because I had never encountered one before. I had no idea how to behave politely with strangers either, and just would not respond to him. The kindly priest was very patient. After we had met a few more times, I succumbed to his gentle persuasion and began to talk to him freely.

He was so very happy to know my family and he brought some of his *gweilo* friends to our boat. They were eager to learn all about the habits and customs of us Boat People. I remember wishing I could speak their language and feeling embarrassed that I could not communicate with them.

After they had heard our story and surveyed our living environment and the dilapidated condition of our boat, they attempted to give my mother some money. "Well, thank you," she replied. "There is no need to help us. We are content with what we have."

2

Swells and Troughs

Through visiting us regularly, Father Edward soon acquired a clearer understanding of my background and family's affairs and so began to discuss with my mother the possibility of seeking medical treatment for my disabilities. She was ignorant of such matters, so she could only trust in Father Edward's advice.

The very first action he took was to make an appointment for me at the Queen Mary Hospital in Pok Fu Lam, a short distance from Aberdeen. He could not accompany my mother and I on the day but he wrote a note to the doctor.

I cannot remember the consultation, but apparently I was examined by Dr. Elizabeth Tang, otherwise known as Han Siuyin, the renowned author of the book, *A Many Splendoured Thing,* among others. She wrote a reply to Father Edward, saying the damage to my eyes could not be remedied but there was a possibility that my curved spine could be treated if I was taken to a specialist.

For a second opinion on my eyes, Father Edward took me to a specialist at the Violet Peel Clinic, a government clinic in Wan Chai. Here, an Indian eye doctor gave me a thorough examination.

He confirmed that nothing could be done about my blindness. I was blinded by cataracts and they were inoperable. This news, of course, was a great disappointment — more so for my mother and Father Edward than for me. I was only about six years old at the time and was rather bewildered by it all. I could not remember ever seeing clearly, so could not imagine what it would be like to be without my cataracts.

The consultation was not entirely in vain. We learned that I needed a number of operations on my eyelids because my eyelashes were growing inwards and were causing further damage to my eyes.

For this delicate surgery, I had to attend the Violet Peel Clinic so often that Father Edward offered to drive us there when he was available. When he was busy my mother had to take me there alone, which was no easy task. I could not walk very far before I became weary. My mother, more often than not, carried me on her back from our houseboat to the bus stop in Aberdeen. Then, when we got off the bus, she hauled me onto her back again and walked from Central to the clinic in Wan Chai. It was a long walk but she could not afford the fare for us to take another bus.

The eye doctor would give me a local anaesthetic to prevent the pain during the operation but I could still feel the movements of the instruments and the blood flowing down my face. I was frightened but I remained calm and did not cry out. My mother sat beside me on a couch. It was very hard for her to witness the surgery, but an hour's rest in the small, simple operating theatre was enough for us both to recover.

Father Edward took me to the eye specialist from time to time, as each of my eyes had to be operated on at least twice. They also had to be examined at regular intervals so it took a long time to complete the full course of treatment.

I remember that some of our journeys to the clinic were not uneventful. On one of our trips in his old Ford Anglia car, affectionately known as the "Puddle Jumper," we suddenly stopped in Deep Water Bay Road. It had run out of petrol.

While we were just sitting there wondering how on earth we could get to my appointment on time, a large lorry had to stop because we were blocking the narrow road. The driver kindly offered to fetch some petrol and return as quickly as possible. There happened to be an empty petrol can in the boot, so Father Edward threw the car keys out of the window to the driver so he could open the boot. Unfortunately, he threw the keys far too vigorously and they landed up in a tree. Now we were in an even worse predicament.

While Father Edward and the lorry driver were trying their best to retrieve the keys, a Rolls Royce pulled up behind. It was driven by a uniformed chauffeur who was wondering what all the commotion was about. Father Edward suddenly had the bright idea to ask him if he could drive me to the clinic and he would join me later. Much to our surprise, the chauffeur agreed. Father Edward admits that he had a chuckle to himself when off I went, a poor hump-backed, blind girl in the back seat of a luxurious chauffeur-driven car. What a ridiculous joke!

Another incident happened when poor old Puddle Jumper broke down in the middle of the road again on the way to the clinic. Father Edward, afraid we might miss the appointment with the eye doctor and also the dentist, confessed that he really did not know how to get us there.

Fortunately, again, a kind-hearted fellow approached and offered to help push the car along the road to a nearby garage. The car was repaired and then we continued our journey. We arrived too late for my dental check-up but were just in time to see the eye doctor, the most important appointment.

The trip that day had taken longer than usual because of the breakdown. As always, Father Edward was very thoughtful and a string is pulled in my heart when I remember him giving me some biscuits in case I felt hungry. He knew that a small child, especially me, could not go without food for long.

The next step Father Edward took was to seek a medical opinion regarding my deformed spine. He took me to see Professor Hodgson, an orthopaedic specialist at the Hong Kong University. From him we learned that years before, tuberculosis had taken hold in my spine and I had developed a condition called kyphosis. Fortunately, the tuberculosis was no longer active, but we were finally told the bitter truth — there was no operation I could have to straighten my curvature. Our hopes were dashed.

Both my kyphosis and my eye disease had been attributed to malnutrition and neither could be cured. It seemed that I was destined to live my life as a blind hunchback forever.

Typhoon Shelter

It must have been at the beginning of 1958 that our houseboat was again moved further east along the channel, this time to the Aberdeen typhoon shelter and still not far from the Seminary.

We felt more secure here because there would be more protection from the typhoons that struck Hong Kong during the long, hot summers. There was another advantage of being moored in this location. We could now take refuge in a factory building just across the road from the typhoon shelter where, for our comfort, food and bedding would be supplied until the typhoon passed. Mother, however, never abandoned our home. She and my eldest brother used to stay on board and bale out water, even during the strongest typhoons.

Our houseboat was anchored in a long row of similar vessels packed side by side along the quay. The shelter was not as busy as the harbour. There were fewer sampans puttering around and small-craft operators only plied their trade around the shelter at high tide, the waters being too shallow at low tide. The boat community either ventured ashore for provisions or stepped from boat to boat to buy from the local floating stores.

Soon after we moved into the typhoon shelter our life began to change for the better, mainly where provisions were concerned. Even I had a treat to look forward to.

Opposite our mooring stood a factory that manufactured all kinds of cold drinks, ice cream and ice lollies. On the days when there had been an over-production of red-bean ice lollies, the workers gave them to the local children. Those delectable crimson lollies were my favourite food. I had no money to buy them, so I used to wait eagerly for news of the free handouts.

Most of the neighbourhood children could not resist the lollies either. So as soon as the workers poured them out onto the ground, we would run up to the pile and try to grab as many as possible. I used to push and shove with the rest of them and in the tussle I would feel around frantically for my favourite treat and make a grab at the cold, red pile. Most of the children were greedy and took as many as they could carry but I did not like to take more than just one or two.

I still wandered alone but these days my father was usually in and around the typhoon shelter. He was unemployed so he kept an eye on my little sister and I while my mother worked in a small factory in Aberdeen as a cleaner. Her wage was not enough for us to live on but she could supplement it by collecting donations of food and clothing from various charitable organisations.

Mother constantly remained alert to hear which organisation was about to give out free vouchers for the handouts. When she heard through the grape-vine she would rush to the designated place, abandoning whatever she was doing at the time. Mother could not read or write, so once she had collected them she had to remember for which days the vouchers were valid and also from where the goods were to be distributed. She often waited all night in long queues at the distribution points. During the summer months, waiting was not so bad for her but in the winter, she huddled in a blanket to keep warm.

These were hard times for my mother. Besides rushing around for the vouchers and donations, she worked long hours at the factory and had to cope with the taxing daily labours on our boat as well.

It was in the shelter that we began to keep chickens. My mother built a wooden chicken coop on a platform in the stern of our boat, next to the cabin on the port side. So now we could look forward to eating eggs regularly and having chicken to eat during the winter and on special occasions in the summer.

Sometimes, when my mother was out, my sister and I used to feed the chickens. How I dreaded this job! As soon as I entered the coop, it seemed to me that the chickens would fly around in a frenzy and peck at my eyes! I would scream as I frantically fought them off. Not only was the experience worse than a nightmare but also my eyes would be sore for days.

Unfortunately, after all my mother's effort, the first coop she built did not last very long. Early one morning, a neighbour happened to step aboard to see her and on leaving, this rather ample lady leaned against the coop; the structure began to creak and groan. Then, to the astonishment of both ladies, it rolled over and splashed into the water. The crash, the squawking of chickens and the cries of dismay echoed around the typhoon shelter, rousing, not only our household, but our neighbours, too.

Bleary eyed, the rest of us on board rushed to the scene only to find our ten chickens floundering for their lives in the murky waters of a high tide. We all stood there aghast, not knowing what to do to save poor mother's investment. We had no way to fish them out and no one was willing to jump into the filthy water to save them. So all the chickens drowned.

Run Aground

One evening my grandfather took me ashore. He clutched my hand tightly as we crossed the road and we then made our way to an alley in Aberdeen that led to the rear of a factory. Opposite this factory, running down the steep hillside, there was a small nullah that cascaded with water after the heavy rain. Here, I could give myself a really good wash in the cool, clear, refreshing mountain water. Best of all, I could use as much water as I liked, unlike the restricted supply on our boat.

While I was absorbed in the sheer pleasure of splashing myself with the abundance of water, my grandfather wandered off to chat to his friends. Soon, I completed my wash and feeling tingly and refreshed I sat on the narrow path, waiting patiently for my grandfather's return. I remember hearing the roar of an engine and then feeling the pain.

My foot had been jutting out into the road and the driver of a passing lorry had not noticed that a wheel of his vehicle had struck it, so he had driven on. Shouts and exclamations grew louder as a crowd of onlookers gathered around me. One of them hurried to call an ambulance while another managed to locate my grandfather. As the ambulance sped its way to the Queen Mary Hospital, I slipped into oblivion.

I was admitted to the children's ward and then a group of doctors examined my foot. They found that the back of my right ankle had been severely crushed, so almost immediately I was wheeled to the operating theatre for surgery. An orthopaedic surgeon put a pin through my ankle and applied splints to hold it in position until it healed. I could not walk at all and I would have to stay in bed for about a month.

This was the first time I had been separated from my family, let alone having to sleep on dry land. So I found my surroundings very strange and I was bewildered by the hospital-life going on around me. The food did not impress me at all. It was soft, watery rice just like baby food, and it did not fill my belly. It was not long before homesickness and hunger engulfed me.

Everyday, I focused my attention on the entrance to my ward, hoping to see the shapes of my family coming through the door. My mother came as often as she could and brought me food — usually just noodles. She also brought toilet rolls, since they were not supplied by the hospital.

There were days, however, when no one came. I remember feeling very jealous of the other children who had visitors everyday who brought them presents and food. I guess these lonely days were probably the days when my father was supposed to be visiting me but never came. My family had assumed that he had been visiting me regularly because he had been asking my mother for money for his fares and to buy me food. In fact, rather than visit his own sick child, the rascal had been spending the money in pursuit of his own pleasures.

Father Edward came to see me a few times. One day he brought me some large green apples, but I was fussy and I refused to eat them because they were not red ones. Really! I wish I had not behaved in such a contrary and ungrateful manner.

About a month went by. Then, a plaster cast was applied from my toes up to my waist after my foot had been X-rayed. Now I was allowed to go home. Father Edward suggested to the nurse that he take me home in his car but I had to refuse his kind offer because I was in a very embarrassing situation — I had no clothes to wear!

My good friend, being very kind and patient as usual, dallied till the sister in charge rescued me from my predicament by finding a dress for me to wear. He then drove me home.

At home, I could do nothing but lie on my bed, which was a straw mat on the floor of our houseboat. I cannot remember how I filled my time but guess I must have been very bored. I do recall the discomfort of the plaster cast in the sweltering heat and humidity of the summer. My skin itched so much that I resorted to using a bamboo stick to scratch inside the cast.

After six weeks, Father Edward was kind enough to take me to the hospital to have the cast removed. I was alarmed by the buzzing electric saw but very relieved when my leg was released from the uncomfortable, reeking cast.

I received no physiotherapy to get my ankle back into working order, but I was advised to swing my leg backwards and forwards. This I did by standing precariously on the edge of our houseboat and while trying to keep my balance, I swung my leg to and fro over the water. On reflection, this was foolish. If I had lost my balance and fallen overboard, I would have been in danger of drowning because I could not swim.

It was a sad coincidence that ten years later, Father Edward himself, while riding his motor scooter, skidded on some oil and was thrown off his machine. He was taken to Queen Mary Hospital for treatment. One leg was broken and was encased in plaster. As soon as we heard the bad news, my mother and I went to visit him. We reminisced about the days I had spent in the same hospital after my accident a decade before.

Along for the Ride

As time passed, my mother accumulated all sorts of donations from many generous organisations and we began to feel quite well-off. So when my mother's eldest sister wanted to bring her husband and three children to stay with us for a while, we did not object.

They came down from their farm in Yuen Long in the New Territories to stay with us because two or three of them needed medical attention and it was more readily available on Hong Kong Island. It did not take us long to realise they were taking advantage of us.

They thought it was their right to lodge with us without contributing in any way to living expenses or to the maintenance of our houseboat. Moreover, my aunt assumed the role of mistress and continually scolded us all. We were very unhappy with this situation and we began to fear they would never go home.

After six months, all their illnesses had been cured and my aunt decided it was time to return to Yuen Long, much to our relief. However, our relief at their departure soon turned to anger.

We noticed that they had left behind their earthenware pot that they used to boil herbs to make medicine. This was definitely a bad omen for there is a superstition that the family who inherits a medicine pot will continue to use it. We firmly believed that by leaving the pot my aunt was invoking illness to fall on our household. My mother, so upset that her sister could do such a thing, called her a black-hearted woman and vowed never to associate with her again.

Another incident had also annoyed my mother. My aunt had promised that her daughter could marry my second brother, Chan Lai Yan, but at the last moment, for some unknown reason, she broke her promise. (Marriage was permitted between cousins but only on the maternal side of the family.) Now, after discovering the family's true colours, my mother admitted that it would not have been a suitable arrangement anyway.

After this upsetting episode, our life returned to more or less the old routine. My father lived his carefree life while my mother struggled on.

Unfortunately, to find the money to support his opium habit and unknown to the rest of our family, my father sold some of the treasured food donations: bags of rice, several sacks of flour and a few tins of oil. This was revealed to my mother by a female hawker who had observed my father carrying out his underhand dealings. On being questioned by my mother, he denied his wrongdoing and scolded her for daring to accuse him.

After her day's work in the factory, my mother fetched water from the hillside waterfalls or from the public tap to wash our clothes and clean the houseboat. She also collected branches and dried fruit pods from the mountainsides to burn in our stove. To kindle the fire, she used wax-coated paper drinking straws that she collected from the local soft drink factory's rubbish bins. These were the sticky, used straws left in the returned bottles. After she had washed them and then dried them thoroughly on the roof, they were kept in a basket near the stove.

I always wondered where she found the strength to carry on with these chores, as well as work and collect the donations. She never complained about her life of drudgery. In working for her family she gained happiness and satisfaction.

Her only respite was in the evenings when my aunts and a few neighbouring matrons would come on our houseboat for a gossip. They loved to consult the "Basket Lady," a fortune-teller who paddled her sampan from boat to boat at high tide in search of clients.

As her name implied, she carried a basket but it was no ordinary basket; it assisted her in telling fortunes. She would be beckoned aboard and for a cigarette or a handful of melon seeds, she would deliver a message from the mystic world in answer to her client's questions. She would place her basket on the floor and cover it completely with a cloth. After the question was asked, the answer would be "yes" or "no," depending on which direction the basket tilted.

This gaggle of women had great faith in this lady's powers because in the past her basket had revealed the identity of a culprit who had stolen from one of them. It had also predicted that if one of my distant cousins married a certain young lady, the union would be extremely fruitful. This prophecy came true. The couple married and were eventually blessed with ten children! Never mind the gossip that the young man's father sold a daughter into prostitution to raise the money to pay for the wedding.

Galley Gourmets

Our good friend Ah Kong still lived with our family but now was employed as a cook in a factory. Apparently, he was considered to be very skilled at his job, though I was not too impressed when he cooked for us at home. He used to cook the most unappetising food such as small turtles, snakes and a selection of weird things that I could not identify. What really put me off his cooking was that he continually sneezed, wheezed and smoked when he was preparing the food. He was not too fussy about cleanliness and sometimes I would vomit up the meal he had cooked. Nevertheless, our family really appreciated his skill in making a meal out of ingredients that cost next to nothing.

At the factory where he worked, Ah Kong used to breed cats and feed them daily until they were plump. Then he would kill them and make cat stew for our meal. We also had a pet cat on board called Meow who had many litters of kittens. They were fattened for the cooking pot, too. Any dogs wandering around the typhoon shelter, especially in the winter, were not safe either. Both cats and dogs were boiled with black beans and ginger and were eaten to protect us from illness during the winter.

Meow was the daughter of our previous cat who had disappeared when we were living in Staunton Creek. No one knew what had happened to her but I can guess. Meow was a short-tailed tabby cat and very intelligent. Her favourite sleeping place was in the basket of straws near the stove. When our meals were ready, she would rouse herself, scamper around our houseboat and call everyone on board.

Sometimes, she stole scraps of meat from our kitchen and when my mother scolded her, she would dart outside and bring them back. She was also extremely adept at catching rats. Some nights, as I felt my way into bed, a rush of horror would strike me as I brushed against the cold and furry body of a dead rat! For some reason, my bed was Meow's favourite place for depositing her dead prey. Perhaps she could sense I was always hungry.

If my mother came across baby mice on board or on neighbouring vessels, she used to put them into a bottle of wine. After about a year, she would either drink it or massage it into her limbs as a cure for her rheumatism. If Ah Kong happened to discover them first, he would gulp them down alive! I hate to say this was not the only unusual delicacy he enjoyed. When he killed a cat for the cooking pot, he would eat its eyes, believing they would improve his eyesight!

In spite of Ah Kong's nauseating habits, I remember him with fondness, as his heart was definitely in the right place. He tried his best to be as helpful to our family as he could and was very kind to us children. He treated us like a father should; he often bought us clothes and even took us to the cinema. He had also taken on the responsibility of being a *kai* parent to a young boy who lived on a neighbouring boat.

A *kai* son or daughter is very similar to a godchild in the Christian tradition, but the custom has no religious connection. If a couple has always wanted a son or a daughter and has remained childless, they may be lucky enough to take on a *kai* child. Sometimes, friends might even *kai* each others' children, or if a child dies, then the next child born to the parents would probably be assigned a *kai* parent or parents to keep away the bad luck that had befallen the deceased child.

In Ah Kong's case, he took a *kai* son as a result of superstition on the part of the boy's parents. They had been told by a fortune-teller that bad luck was hovering over the family because they had chosen the wrong names for him. To ward off this bad luck, they had to *kai* their son and Ah Kong was chosen. He took his *kai* duties seriously and at every festival he and the boy's family would exchange gifts.

Traditionally, when a *kai* child is grown, besides helping to support his natural parents, he would do the same for his *kai* parent or parents; if not by a regular monthly monetary contribution, he would at least pay what he could afford now and again. Sometimes, on the death of a *kai* parent, a *kai* child would help make the funeral arrangements. Unfortunately, in later years, poor Ah Kong did not receive any help from his *kai* son.

Cloud Banks and Sunbeams

When I was almost eight years old, an abscess developed on the lower right side of my back. My mother took me to a local private clinic but the treatment I received did not help. Soon I had a raging fever and my face looked so gaunt and sallow that my mother sensed my condition was critical. Day by day she sank deeper into despair as she saw my health deteriorate. Fearing that my death was not far away one day, in a panic, she contacted Father Edward. He was the only person to whom she could turn to find help for her poor sick child.

On seeing my poor state, Father Edward was very worried, too. He asked my mother: "Will you allow your daughter to be treated in a hospital? She may need to stay there for a long time."

"Yes," my mother replied. "No matter how long it takes, she must be cured."

To this day, my mother is convinced that without Father Edward's intervention, I surely would have died. Within two days he drove us to keep an appointment with Professor Hodgson at the University Faculty of Medicine.

Immediately, X-rays were taken of my spinal column. Then a junior doctor examined my body, paying particular attention to my hands and feet. It was discovered that the tuberculosis in my spine had become active. I would need extensive chemotherapy to cure the disease and this would require a long stay in hospital.

After the consultation, Father Edward drove us directly to the Children's Convalescent Home at Sandy Bay, on the northwest coast of Hong Kong Island.

As soon as I was admitted, the nurses helped my mother with the registration procedure while an *amah* carried me to the bathroom to give me a bath. I was then placed in a large cot in the young children's ward.

When my mother finally left, I was frightened and filled the ward with my sobs but soon I calmed down and was given a cursory examination. Then came a sleeping tablet and within a few minutes, I was fast asleep. During this sedation, an incision was made to drain my abscess.

When I woke up, I found I had an incision on the right side of my lower back that needed to be dressed twice a day. Painful injections and bitter medicine were given to me daily. The medicine was so horrid that on one occasion I just refused to swallow it. I choked and spluttered and made a big fuss but the nurse had no sympathy for me. She quickly gave me another spoonful and made sure I swallowed it. Though I was so young, I soon came to realise that I had to bear the awful taste, for if I refused to take the medicine, even only once, it would jeopardise treating the disease effectively.

Fortunately, my lungs were free of the tuberculosis, so the risk of infecting those around me was not high. Still, the nurses exercised great caution when tending my wound.

Most nurses were gentle in giving me injections in the back of my thigh, but a few were careless and rough, paying no heed to my feelings. I suffered when some nurses disregarded the fact that the injected patch was becoming sore and continued to jab it with their needles. This caused the patch to become inflamed and swollen, and soon it deteriorated into another abscess. The Sister in charge, a Missionary Sister (a few sisters of the Missionary Sisters of St. Columban worked at the hospital at this time), scolded these nurses severely and with my gory new abscess as evidence, they could hardly deny their carelessness.

This new abscess was examined by a group of doctors, including Professor Hodgson who was holding a clinic at the hospital at the time. They concluded that I should be sent to Queen Mary Hospital to have urgent surgery. I did not understand the matter clearly but the superintendent of the Queen Mary Hospital must have signed for my operation to go ahead because my parents had no telephone and could not be contacted urgently. That night, in a really poor state, I was wheeled into the operating theatre. A rubber contraption was placed over my mouth, I was asked to take three deep breaths, and that was all I remembered.

When I came to, I found myself lying in a camp bed in a very crowded, noisy ward. Despite this, and the milling of white uniforms around me, I felt terribly alone.

Soon, amid the cacophony, I detected a special sound nearby. It was a baby whimpering. I filled with a sense of foreboding, as the whimpering grew fainter by the hour. Then suddenly, the sound stopped — the little soul had passed away.

Fearing it would soon be my turn to die, I became panic stricken. At the top of my voice I wailed, "I don't want to die! I don't want to die!"

I could not understand why the doctors and the nurses were amused at my cries. They made no attempt to soothe me, so I wailed even louder. Then, just as I was beginning to think that everyone had forsaken me, I heard a strange voice saying: "Don't be so foolish. You will not die. You will live!" Instantly, a feeling of calm came over me and I was no longer afraid.

Sure enough, I was still alive two days later, and well enough to be sent back to the Sandy Bay Hospital.

Two incisions had been made to drain my latest abscess and I still had the incision draining my original abscess. I dreaded the daily changing of the dressings but it was an ordeal I would have to bear for months to come, as the latest abscess was very deep and would take a long time to heal.

To fill the long days sometimes the Red Cross teachers would attempt to teach me to read and write. Although I was almost blind, I could vaguely see the English letters and Chinese characters if they were written very large and I held them close to my eye.

Voluntary organisations arranged entertainment programmes, such as film shows for us patients and the American Women's Association came once a week, bringing all kinds of toys for us to play with. These toys filled me with awe and wonder for this was the first time I had come across real toys. Only stones and shells had been my playthings at home.

On bright, sunny, winter mornings, we were taken outside to sit on the lawn to enjoy the sun, and during the summer we were sometimes taken to the beach, only a few minutes walk from the hospital.

At Christmas time, to my surprise, we were given presents, food and clothing, too! I had never heard of Christmas or of any other Christian festivals for that matter, so I did not fully understand the significance of the celebrations in the hospital. Nevertheless, being a young child, Christmas seemed like a good idea to me if presents and the like were meted out. During Chinese festivals, only *lai see*, "lucky money" in little red packets, is given, and there is no exchange of gifts as such, except traditional food. Such joyful occasions as these I had not even imagined. This was all a new experience for me and I thoroughly enjoyed those happy days.

For a few weeks when my health was really poor, I was removed from the ward and isolated in a private room. I was so lonely. I longed for company and my parents to visit. Once again, I envied the patients in the general wards whose parents visited them regularly and brought them food.

My mother seldom came to see me at this time because she was pregnant with a baby girl who sadly died when she was only a few weeks old. She also had to look after my young sister, Choi Ha. My father came a few times but he only stayed for a few minutes, giving me some small food items and a roll of toilet paper.

Father Edward came to visit when his schedule would allow. He knew some of the Irish nuns who were tending me. They were very kind and demonstrated their love and compassion towards the patients in their care, especially to the orphans.

I recall with emotion, the day Father Edward brought some toy cooking utensils for me to play with. Yet again, he had shown his understanding of the needs of a young girl. Now I would not be so bored and could while away the time more happily. He also gave me a rice bowl and chopsticks of my very own. These simple gifts I treasured and used for years.

I continued to stay in the Sandy Bay Hospital until the summer of 1959, about a year in all. Though I had longed for my discharge day, when it finally arrived, I recall feeling quite sad. I did not want to leave my friends or the nurses either, since my stay with them had been a happy one.

Some of the staff presented me with a box of sweets and a beautiful doll. I was so overcome that I did not know what to say. "Thank you. Thank you," I repeated emotionally, as they escorted me out of the ward to Father Edward's car, waiting at the hospital entrance.

I must confess that I was not entirely happy when I settled myself down in Father Edward's car. In fact, I had left the hospital feeling very apprehensive, for this time I knew I was not going home. I was going to school for the very first time — a boarding school for the blind.

Father Edward had made all the arrangements and explained everything as simply as he could to my mother. As for me, I did not have much of an idea of what going to school was about for the only learning I had experienced was a few lessons from the Red Cross teachers in the hospital. Really, I did not know what to expect. What concerned me most, though, was that I would be a boarder and would only go home for the Chinese New Year and summer holidays.

Waters To Swim In

So it was a late summer morning in 1959, when I was almost nine years old, that Father Edward came to take me out of the hospital and drive me to school.

With a few plastic carrier bags of my belongings, he drove me straight to Honeyville Convent. This was a school for blind girls and a home for homeless, blind spinsters; it was about a five-minute drive from the hospital and run by the Canossian Daughters of Charity, an Italian order of nuns. The car seemed to crawl down a long driveway before we came to the main entrance of the honey-coloured, colonial-style villa where a nun stood waiting to greet us. She led us into the parlour where I was interviewed by the headmistress before being shown around the school.

Honeyville was then a large, two-storey villa on the lower slopes of Mount Davis overlooking the Lamma Channel. The area was peaceful and the house was secluded by trees and gardens. It had been donated by a wealthy man for the Canossian nuns to use as a convent and a boarding school for more than sixty blind girls. It was as well provided for as Hong Kong's other school and home for the blind — the Ebenezer, located less than ten minutes drive away on Pok Fu Lam Road.

The top floor of the convent housed the nuns' living quarters and was strictly out of bounds for students. The ground floor was divided into two parts: the parlour, the classrooms, the sitting room, and the spinsters' handicraft room on one side; and the guest accommodations, several nun's rooms, including their kitchen and dining room, on the other.

The students' dining room was at the rear of the building, together with a laundry and a garage. Our bedrooms and bathrooms were in the basement. Though rather dark and gloomy, it was spacious enough for us to move around safely.

A long driveway led from the road to the front of the house where the garden was mostly set to lawn, shaded by shrubs and trees. The back garden, being on a slope, was terraced. At house level spread a large grass lawn bordered by flowers, shrubs and trees. Chickens and their pens shared this level of the garden, too.

The gardener's house was further down on a lower level. We often went down there to play with his children. The gardener's wife was a kind-hearted lady and did not mind being friendly with us blind girls.

There were only two classrooms for six grades. Primary 3 to 6 were in the largest of these rooms. It was extremely cramped — the pupils squeezed in with more than forty desks and chairs. The other room housed Primary 1 and 2. It was furnished with small tables and chairs, just like a kindergarten.

In my class, Primary 1, there were only six pupils. On fine days, lessons were held on the balcony of the living room to make more space for Primary 2. Our teachers, Miss Kam and Miss Ho, were mainly responsible for teaching the higher classes, so two senior girls assisted them by giving us simple lessons.

I was rather nervous of the venture, it being the first time I had attended normal school lessons but nervousness did not bother me where the nuns were concerned as I had become accustomed to nuns when I was under their care at the hospital. However, I did not know anything about their religion. My family worshipped our ancestors and Taoist gods and Father Edward had never mentioned anything about Christianity or Roman Catholicism to me. Consequently, I was baffled by all the praying and attending Mass that I was required to do. It was all a complete mystery to me. I just recited the prayers along with the rest of the girls, but in parrot-fashion, not knowing what on earth it all meant.

It was at this first school that a teacher gave me the name Ma-lai, but I preferred to be called Mary as soon as I learned it was the English equivalent. Before then, I did not have a given name except Ah Ngan meaning "tiny and thin."

At first I could hardly cope with my new, blind classmates because they delighted in teasing me for coming from a "Boat Family." Though I had already learned a great deal about handling such occasions in my childhood, I squirmed when they ridiculed me for reciting my prayers with a pronounced Tanka accent. So I tried very hard to lose my accent and speak the Cantonese acceptable to them. Eventually, we all became friends having many common difficulties to overcome. An immediate one was learning to inscribe Braille with a stylus and a writing frame, and this proved to be a daunting task.

Braille consists of sixty-three characters, including the twenty-six representing the alphabet, each made up of one to six embossed dots. "Writing" entailed pushing holes through sturdy paper with the metal stylus, working from left to right. To read what I had inscribed, I had to turn the punctured paper over and feel the raised dots with my fingers, going from right to left.

I could not concentrate sufficiently to master the skill. This was probably because I was in new surroundings and coping with the new experience of being in a class full of students. Also, I had never had to concentrate on anything in my life before and I became easily distracted. I just gazed around in a dream, mesmerised by the strangeness of it all and paid no attention to my teachers' instructions. Soon they became annoyed with my lack of attention, so to encourage me to learn they bound my eyes with a length of black cloth for a few hours a day.

It took me about a year under this strict supervision to master Braille in both English and Chinese. I still found inscribing Chinese Braille extremely difficult, mainly because of the many tones in the language, represented by tone marks. There were more than seventy initial and final symbols to remember as well. I was much more interested in inscribing English Braille as it was less complicated and much easier to remember.

As for the other subjects, I tried really hard to learn but nothing seemed to filter into my brain. The teachers blamed my lack of progress on my laziness and on my inattentiveness in class.

It was at the end of 1959 that Father Edward went to Rome to study for a doctorate in theology. Up until then he had come to see me regularly and constantly inquired about progress in my studies. He was particularly concerned about my attitude, so besides forever urging me to be diligent, he would tirelessly caution me not to be a "lazy bones." He would then turn to chat with my friends. Charmed by his gentle voice and fluent Cantonese, after each of his visits they never failed to confess that they envied me for having such a very good *gweilo* friend.

I was one of the six youngest girls in the school and the nuns showered us with loving care. During the summer holidays they arranged for us to go swimming, and took us on picnics and leisurely evening walks. Such outings were quite beyond my experience and they brought joy to my childhood. I had not forgotten the days when I had wandered alone.

Sometimes, the nuns gave us a few cents to buy ice cream and ice lollies from the seller who rode by the convent on his bicycle. Knowing we found his wares irresistible, they would stop him for us and we would crowd around his bicycle, eagerly pushing our money towards him. We would jostle of course, to be the first girl served but at least I did not have to scramble for my favourite snack as in the typhoon shelter.

If we had coughs when we attended morning Mass, the nuns would give us some ginger or mint sweets to help soothe our throats. This caused the older girls to envy us. After one such occasion they scolded us vehemently, and accused us of pretending to have coughs in order to attract more attention from the nuns but at that time — if not on other occasions — our coughs were genuine. So we young ones took umbrage at their false accusations, feeling we were entitled to this attention from the devoted nuns.

There was, however, an unpleasant and humiliating incident involving a nun that has remained vivid in my mind to this day. It happened near the feast day of the Superior of the convent. The nuns had planned a programme for her party and we were rehearsing a play on the stage. I was given the part of a beggar who behaved like a clown. One of the nuns, who was crippled and walked with crutches, thought to exaggerate my abnormal posture by putting a large bag on my humped back. "Ma-lai, put this bag on your back," she said. "I'm sure it will help make your act more amusing to the audience."

My heart sank. I had been so thrilled to have a part in the play but now this! What a humiliation!

In tears, I flatly refused to perform. I did not want to look even more ugly and be ridiculed by all. "No, I won't do it — I won't do it!" I cried.

To solve the problem, one of the blind spinsters was told to take my place. She was not at all happy. "Ma-lai, you are a naughty girl," she snapped. "Because of your stubbornness, I have to play the silly beggar now. I don't want to play him either." Then she furtively pinched me!

When Christmas approached, I was selected to perform a Chinese folk dance with some other girls in my class. We wore colourful traditional costumes and sang as we simulated rowing small boats on the sea. Our performance won enthusiastic applause, especially from the Westerners in the audience. A party ended the afternoon, and we were given tiny toy bicycles. These fascinated us for when we wound them up, they ran in circles!

After we had attended Mass on Christmas Eve, a group of foreign sailors arrived and distributed bags of gifts among us. To our delight each contained sweets, walnuts, chocolates, peanuts, bars of soap and a variety of other carefully chosen things that girls would appreciate.

On Christmas morning there was another distribution of gifts, followed by pocket money given by the Superior. After the excitement had died down, we filtered into the dining room and heartily consumed a festive lunch.

Another happy event was our visit to a large American warship in the winter of that year. Those who were overweight were not allowed to go for fear the sailors would have difficulty lifting them up onto the warship. I was one of the lucky ones.

More than one hundred blind girls, including some from the Ebenezer School and Home for the Blind, assembled at Queen's Pier in the Central District. Soon we were aboard motor boats that ferried us to the warship anchored way out in the harbour. Once safely on board, we were led in small groups by the sailors who were very eager to show us around. I remember feeling ashamed my English was not good enough to communicate with them.

The ship was vast. It consisted of four decks and among the facilities we were shown was a large library, a huge galley and an abundance of bunks for the sailors. I was amazed.

One cheerful sailor showed me the warfare equipment carried on board. Everything was strange to me. There were helicopters, shells and guns of all kinds. I paid careful attention to my guide but I was too young to understand everything in detail. Nevertheless, I was very interested in learning all I could about this magnificent ship.

After taking an hour or two touring the vessel, we were invited to have a meal. I was rather apprehensive, for this would be the first time I would sample a Western meal. I did not know what to expect and I wondered if I would enjoy it.

We were given a tray that was generously adorned with sliced bread, roast beef, fried chicken, carrots, potato chips and a selection of fruit. We drank tea or coffee and had ice cream for dessert. I struggled with the knife and fork but I was pleasantly surprised by the food and enjoyed my first *gweilo* meal.

After lunch, we were presented with gifts, which added even more excitement to our day. Then we sang, played musical instruments and enjoyed a hilarious time imitating the sounds of animals. Later, a magician performed. I thought this was a strange entertainment for the blind until I realised there were other tour groups in the audience as well as ours. However, the magician explained his tricks in detail for our benefit and he earned a rowdy applause from us all.

Finally, we thanked the sailors heartily and lined up to leave the warship. Our boarding had been carried out with no consternation but our disembarkation proved otherwise. It was hazardous being carried down the steep steps to the waiting boats.

Though we had trust in the strong arms of the crew, being in high spirits, we took great delight in exaggerating our fear of being dropped into the sea. We gasped and giggled nervously and even cried out in alarm, but we were soon scolded by our leader for making such a fuss. Thereafter, we left calmly and without incident.

The hospitality and enthusiasm of the crew had impressed us all. Perhaps we had contributed a little happiness to their day in return. No doubt many of them were missing their families back home.

New Horizons

In 1960, the Canossian Sisters decided to move the school to a larger building in St. Francis Street, Wan Chai, which had been the St. Francis Hospital run by the same order of nuns. Honeyville was too cramped and there were insufficient facilities for us to study satisfactorily. The Canossian Order had recently replaced this old hospital with a new one called the Canossa Hospital in Old Peak Road in the Mid-Levels District. So now the old hospital building in Wan Chai became the Cannossian School for Blind Girls to cater for the increasing number of girls who needed to study at a specialised school. When summer arrived we moved into the new building.

Although we felt sad at leaving our former school, the new one had an advantage — it was more spacious and easier for us to move around in. The environment, however, was not as peaceful and the air not as clean as we were used to. Honeyville was in a country area near the coast and this new school was located in a narrow street which ran up the steep hill between Queen's Road East and Kennedy Road, a busy area full of noise and traffic.

We were uneasy about moving to an unfamiliar area of the city, of course. It would take us a long time to find our way around before we would feel secure in our new location.

Three coaches and three removal lorries transported us and our belongings to the new school building in Wan Chai. As soon as we arrived,

in our anxiety to feel our way around our new school, we alighted in a
hurry. We rushed towards the four-storey building, but were dismayed
when we found we had to negotiate two flights of steps before we could
reach the main entrance!

Inside, opposite the main door, a staircase led to the three floors above.
On a landing between the ground floor and the first floor was the
headmistress's office. At one end of this large room stood a huge, glass-
topped desk flanked by a couple of chairs for visitors. At the other end stood
a large, round marble table. Lining the walls were four long cupboards that
contained models of objects to teach recognition by touch.

To the right of the main entrance was a large assembly hall furnished
with rows of metal chairs. A long table stood at one end and a large,
wooden stage stood at the other. Beyond the hall there were two small
rooms; one was for typing instruction and the other was the staff room.
Leading off to the left of the hall was the domestic science classroom
furnished with old-fashioned appliances.

Although there were six classes, there were only four classrooms — all on
the ground floor and furnished in the same way. In each there were fifteen desks
and chairs arranged in three rows. There was also a teacher's desk, of course, and
sturdy shelves, which held the heavy Braille exercise and textbooks. Two walls
were hung with large notice boards. It was important for a blind student to
learn the positions of all the objects in a room, especially in her own classroom
where she must count the desks in order to find her own.

At the rear end of the building to the left, there was a long hall divided
into two rooms — the kindergarten and the remedial class. Outside, along
the length of this hall, was a long narrow verandah where students lined up
for the afternoon session.

Also on the ground floor to the rear of the building were three dining
rooms — one for the blind spinsters, one for the boarders and the other for
the day school pupils. There was also a large kitchen — it's staff provided
three meals for us daily. They also prepared the nuns' meals, which were
sent up to their dining room on a dumb waiter. Outside the kitchen was an
open space where we could dry our clothes and bask in the winter sunshine.

The dormitories for the boarders were on the second floor. There were
six in all, each furnished with six beds and six lockers. Adjoining these
rooms was a very large room containing six bathrooms and six toilets. The
headmistress's bedroom was also on this floor.

As at Honeyville, there were no ceiling fans in the bedrooms or in any of
the rooms used by the students, except in the assembly hall.

To the right of the staircase on the second floor was a small chapel that housed an ancient organ and ten rows of pews. Next door was a little room for the priests to change their vestments. Adjoining this was the library and two rooms where the blind spinsters could sew, knit and make handicrafts. The third and fourth floors were the residential areas for the nuns and they were strictly out of bounds to students.

There was a strict routine. We were awakened every morning at 5:30 a.m. by our "big sister," an older student who was in charge of the dormitory. Usually, I was in such a deep sleep that to rouse me she would drag me out of bed onto the floor.

Our beds were metal frames with wooden bases. We had neither the luxury of a mattress, nor even a sheet on the bare board, though in the coldest months we were issued two blankets. By Western standards our beds were very spartan, but I considered my bed to be the most comfortable place in the world.

After prayers, led by our big sister, we washed, dressed and made our beds very quickly because we had to attend Mass in the chapel at 5:45 a.m. If we tried to avoid this duty we risked being punished.

I hated to wake up so early and in my drowsy state during the Mass I would sometimes float away, but I would usually jerk myself awake when I sensed I was falling from the pew. Once I was just about to fall when I felt a nun's tight grip on my arms. She scolded me soundly for dozing and pulled my ears!

At 7 a.m. we drank milk and ate bread for our breakfast. Then we were required to clean and dust the dormitories, and generally tidy up.

Morning school started at 8:30 a.m. and consisted of six periods broken by a fifteen-minute recess after the third period. Lunch was served at noon. After we had cleared the tables and washed the utensils, we relaxed for one and a half hours. At about 1:45 p.m., we began our afternoon lessons of three more periods.

At approximately 3:30 p.m., we finished lessons for the day. The day students went home and we boarders climbed the stairs to take baths and wash clothes. With all chores done, we revised our day's lessons for a short time and then we would chat till dinner. In the dining room we sat around six rectangular tables, each seating eight. Two older girls were responsible for distributing the food.

Sometimes, our meals were not very palatable because some of the food was donated by hawkers. It was usually the food they had failed to sell that day and it was not good quality. However, we could always look forward to Sunday meals when there were noodles for lunch and fresh green beans and roast pork for supper. Most of Sunday was spent playing games or in other recreation.

In the evenings we took turns to carry out household duties. A two-hour homework period followed, supervised by one of the nuns. We retired to bed at about 9 p.m. All the lights were switched off and no one was allowed to talk.

On Saturdays there was no school but we were required to clean thoroughly. We dusted and cleaned the dormitories and bathrooms from morning till late afternoon just before the evening meal. We were always exhausted when we finished these chores, but no girl could escape her turn, otherwise, she would be punished.

Usually, the penalty for disobedience was being served only plain rice and water at mealtimes. Or we might be punished by having to carry heavy metal buckets or books upstairs alone when it was dark. I was scared of the darkness; I had heard stories about ghosts.

Our school life was tightly organised by the headmistress and we could not get away with being lazy. Even during the school holidays we were kept busy. Another school donated unwanted exam papers and we helped our teachers make books for writing Braille by folding twenty pages and stapling them together.

At this stage, I got along with my schoolmates quite well. I was always prepared to offer my limited sight to help them explore and my hands to guide them, especially to those who could not see at all. On occasions, though, some became too excited to hold hands and they would run through the rooms, often hitting against objects, walls and doors. Sometimes, they hurt themselves badly and bled. Though they did not blame me, these accidents upset and worried me as I felt responsible for their safety.

I was gratified that I could help my friends and I enjoyed the companionship they offered me, but some aspects of my school life made me very miserable. I was very self-conscious of my camel-shaped back and felt that because of my deformity, I was not selected to take part in some of the school activities such as the Girl Guides and dancing performances. I was also excluded when groups of pupils were sometimes taken to their teachers' homes. This really caused me to feel left out and lonely.

The teachers sometimes took their pupils on excursions but I was excluded from these, too. "Why was I not included?" I continually asked myself. I always concluded it was because I was a hunchback.

The only outings I could look forward to were those with my mother when she came to visit. We liked to wander around Wan Chai market where she would buy me a few things.

Most pupils were orphans and I was treated as one, too. The school provided my daily requirements and my clothes were allocated to me from donations. How I dreaded the day I was expected to change clothes for the new season.

I never failed to work myself up into a panic when it was my turn to collect my clothes from the headmistress. She could not always find suitable clothing for me because of my deformed shape and I feared I would end up with something horrid. I remember the time when she found an old, torn cardigan, had it dyed dark blue and then tried to give it to me for my school uniform. Despite having nothing else to wear and the weather being chilly, I adamantly refused to wear the awful thing. It was shabby and way too big for me.

The headmistress was very cross with me and I found myself in trouble. Still, I was stubborn. I would not obey her and promised myself that no matter what the pressure, I would not give in.

In the end, my dear mother came to my rescue. She bought me a suitable cardigan in Wan Chai market. I have never forgotten the immense relief I felt.

I formed the impression that the few pupils whose families were considered well-off and could pay towards their schooling were treated more favourably by the headmistress. She did not seem to scold them nearly as often as she did the rest of us. Whenever they asked to take extra lessons, such as piano lessons, it seemed they were given priority. I longed for piano lessons but dared not ask.

I tried to avoid the headmistress. The way she disciplined some girls created within me a great determination not to upset her. I also noticed that she was sometimes unfair to the girls she did not like. So knowing I was not one of her favourite students and she did not have much time for me, I kept a low profile when she was around and rarely talked to her. The times I did happen to incite her wrath, I have to admit she did not punish me as severely as she did some of the other girls who were not her favourites.

As far as I can remember, besides the headmistress, only one or two nuns were Chinese and they were teachers. The remaining ten to fifteen nuns were Italian and did not teach. Apart from one or two of these Sisters supervising our evening homework, we did not have much contact with them. It was the headmistress who controlled everything, even down to washing and bedtime. She seemed to be on duty twenty-four hours a day and there were times when I felt she should have taken a break!

Making a Splash

When my mother came to see me during this period, we had exciting forthcoming events to discuss. My adopted brother, Chan Sum, now twenty-five years old, was about to be married and my mother was busy preparing the dowry.

A matchmaker, a man who was a friend of our family, had found him a bride. Her name was Li Ho, a young woman from a Tanka boat family in the Castle Peak area of the New Territories.

The engagement of a couple is confirmed when the groom's parents present a dowry to the bride's parents. It is customary for the bride's mother to send the groom's mother a list of things she expects the dowry to contain. If it is within the means of the groom's family, there will be no bargaining and the dowry will be delivered between three months down to two weeks before the wedding.

Unfortunately, Li Ho's mother upset my parents by demanding an excessive dowry. There were heated arguments and a great deal of vicious bargaining all round before the content was agreed.

My mother did her utmost to comply with the list, and finally, our family and relatives assembled on our houseboat to make an occasion of packaging the dowry. It was to be delivered by one of my relatives on a day deemed as propitious by my great aunt, who was the go-between.

The dowry consisted of a selection of expensive dried seafood, live chickens, wine, clothes for the bride's brothers and sisters and money. In keeping with tradition, four coconuts and a pair of lotus roots tied together with a red ribbon were included. The coconuts symbolised that many children would spring forth from the union and the lotus roots meant a lasting relationship. Gift vouchers for cakes were also sent with the dowry. These were for the bride's family to distribute to friends and relatives to announce the betrothal.

Unfortunately, when the dowry was delivered to Li Ho's boat, her mother accused my mother of being frugal. She complained that the food items were not in the quantity she had demanded, nor in the correct proportions. My mother insisted that everything in the dowry did comply with the list and another heated argument ensued.

Eventually, my great aunt, who had much experience in the settling of dowries, was called in to help solve the dispute. She confessed she had never had to deal with such a greedy woman as Li Ho's mother in all her years as a go-between, as even she could not lessen the demands. In the end, she advised my mother to send some more money to save more bitterness. The incident really upset my mother and she has rarely spoken to Li Ho's mother since.

The marriage took place just before the Chinese New Year of 1962. I was invited and my second brother came to take me home from the boarding school two days before the ceremony. I was thrilled when my mother showed me the red tunic with a mandarin collar and trousers she had bought for me to wear to the wedding. I thought the suit was beautiful.

The evening before the wedding day, the Candle Ceremony was performed. My mother placed two thick, long, red candles before our ancestral altar and then decorated a small branch of a tree with peanuts and dates to bless the couple with many children. The oldest married couple in the area was found to sit vigil at the candles. They had to catch each droplet of wax with chopsticks and place it into a bowl of salt, averting a short marriage for the couple. This ceremony was watched by a happy gathering of our relatives who sang, joked and ate rich food throughout the night.

Early on the marriage day, the Combing Ceremony took place. A woman called a Tai Kum Che uttered good luck incantations while she brushed my brother's hair. Afterwards, everyone ate a sweet soup for breakfast called tong yuen, a tradition that called for a strong union for the couple.

At the same time, more or less the same rituals were being performed on the bride's boat at Castle Peak. In addition, she would perform the traditional farewell rituals because she was leaving her family to become a member of her husband's.

According to the Chinese almanac, the most auspicious time for Li Ho to make her formal visit to our family would be 9 a.m. in the morning. So after the Combing Ceremony, my brother, accompanied by his best man, travelled to Castle Peak to claim his bride who he had met only twice before.

The bridesmaids would not allow my brother to claim his bride until he paid them a "ransom" of $99.90. By custom, the amount is made up of as many nines as the groom can afford. Nine is significant because the Chinese word *gau* has the same sound as the word meaning "everlasting" and would imply a long married life for the couple.

So when my brother handed the bridesmaids a red envelope containing the ransom, he was permitted to claim his bride. The couple then offered tea to the bride's parents and shared cakes and pastries. Finally, they left the boat with money and gifts from the bride's parents to the sound of firecrackers.

Our houseboat was decorated to the hilt. From prow to stern it was hung with red paper scrolls and banners embellished with symbolic inscriptions in gilt. Drink and festive food were plentiful and our spirits were high as we waited anxiously for the arrival of the bridal pair.

At last they arrived. Li Ho wore a red wedding garment embroidered with dragons. She was accompanied by her bridesmaids and her unmarried brothers and sisters. As they stepped onto our gangplank, the sound of firecrackers and the cheers of the guests and onlookers resounded through the typhoon shelter.

This visit was for the bride to formally meet her husband's parents and family. In compliance with tradition, her parents stayed at home.

The entourage stepped down into our sitting room and the guests looked on as the couple knelt before our family altar and bowed before the ancestors' tablets, then the bride turned to greet the elders and guests in order of seniority. She invited them to take a cup of red date and lotus-seed tea. The date signified a sweet and peaceful union for the couple; the lotus seed meant a child would be born within a year of their marriage. During this tea ceremony, gifts of money, blankets and jewellery were presented to the bride.

The celebration lasted for more than an hour. The twenty or so guests and the bridal party were seated on the floor and in their midst were seven-year-old Choi Ha and I, enjoying ourselves and occasionally delving into the selection of cakes and pastries offered on a red cloth.

I listened intently to the hilarity going on around me and blushed for the bride when embarrassing jokes and teasing began, mainly delivered by the elderly, commenting on her appearance. It is the custom to criticise a bride's appearance during her wedding celebrations.

When the newlyweds retired from the party, they began preparing for the banquet, which was to be held in a restaurant in Aberdeen at 4 p.m.

In those days, it was very unusual for a boat family to hold their wedding banquets in a restaurant ashore. They would usually be celebrated in one of the less ostentatious floating restaurants in the harbour but my father happened to know the manager of this restaurant in Aberdeen and was given a special deal.

On the way to the restaurant, spruced up and feeling rather uncomfortable in our finery, our family walked tall. We were convinced that our social standing was about to soar, as everyone would think we were very prosperous being able to splash out for a banquet in an opulent restaurant ashore.

As the guests arrived at the restaurant, they handed Chan Sum the red envelopes containing gifts of money. They then proceeded to the "Bride's Room" to be greeted by Li Ho. She was dressed in the same red, embroidered wedding garment and wore the jewellery she had received from both sides of her family. When everyone had been welcomed, the chaotic ritual of posing for photographs began.

Eventually, we were seated for the banquet. I was at one of the many large, round tables with my family and the bride and groom. Li Ho's parents, brides-maids and brothers and sisters sat at the next table.

After two courses had been served, the couple rose to toast their parents and thank them for all they had done for them and then proceeded to visit each table in turn to toast their guests and thank them for coming. At each table the guests stood for the toast and teased the couple with such remarks as: "Don't forget to invite me to the celebration next year," hinting the couple would soon give birth to their first child.

At the end of the twelve-course feast, Li Ho changed from her wedding dress into a smart, Western day dress. Then the wedding party assembled at the restaurant door to say farewell to the guests. When all had left, my brother settled the restaurant bill.

Our family, including the married couple, then returned to our houseboat, feeling relieved that it was all over and all had gone well.

Shipmates

After their marriage, my brother and his wife lived with my parents. An unsuccessful attempt to acquire his own fishing boat had left my brother unemployed and Li Ho had no job either, so both spent their time idly at home while my mother supported them.

After a while, through the help of my father's friend, Li Ho started working part-time sorting fish at the fish market with my mother. They had to be at the market in Aberdeen at 3 a.m. where they waited for the fishing boats to be unloaded. Sometimes, if they were lucky, they could earn about HK$10 a day, but other days they could be kept just hanging around waiting for the boats to come in.

The fish-sorters were permitted to keep a few of the smaller fish free of charge. Soon, much to my mother's dismay, she was told by some fellow workers that Li Ho was taking much more than her allowance. Li Ho had persuaded her elder sister to moor a small boat nearby and furtively she would fill it with fish that she would later sell.

My father's friend soon found out what was happening, too. Li Ho lost her job and the whole affair caused great embarrassment to my parents. I'm sure Li Ho had reasons for her actions, but as far as the family was concerned she was untrustworthy.

My new sister-in-law was rather plump and was frequently called *Fei Paw* meaning "Fat Woman." She also proved to be selfish and lazy. She slept a great deal and rarely offered to help with the housework. When my brothers came home late and we had already eaten, she would prepare her husband's food only and refuse to cook for my youngest brother.

After two months, Chan Sum and his wife moved to Kowloon and made their home in a small sampan in Cheung Sha Wan Harbour. Both worked as labourers in the fishing port with my uncles and aunts who still lived there. According to these relatives, the couple was able to earn a good wage.

It is the Chinese tradition to help support parents even after leaving the family home but they gave my parents only thirty dollars just now and again, claiming they were earning very poor wages and could not afford more.

Afloat Again

I had been at the new school for about two and a half years when the headmistress introduced a policy that changed my status from boarder to day pupil. More and more girls were arriving and many lived far away in the New Territories so it was decided that those who were partially sighted and had homes to go to should become day pupils.

In the opinion of our headmistress, by living at home we would be able to communicate with our families more closely and they would come to understand more fully the needs of the blind.

She also suggested that day pupils should invite the orphans to stay in their homes during the Christmas and Chinese New Year holidays to give them an opportunity to experience family life.

I invited an orphan named Ann to stay on our houseboat at Christmas 1962, and another, Maria, at the Chinese New Year Holiday of 1963. Both were very excited to be able to explore the outside world after being closeted in the boarding school for so many years.

Ann was a totally blind Chinese girl from Johore Bahru in Malaysia. After being abandoned by her parents when she was very young, she was found wandering in Singapore by a lorry driver. He took her to the Canossian convent in Singapore and eventually she was transferred to Honeyville. She had lived there for a short time with me before we moved to our present school.

Ann, a sturdily built girl with short black hair, was rather obstinate. She was also very forthright and never held back her opinion or criticism of others.

Her faults were significantly outweighed by her virtues. She was sincere and possessed an endearing innocence. She had an open, cheerful heart and her zest for life often caused a great deal of merriment among her peers.

Besides entertaining us on the piano sometimes, she used to mimic what she considered the strange voices of others. Her thunderous laughter never failed to be infectious, so the people around her also shared in her joy.

My family made her welcome and gave her the best food they could afford. At first, she was extremely active and very curious in touching her new surroundings but soon she became bored. She found she could not move around our houseboat safely because the waves caused it to lurch from side to side and she could not see or anticipate its movement. So to entertain her while on board, I encouraged her to remain seated by singing with her and talking about our life. We explored outside now and again but only as far as our sightlessness would allow.

Despite the "seesaw" experience, I believe Ann enjoyed her first taste of family life. Her stay with a boat family had given her an occasion to remember.

My other guest, Maria, came to St. Francis Street from the Canossian orphanage in Macau. Only one of her eyes was sightless, so she could see to walk wherever she liked.

She was not the least bit shy and her delight in playing tricks on her peers proved she was a rather cheeky girl, too. Maybe it was unintentional, but sometimes she took advantage of her friends by expecting a share of their good fortune. Her faults were minor and she demonstrated a warm heart when she lent her hands and sight to others.

As she stayed with us over the Chinese New Year holiday, she could celebrate with a family for a change. She was thrilled when she received lucky money from my parents and from my relatives who lived in the neighbourhood.

The rocking of our houseboat did not bother her and each time she explored Aberdeen and the typhoon shelter she could find her way back to my home quite easily, much to the relief of my family.

Her visit proved to be a joyous occasion for her — a precious time. She had never stayed with a family before or even anywhere else since she had entered the boarding school.

When Maria left school she worked as an *amah* and eventually married a sighted man. They now have a son and a daughter.

It was an anxious time when I became a day pupil. Both my mother and Father Edward were worried whether I would manage to find my way to and from school on my own. They doubted I was even capable of crossing roads safely much less catching the correct bus.

My schoolmistress gave me a wooden cane but I refused to use it. I was afraid of being ridiculed by sighted people who might call me a *mang mui*. Depending on the tone used, this could mean just "blind girl" or "blind slave," which was hurtful. In China, blind girls used to be sold into slavery to be trained as street singers or entertainers and the carrying of a cane signified the girl was a beggar or prostitute.

Each morning my mother woke me but usually I would just lie there, snatching a few more minutes of sleep. Soon she would become very annoyed at my idleness and would shout in an angry tone: "Tomorrow I shall not call you. It's your own business whether you want to study or not."

Only then would I jump up from my straw sleeping mat and force myself awake. Despite her threats, the next morning she would wake me up as usual.

It took me a long time to get used to travelling to school after being a boarder from the beginning of my school days. I used to cross our gangplank, climb a flight of steps to the road and then walk for about half an hour until I reached the Aberdeen bus station.

Crossing the busy main road was nerve wracking. Rarely was I helped across. Luckily, I could just about see the shapes of vehicles if they were near enough and I could of course hear them approaching.

I recall being very drowsy in the mornings when I lined up in the long queue at the bus terminal. As soon as I was seated on the bus, I fell asleep and would sometimes use the next person's shoulder as a pillow. On one journey, I was startled out of my slumber when one man complained sternly: "Wake up! Don't use my shoulder as your pillow. Your head is so heavy I can't bear it!" I mumbled an apology and in order not to induce another embarrassing protest, I forced my eyes to stay wide open for the rest of the journey.

Usually, I caught the school bus to and from the Central Ferry Pier, but on the occasions I missed it I had to face the problem of getting to St. Francis Street on the public bus. I had to rely on the people in the bus queue to tell me the numbers of the approaching buses and then I had to ensure I alighted at the correct bus stop in Wan Chai.

Learning the Ropes

Primary 1 had been a great struggle for me but by the time I entered Primary 2 in September 1960, I had adapted to the discipline of school life and found it easier to concentrate on my studies. My grades were improving steadily and on one memorable occasion my Chinese language teacher praised me for an article I had written in Braille. I was thrilled when she put it up on the notice board for all my classmates to read. She also helped me write it in Chinese characters for the sighted to read. I was surprised I had been complimented on my work, for seldom had this happened before.

I also made steady progress in all my subjects throughout Primary 3 and 4 and my average marks for each were quite balanced.

I had improved significantly in arithmetic and Chinese, thanks to Miss Kam, the teacher of these subjects in both these school years. During our mathematics lessons, she used to instruct us with teaching models — ice-lolly sticks, ice-cream spoons or beads — which we touched in order to learn more easily. Many blind students had benefited from her teaching methods and due to her encouragement, I became more interested in arithmetic and was able to score quite high marks. As the weeks passed, colourful stars — rewards for a good effort — appeared more frequently in my exercise books. At last, I could feel heartened by my progress.

Though I was not a remarkable pupil, it was encouraging that each year I was promoted to a higher class. Despite this, anxiety over my capabilities had not diminished. I was still scared of being left behind.

For me, it was not simply a question of overcoming my learning difficulties; the antipathy and discrimination I had faced since my early years because of my deformities and background had left their indelible mark. One symptom of this was a fear of being ignored. As a result, I tried to attract attention by shouting or talking loudly in class. The teachers tried to quieten me by forever chiding: "Your bellowing will be heard on the ninth floor. So please speak softly." There was no ninth floor and I did not even attempt to heed their requests.

Though they sometimes grew weary of chastising me, usually they could not help but smile at my antics. My behaviour also amused my classmates and they gave me the nickname, *Hoi Sum Gwo* meaning "Happy Heart." I was delighted to be called such a lovely name and as a consequence, decided to live up to it and continued to indulge in my favourite pursuit — attracting attention by disrupting lessons.

Everyone seemed to assume that I had no worries at all and only I knew they were wrong. I was terribly worried about my future. I knew it would be difficult for me to fit into society and find a job because of my abnormal appearance and diminished sight.

On the other hand, my peers — all burdened with a handicap that would have induced such worries as mine — like me, said nothing.

Blind girls, perhaps because we could not see the events going on around us, were always interested in the smallest snippets of gossip.

Our teachers were very understanding and sometimes gave us an insight into their family life. Invariably, these discussions diverted our teachers' attention from our lessons; we were very bold in using them as an excuse to take a break from studying.

Of course, some embarrassing incidents occurred because we students could not see. One took place during a music period. The lesson was so boring that some of us began to whisper among ourselves, and others fell asleep. Therefore, few were paying attention when the teacher began to sing in a hoarse, loud voice.

In her drowsy state, a student named Philomena mistook the voice as that of a classmate Ah Jing and shouted sleepily: "Ah Jing — why are you singing so badly and so loud? It sounds terrible!"

We were startled by this sudden remark and when we realised what had happened we fought hard to stifle our giggles. Poor Philomena, we dared not even whisper to her that it was our teacher who was singing and not Ah Jing — a mentally retarded girl who always made strange sounds when she attempted to sing.

Our teacher was furious with Philomena and extremely embarrassed but she did not chastise only Philomena. Having realised that she was not the only student being inattentive, our teacher shouted angrily: "Girls, this is a singing lesson; please concentrate, otherwise marks will be deducted in your reports."

Luckily, the teacher was a broad-minded lady and she did not take Philomena's rudeness to heart. In fact, not long after the incident, she bought us ice cream after school. I was always impressed by this teacher's generosity and her fair treatment of all the pupils in our school.

I recall another incident when we were caught not paying attention, and several classmates, including me, were punished. On that day, during the physical training period, a group of us chatted among ourselves not paying attention to the teacher. At the time, she was describing some exercises, but we did not bother to listen and continued talking. This annoyed her immensely, so she commanded very sternly: "The six of you who were not paying attention must run around the playground ten times without stopping, otherwise you will feel my ruler. If you have not finished the ten laps before lunch time, then you will have no lunch."

I remember we were so alarmed at the threat that we dared not talk any more and assembled to obey her orders.

As soon as she blew her whistle we began running in earnest. I dared not run only part way round because I knew we were being watched by her sharp eyes but some of the other students did try to cheat and escape her notice. She was a clever and discerning lady and recognising their cunning, she ordered the cheats to start running from the beginning again. The rest of the class stood by giggling, highly amused at their schoolmates' silly pranks.

We must have looked a strange sight — a group of giggling, blind girls running around in circles. We soon failed to see the funny side of the occasion when the giggles were replaced by heavy pants and gasps. In the end we found ourselves completely exhausted; we had been taught a lesson.

The Tide Turns

The American Women's Association had given an invaluable service to our school — the translation into Braille and the printing of many of our textbooks and library books had been funded by them. So to show our appreciation we tried our best to provide entertainment for them every Christmas season.

One Christmas we performed a Nativity play and a traditional Chinese dance; the younger children played musical instruments and sang carols.

Most of us had been given the chance to take part in the show and I had been given the role of an Australian girl in the Nativity play. I had to carry a toy kangaroo onto the stage and quote a text from the Bible. I was thrilled; but being the first time I had been asked to read English and perform in front of an audience, I was self-conscious and extremely nervous. My heart pounded and my face flushed. I could also hardly contain my excitement — this was the first time I had ever worn such a beautiful costume, or in fact, a costume of any kind.

My performance went well and I was pleased when my teacher complimented me on my English. I gained more confidence through this experience and from then on I worked much harder to perfect the language.

I entered Primary 5 in September 1963, and it was not long before my teacher, Miss Kwok, was surprised to notice a sudden improvement in my written English work. She was very pleased and encouraged me to go on working hard.

I began to score high marks in dictation, general English knowledge, composition and reading, and I earned an average mark of eighty in the examinations. Miss Kwok was delighted and gave me a piece of chocolate as a prize.

Miss Kwok was always ready to help me with my English and I was forever asking her questions. In fact, I treated her just like an English dictionary. Even one of my classmates teased me one day and suggested, "Why don't you make a large bag and put Miss Kwok inside? Then whenever you need to ask the spelling or meaning of a word, you can simply open the bag and get the right answer."

I laughed at her silly suggestion and exclaimed: "What a ridiculous joke!" — but I wished I could do it.

Father Edward had returned from Rome by now and had moved from the Aberdeen Seminary to Wah Yan College in Wan Chai, run by the Jesuits. Every morning at 7:30 a.m., he celebrated Mass in our convent chapel for the pupils of the St. Francis' Canossian College, just two flights of steps up the hill from our school. We now had the chance to meet each other more often.

Most days, while we pupils were lining-up to go into the assembly hall to pray and to hear the boring pep talk given by the headmistress, I used to catch a glimpse of Father Edward leaving through the convent main entrance. He was on his way back to his office in Central District. He always greeted me and if we had a chance to chat for a few minutes my spirits would soar.

Due to my diligence in the study of English, my teacher asked me to make a speech in English at a farewell party for the Superior of the convent.

Since I was standing on a stage and the speech was quite long, I was extremely nervous. My voice quavered a little at first, sending prickles down the back of my neck, but within a few minutes I overcame my stage fright and did not falter for the rest of the speech.

During the ensuing party, to my surprise, the Superior congratulated me on my performance. "Well done!" she exclaimed. "You delivered your speech very well. Your pronunciation was perfect and very clear."

Miss Kwok was very pleased to hear this comment. She was a former student of the Superior so she was especially proud that her own student had impressed her.

After that success, I was given further opportunities to speak English on the stage.

One of these was at a Christmas celebration. I was asked to give the opening speech before the programme began. Unknown to me, Father Edward had been invited by our headmistress to come to hear my speech.

After the programme, he came up to congratulate me. "Your pronunciation has improved a lot," he said. "You speak accurately and you presented your speech very well. I am amazed at your achievement."

By now, I began to feel that maybe God had given me a special talent after all.

Over the next few months, Miss Kwok became so satisfied with my progress that she wanted me to take part in the School Music Festival. It was held annually between February and March. All schools were asked to participate in a variety of programmes, both in English and Chinese, such as: verse recitation, prose reading, singing and playing musical instruments. I was encouraged to join the English-prose reading group.

The story I was to recite had been recorded on tape by an English lady. I listened and practiced diligently, but I found distinguishing the voices in the conversational piece difficult and remembering where to put the correct emphasis even more so.

We contestants had to score more than eighty marks in order to be awarded a Certificate of Credit, which was the most honourable prize. I took part in the programme a number of times and usually left with a Certificate of Credit. I treasured the experience I had gained in taking part in the programmes and with each certificate I was awarded, I became a little more confident and content.

Miss Kwok had given me many opportunities to improve my second language. She was my favourite teacher in primary school. She was sincere and very kind to all her blind pupils, always endowing us with care and affection. If a girl was not well behaved, then Miss Kwok would talk to her privately and advise her well.

When Miss Kwok had spare time after lunch, she liked to come out of the staff room to talk and sometimes she would sing to us in Mandarin. Her clear, sweet voice charmed us and we would cry: "Go on, Miss Kwok. Please sing some more. We enjoy hearing your songs."

There was no gulf between us students and Miss Kwok. In fact, she considered us her friends. It meant a great deal to us when she invited us to her home to share a meal with her family and she moved us deeply when she presented us with gifts at Christmas.

On one occasion, she took us to Victoria Park for a picnic. We explored the grassy areas under her guidance and she helped us feel all kinds of plants. We chatted and frolicked and in an atmosphere of joy, we played games in English. Those who lost the game would be required to act out a scene in English, while her giggling classmates looked on.

The Magistrate's Court happened to be nearby, so we took the opportunity to visit. The court was in session and we were permitted to enter as long as we remained silent. A magistrate was sentencing a prisoner at the time. I listened with fascination. Witnessing court proceedings was a rare opportunity for girls like us. It was truly an experience to remember.

When I had completed Primary 6 in July 1965, Miss Kwok left to take up a post in another school at the beginning of the next school year. I felt sad at her departure, looking back at the happy years I had spent with her. The day before she left our school, she took me aside and offered to give me her advice and support at any time. Then, to my astonishment, she proceeded to tell me in confidence: "Because of your constant diligence, I have given your name to the headmistress and suggested that you be chosen to study with the sighted students at the St. Francis' Canossian College. If you can study there, it will help you build towards a better future. I wish you every success."

My heart leapt with excitement. I had been so worried about my future prospects and now Miss Kwok had kindled hope and with it, a sense of relief. Maybe it was possible that I could have a bright future after all.

Plotting My Course

Each year, my headmistress could not obtain more than three places for her blind girls to study in the St. Francis' Canossian College. Before I could have a chance to enter, I would have to remain in the Blind School for two more years.

The standard of the college was very high and some of the blind students who had gained entrance had found it very hard to cope.

I worked extremely hard during the next year. I was rewarded when I scored high marks in all the end of year examinations, except mathematics. I had also won the first position in my class for the third time that school year. For this achievement, I was awarded a coveted prize — a Swiss watch for the blind. Charitable organisations donated these watches to the school to award to those who achieved the highest marks in their examinations.

Meanwhile, my parents and my second brother had asked Father Edward to help me. Since the day he had driven me through the gates of Honeyville, he had shared in my joys and offered me his support through all my troubles.

He had always wanted me to go on to secondary school and the main reason he had encouraged me to excel in English was because most of the good secondary schools in Hong Kong taught in that medium. So my good friend did not hesitate to help me obtain a place at the college; he wrote a letter to the headmistress, an Italian nun, to explain my case.

Though I was first in my class, I had to wait quite some time before I was informed that I had gained a place. At last I could rejoice.

My excitement was soon dampened when my headmistress, who was still not satisfied with my performance, said: "Actually, I was not willing to let you study with the sighted students but because Father Edward spoke up for you, I will give you this special chance."

Her words depressed me. Over the years, she had not shown a liking for me and we did not have an easy relationship.

On the other hand, maybe she feared that I could not compete with sighted students and would fail to reach the required standard.

To further dampen my excitement at this time, I soon discovered that some of my blind classmates were jealous of my achievement. They played pranks on me and I became very annoyed with them. One of the girls actually hit me on my head with a pile of thick Braille books!

Later, a group of classmates shoved me into an empty bookcase and closed the glass doors. I could not get out and soon I could hardly breathe. What a terrible joke! Frantically, I tried to force open the doors and screamed so loudly that the girls became alarmed. They feared I would smash the glass doors, then they would really be in trouble.

At last, in a panic, they set me free. I was very cross with them, of course, but as usual it was not long before I forgave them and we were friends again.

Landlubbers

While I was struggling away trying to gain a place at the College, exciting events were unfolding at home. About two months before I left the Blind School, my parents heard from the Housing Authority that they had been allocated a flat in Shek Pai Wan, Aberdeen. The typhoon shelter was to be reclaimed from the sea to make more land for development and the Boat People were being relocated.

It was a few weeks before the Chinese New Year of 1967 that we were scheduled to move and we waited eagerly for the day.

During the last night on our floating home, in anticipation of living in a more stable and healthier environment, our family was restless with excitement. At last we could escape the demands of our boat-life. There would be no more carrying water and fuel and no more emptying slops overboard. Instead, we would have running water, electricity and toilet facilities. We would not have to worry about typhoons anymore, either; my mother could now throw away her baling bucket.

For me, it was a relief that I would be nearer to the bus station to travel to school. Although I would have to go down a few flights of steps to the main road, the route would be easier. It would however, take me just as long to walk because I would encounter more pedestrians.

We had very few belongings to load onto the lorry the next morning — just a few folding tables and chairs, clothes, bedding, kitchenware and the most important item — our ancestral altar.

We said farewell to Ah Kong who was moving in with friends and also to our two cats. Pets were not permitted in the flats so we had to leave them behind to fend for themselves. We were confident that they would soon find a home among the remaining boat-dwellers — unless Ah Kong had other plans for them.

I felt a pang of sorrow as the lorry pulled away from the typhoon shelter. We were Tanka, and living on a floating home had been the only lifestyle my family had known for generations. We were abandoning our familiar living environment for a life in a confined unit in a high-rise, concrete block — and we were happy.

We were the second group of Boat People to leave the typhoon shelter for government housing, and our houseboats were left to be destroyed by the Government.

Our new home was a unit of about 150 square feet on the seventh floor of a seventeen-storey block and our view was the slope of a steep, green mountainside. We had our few pieces of furniture, but no beds or electrical appliances. We were accustomed to sleeping on the floor, so we did not mind in the least waiting for the time when we could afford the bits and pieces to make our new home more comfortable.

At one end of a small balcony there was a kitchenette, and at the other end a squat toilet, a porcelain hole level with the floor in a very small cubicle. There was no shower or bathtub — just a tiny washbasin. The bedroom was a cubicle where eventually, when we acquired a bunk bed, I slept on the top bunk and my parents slept underneath. My brother and sister slept in the sitting room.

No one knew why but a couple of years before we moved, my father had decided to give up smoking opium. He also surprised us by finding a job in a godown, a warehouse, in Wah Kwai, quite near Aberdeen. It was curious that he was now eager to spend some of his earnings on buying appliances for our new home. Among the items he bought were an electric rice cooker and a gas ring. These were sheer luxury to a family who had only ever known a wood-fired stove.

My brother Chan Lai Yan was also contributing to the family expenses at this time. He had worked for a while in the fish market after leaving school and having recently learned to drive, he was now employed in a more stable and lucrative job as a driver with the Government's Urban Services Department. So, with three members of the family earning, the pressure on my mother in supporting the family eased. There was no reason our future in our new home should not be brighter.

3

Choppy Waters

My summer vacation in 1967 was the busiest period of my school life. I spent weeks transcribing Chinese Literature and Chinese History textbooks into Braille in preparation for my entry into the St. Francis' College. To assist me in this daunting task were volunteers who kindly gave up their time to dictate the texts to me. These were students from the college who were members of a Roman Catholic sodality, The Legion of Mary. They read to me in turn, according to a rota drawn up by their headmistress.

Five days a week, I met my friends Magdalene and Yvonne, two blind girls already studying at the college, at the bus terminus in Central District where we took the public bus to the Blind School. We then walked a short distance up the hill, usually arriving after the morning assembly. We often met Father Edward coming out of the chapel. He had been celebrating Mass and was on his way up to the convent for his breakfast. He would pause for a chat and as always, express his concern and care for me. I was the only blind pupil entering Form 1 of the college that year — my two friends had already been studying there for a year and were about to enter Form 2. They were also preparing for their impending school year in the same onerous way. This exercise kept me so busy that I had no free time to revise my new English textbooks or to do any other preparations for my entry into the college.

In September of that year, aged seventeen, I entered Form 1 of my new school. It was the first time I was to study with able-bodied students and I felt very uneasy, not only because I was blind but also because I was the only deformed student in the school. I just prayed that my fellow students would not look down on me, or even pity me.

One or two blind students a year had been entering the college since the Blind School had moved next door in 1960. So my form-mistress, who specialised in teaching English, had taught blind students before. According to some of my blind schoolmates who had been her students, she had considered their needs and treated them well. In fact, before I even arrived in her class, she had assigned a student to help me during lessons. This student, a prefect, was a Portuguese-Chinese girl named Louise Da Rosario. Her features were predominantly Chinese and she wore glasses. Along with having a genial character, she was considerate towards her peers and was always ready to help them.

Rather than participate in sport or other social activities, she preferred to spend her time drawing and writing articles. In fact, after finishing her studies at the college, she became a journalist. We still keep in touch, as she works in the Far East and her husband is with Reuters. Louise was very keen to help me.

She had the advantage of studying in the English section of her primary school and was a very competent student. So when the teachers wrote notes on the blackboard, she could copy them down and at the same time, dictate them to me while I wrote them in Braille as fast as I could.

Besides helping me in class, she usually gave me a hand with my schoolwork after we had finished our school day. I greatly appreciated her kindness in helping me, for this considerably reduced my anxiety over not being able to keep up with the rest of the class.

My form mistress was a tall, slender, middle-aged, Chinese lady of elegant appearance. Fortunately for us students, she spoke loudly and clearly in class. Even the students in the adjacent classrooms could hear her.

To me she seemed a very rational lady, but I soon learned that she was fanatical about hygiene. She surprised us all one day by suggesting that we should encourage our families to break with tradition and not use their own chopsticks when taking food from common bowls. At home, she disinfected everything her guests had used.

Unfortunately, she was inclined to be prejudiced against some of the pupils who came from the Chinese-language oriented primary schools, mainly because their English was so limited and they could not learn easily.

In previous years, the St. Francis' Canossian College primary school had been divided into two sections — the English section and the Chinese section. Now, there was no Chinese section in the primary or secondary school. Therefore, the new intake of pupils into Form 1 in both schools had no alternative but to learn in English if they wanted to study at this reputable college. Approximately half of the students in Form 1 of the senior school had studied in primary schools that taught in the English medium and the other half had come from primary schools that used mainly Chinese. Those who came from the Chinese section, like me, found it very hard to cope.

The School for the Blind's standard of education was also much lower than in other primary schools. We students from the Blind School entered the college with this disadvantage in addition to our handicap. This usually resulted in a very low success rate in our examinations. At the Blind School, we had used only two English grammar books and these were not difficult to understand at all; but now, the standard of English in the college textbooks was much higher. I realised that it was going to be very difficult for me to attain the standard expected in my new school. What a shame it had been that during the summer holidays I could not employ a tutor to coach me in English. I had neither the time nor the money. Furthermore, I felt that the headmistress of the Blind School had not advised me of the best way to prepare for study at my new school. She had been concerned only that I transcribe the two Chinese-medium textbooks into Braille. It was for this reason that I was compelled to go to the Blind School during the summer vacation everyday from 9 a.m. to 5 p.m. to complete the mammoth task. I had been very tired and bored with transcribing, especially in Chinese, because I believed the text would not be very useful in my studies because they would be taught mainly in English.

My blind friends in the same predicament also thought we should not have concentrated so much on Chinese, because Chinese in Braille is not easy to understand. Many Chinese words sound exactly the same but they have different meanings. In written Chinese, these same-sounding words are represented by different characters so they can be distinguished from each other. On the other hand, Braille is based on phonetics — words that sound the same have the same pattern of dots. This caused confusion sometimes, especially in examinations. In the college, blind students used to write Braille in the Chinese language examinations, then afterwards dictate them to a sighted classmate who wrote them down in Chinese characters for the teachers to mark. Then panic would assail us sometimes when we found we could not read back some of our Braille. All we could hope for was that the classmate, who would have just taken the same exam, would be able to make sense of what we were trying to say.

Buffeted Back And Forth

My results during my first term at the college were not good at all. I was despondent. At first, I dared not mention my poor standard to my sighted classmates for fear of being scorned, but later I plucked up courage to discuss my worries with those who had come from the Chinese-medium primary schools. I found they were also getting low marks. So I was relieved that I was not the only one who could not cope. The form mistress could not criticise only my application. I took heart in any sign of improvement in my schoolwork. There were occasions when I was very dispirited.

I recall that the teacher who taught us geography and science was a very impatient and quick-tempered lady. She displayed a stern demeanour and did everything in a hurry. She would fire a question at a student very suddenly, sometimes startling her into speechlessness. No matter how much the student stammered, we were strictly forbidden to prompt her and our full attention was needed to stay alert in case we were the next in the line of fire.

One morning, as soon as she entered the classroom for a double science period, she asked me a question. I was startled. I did not expect her to pick on me first, but remembering that this teacher was so impatient that sometimes she did not notice if an answer was slightly wrong I answered as quickly as I could. My heart thumped and I became a little tongue-tied, but to my relief she was satisfied with my answer.

I had no geography book in Braille but fortunately this teacher made allowances for me. She assigned a student to read me the notes on the blackboard so that I could inscribe. She also reserved ten to fifteen minutes during each lesson for a student to dictate passages from a textbook to me. Furthermore, when my classmates were noisy, this teacher would often say: "Girls, don't be so selfish. Don't disturb Mary Chan. Please keep quiet, otherwise she can't hear her helper clearly. You should all be ready to give her help when she needs it, too." On hearing that, I used to blush, and then shrink into my chair with embarrassment.

The teacher who taught Chinese and mathematics was very kind to me and often gave me a chance to speak in class. She was a pleasant lady who treated all her students with the same consideration. I was certainly impressed by her patience and thoughtfulness.

I remember her being quite plump and having fair skin. Her legs were the same shape and colour as a chicken drumstick, prompting her students to give her the nickname, "*Gai Bei*," which means "Chicken Thigh!"

In the end, my performance in Form 1 proved to be quite good and after the usual preparation of my Braille books during the summer holidays, I entered Form 2 in September.

My form mistress, a graduate of Hong Kong University, was a tall, slim, good-looking lady. She was very kind to me and she treated me as a normal student in her class by giving me many opportunities to read aloud and answer questions. She taught English and English Literature but where the latter was concerned, she was more interested in asking meanings of words than giving an explanation of the text. This worried me because my vocabulary was very poor.

I soon came to realise that the only way I could improve my vocabulary was to ask for help other than from my teacher. So everyday after school, I asked some of my classmates to dictate vocabulary and it's meaning to me from a dictionary. I wrote the words and meanings in Braille and then learned them by heart.

Although this was a slow process, it was the only way I could improve my chances of answering my teacher's questions correctly.

My fondest memory of her is of her kindness when I had missed the chance of taking English Oral in the end of the school year examinations. I had been late for school that morning and by the time I had reached my classroom, the English test was over but when I received my report, I discovered that she had given me seventy marks! This surprised me, for not only did I not take the exam but during most English lessons she had remarked: "Your voice is so soft that even the flies cannot hear your spoken word! Please, speak louder in class."

The blind students studying in the college still had very close contact with the Blind School next door. We used to have lunch there and continually borrowed and returned Braille books. Also, after school, we used the typewriters to type some of our homework and our helpers would come there, rather than read to us at the college. Consequently, we felt we did not fully belong to either school. We were not encouraged to join in any of the college programmes or extracurricular activities because not only did we not have enough spare time, we were still considered to be students of the Blind School.

Sometimes, the impression we received from some of the teachers was that the headmistress of the college was only doing the Blind School's nuns and us a favour by letting us study there because we would never be able to keep up with the standard of the sighted students.

As for the Blind School, both pupils and staff considered that we held a privileged position and we should be proud of ourselves for having the opportunity to study at the college. Little did they realise that we were ashamed of ourselves for being at a lower standard than the sighted students.

Personally, for years after I had left the college, I would never tell anyone that I had studied there. They would not have believed a blind girl would have ever had the chance to study at such a prestigious secondary school. Keeping quiet saved me from the embarrassment of people thinking that I was lying.

Floundering

When I entered Form 3 in September 1969, I found it even more difficult to reach the standard expected. I was now in Form 3B and most of my classmates who had been my helpers in Forms 1 and 2 were now in Forms 3A and 3D. I really missed them, as I was not having much success in finding new helpers. When I did find students to help me, at first they would be quite fascinated that I was blind but after a while, the novelty of reading to me would wear off and they would not be so keen to help me anymore.

There was also another obstacle to overcome — not having Braille textbooks in some of the subjects I was taking. I could not take economics and public affairs in the final exams because I did not receive the relevant Braille textbooks until just before the examination, leaving me no time to revise.

Coping with the complex schoolwork exhausted me and coupled with travelling to and from school while lugging my heavy Braille books I found it increasingly more difficult to find the energy to revise my schoolwork at home. I persevered, but no matter how hard I tried at home or in school, I just could not keep up. There was no way I could afford to employ a private tutor and my family could not help me, either. Day by day, I sank further into depression.

During all this anxiety and frustration, I really had been thoughtless. The headmistress of the Blind School had already taken the trouble to prepare all the exam papers for me in Braille. I should have told her that I would not be taking all the exams due to my lack of textbooks. Understandably, she was rather upset that I had caused her needless work and this time she was justified in complaining.

I had not taken all the examinations, so I would be compelled to repeat Form 3 the following September. It had been a very unhappy and frustrating school year and I had achieved practically nothing.

Though I would be repeating the school year, the syllabus was different. So yet again, I spent my summer holidays transcribing new Chinese textbooks into Braille while the Legion of Mary girls gave up their time to dictate them to me. As usual, what with all the travelling to and from the Blind School, I had neither the time nor the energy to prepare any other subjects for the term ahead.

This school year proved to be as disastrous as the last, for I had come up against the same obstacles. My school life was not much fun and I feared that a bleak future was looming on the horizon.

Battened Down

The year 1970 was drawing to a close when an orthopaedic specialist at the Duchess of Kent Children's Orthopaedic Hospital and Convalescent Home, formerly known as the Sandy Bay Convalescent Home where I had spent a year before I entered the Blind School in 1959, informed Father Edward that a new technique for straightening the spine had been perfected at the hospital and wondered if I would be interested in undergoing the treatment.

For years, I had longed for this chance. So after listening to Father Edward's explanation of the technique, I gave serious thought to the matter. If I opted for the treatment I would have to spend many months in hospital without the support of Father Edward, my mentor and friend. He was about to embark on a three-year assignment in Vietnam.

I talked to my relatives and friends and then decided to go to the hospital for tests to see whether I would be a suitable candidate for the spine-straightening technique. At this time, I was approaching the age of twenty-one and it was more than sixteen years after the fall which had injured my spine.

An Australian orthopaedic surgeon, Doctor O'Brien, gave me a thorough examination and soon afterwards I was overjoyed to hear from him that I was a suitable candidate. I wanted to ask a thousand questions — but I could not find the courage to do so. Dr. O'Brien had many other patients to see that afternoon and I feared that my stumbling English would only delay him.

I had been told that the treatment involved months in traction and a number of spinal operations; I would need to stay in hospital for at least six months.

I yearned not to be despised and ridiculed for my appearance any more. I was tired of being called hurtful names such as "camel back" and tired of not being able to wear nice clothes because of my awkward shape. So I plucked up courage to meet the challenge and in May 1971 I entered The Duchess of Kent Children's Hospital for a second long stay.

After I had undergone at least a month of extensive tests, the nurses prepared me for the fitting of halo-pelvic traction. I remember clearly the night before the operation being shaved, bathed and undergoing an enema. As I had not known what to expect, these procedures took me by surprise. I thought they were very strange — and very embarrassing!

The next morning, July 3, 1971, apprehension struck me the moment I awoke. I also felt terribly alone, but the nurses soon were milling around and preparing me for the operating theatre, all the while trying to cheer me. A trolley then appeared at my bedside and I was wheeled along the corridor to the operating theatre.

Although I was feeling very dozy from the effect of the pre-medication, I became alarmed when I was pushed through the door of the theatre. Booming laughter filled the room! I soon realised, to my astonishment, that the person roaring like a giant was Doctor O'Brien!

"Wah! This *gweilo* is very strange," I thought, "laughing so heartily when he's about to operate on me."

Then came the anaesthetic and I drifted away. When I came to, I found myself rigid, enclosed in a metal frame. It was held in place by metal pins embedded into my cranium and pelvis. The pinholes were bleeding and I was in such pain that it was impossible to relax or even get into a comfortable position.

Just helplessly lying there, hemmed in by this dreadful cage, I remember thinking that if I had known how it would feel I would never have agreed to go ahead with the treatment.

From the moment of that brutal shock, I understood I would have to suffer a great deal in the months ahead if I wanted to see any improvement in my spine.

Ten days later, I underwent an A.S.O. — Anterior Spinal Osteopathy. Doctor O'Brien and a fellow orthopaedic surgeon, Doctor Yau, performed the operation while I was still enclosed in the traction. This surgery added to my discomfort and I continued to experience considerable pain.

I stayed in the Intensive Care Unit for four days with no desire to eat. Two weeks later, my appetite returned and I became strong enough to get up and walk around, though with considerable difficulty as I was still enclosed in the metal frame.

Halo-pelvic traction looked like a form of torture. My torso and head were held rigid by a steel frame consisting of four adjustable vertical bars — two in front of me and two behind — attached to a ring around my head and a girdle around my hips. Six steel pins embedded one inch deep in my skull held the halo in position and four in my pelvis held the girdle. Each night, a nurse extended the bars with a screwdriver and strangely, I was always asked if I had any double vision! Once a week, I was X-rayed to measure the degree my spine had straightened.

The pinholes bled continually at first and some became infected. I knew the nurses tried to be gentle when they dressed them, but the holes were so tender that it felt as though they were being scrubbed on a washboard. How I dreaded the pain!

All my movements had to be performed in slow motion; any sudden movement could jar the pins and cause me to wince with pain. Furthermore, I could not twist my neck because it was held rigid by the traction. To look around, I had to turn my whole body.

I dreaded using the toilet — the frame made it a very precarious activity. I had to be very careful not to lose my balance and fall on the floor.

Taking a bath was a nerve-racking and wearisome task, too. I stood in the tub and used the shower to wash from my hips downwards, always making sure the water did not splash the pelvic pinholes, otherwise infection might set in.

Washing my face and the top part of my body through the bars was even trickier. I had to be very gentle. Some of the other traction patients could not manage to wash themselves gently, so the nurses had to assist them, but no matter how difficult I found the struggle, I would wash on my own rather than be bothersome to anyone.

Dressing was an awkward affair. Open-fronted clothing had to be threaded through the bars and pants could only be pulled up as far as the girdle.

Negotiating stairs was nerve-racking; I would grasp the banister very tightly and holding my breath, try my utmost not to make any sudden movements. My poor vision hindered me and I had to be very careful not to fall.

In bed, I reclined on six pillows supported by the bed's adjustable headrest and it was impossible for me to change my position.

The contraption hindered my sleep, and sometimes the pinholes were so painful that even medication did not help. I remember the subdued groans of other traction patients keeping me company throughout these pain-racked nights for they were also in agony.

I still have nightmares about the torturous nine months I spent in the "cage." Looking back, it was the most physically painful time of my life.

On September 14, 1971, about two months after I had been fitted with the traction, I underwent the second operation, again performed by Doctor O'Brien.

After this two-and-a-half-hour operation, which combined a P.S.F. — Posterior Spinal Fusion — and a P.S.O. — Posterior Spinal Osteopathy —

my camel back had disappeared! My joy was immense; my suffering had been worthwhile.

Deservedly so, Doctor O'Brien was very proud of his skill and the successful outcome of the surgery. The deep gratitude I felt towards him could not be measured. Not only had he rid me of my deformity, he had always found the time to visit my bedside to show special concern for my progress, despite being a very busy surgeon.

My spine was straight, but could not support itself so I was not yet out of the woods. I was to remain in traction and further treatment lay ahead.

Two-and-a-half months later, my last operation took place. This was performed by Dr. Yau and another orthopaedic surgeon Doctor Hsu, and was called an A.S.F. — Anterior Spinal Fusion. Unfortunately, Doctor O'Brien could not participate because he himself had been hospitalised with a spinal problem.

Despite being in a plaster jacket and bedridden, he was still concerned about me. He phoned my ward Sister to ask about my condition and also conveyed to me his best wishes. I was very touched, as I had not been the only patient to have surgery on that day. When the story of his concern for me spread among the hospital staff, they concluded that I was his pet. I remember blushing with the embarrassment of it all.

In the Same Boat

During this stay in hospital, I had come to know a group of girls about my own age, most with spinal problems similar to mine. At first we were not bedridden or in halo-pelvic traction, so we were able to move about freely and enjoy ourselves. We chatted and joked to keep our spirits high while we waited for our surgery.

The staff members in the ward were very considerate. Understanding that this was an anxious time for us, as a special concession, they allowed us to make our own breakfasts and even late suppers. We used the kettle and utensils in the kitchenette attached to our ward.

While sitting in a circle we ate and chatted away, telling our own stories, confiding our ambitions and imagining the lives we would lead when we were cured.

These gatherings created a pleasant atmosphere in the ward, but sometimes, when we continued after the lights were out, the nurses scolded us for being noisy and keeping the other patients awake.

My neighbour in the next bed, sixteen-year-old Lai Wai was originally from Shanghai. She was a big girl by Chinese standards — around five-feet, eight-inches tall and she weighed about 133 pounds. Her face was chubby and many remarked on her jolly appearance. She was so shortsighted that she could not see clearly even through her spectacles, and being rather lazy, she loved to spend a great deal of time lying in bed with a white sheet completely covering herself, just like a corpse!

Lai Wai did not have much regard for her parents because she felt they were more affectionate towards her sister. She was, in fact, brought up by her grandmother, a very kind lady who treated her so dearly that she was spoiled and expected everything her own way. Her appetite could not be satisfied by the hospital meals, so she used to insist that her grandmother should visit on specific days to bring her extra food. The poor old lady dared not argue with her granddaughter and she never failed to meet her tiresome demands.

Another large-framed girl in our group was Lau Foon. She was twenty-three years old and suffered from a curved spine caused by tuberculosis. Her home was a large farm in Yuen Long in the New Territories and she told us many stories about the habits of pigs. Though she was experienced in the rearing of these animals, we learned she was reluctant to give her father a hand in the delivery of piglets. She said it was a messy job.

During her stay in the hospital, she was lucky enough to be visited by six aunts in turn. They treated her kindly and brought her special soup, which they thought would help cure her. About ten years after she left the hospital, I heard that she and her family had emigrated to America.

A twenty-six year old called Ada, who was employed as a government clerk, was a young lady with the same disability as myself. Her hair was cropped very short and she wore spectacles. She was quiet, gentle and always very kind and generous to everyone.

Every Saturday afternoon, her boyfriend came to visit. We patients delighted in teasing the courting couple as they sat on the verandah, whispering to each other while they listened to music. Some years later, I heard their romance had ended. Ada's boyfriend had decided to emigrate to Canada and Ada had refused to go with him.

In the bed opposite mine, was my friend Ah Yung. She was a small, thin girl, weak in health. Her short, almost black hair that framed her waxen face emphasised her frailness. Tuberculosis had taken hold in her neck and she was unable to talk loudly. Nevertheless, she was very eloquent and amazed us with her sense of humour and her skill in telling jokes. Her jollity, however, belied her worries. She had noticed that the lifeline on her palm was very short and she confided in me that she had a sense of foreboding concerning her impending operation.

Sadly, Ah Yung's fears turned out to be justified. She had caught a chest infection and during surgery she experienced difficulty in breathing. Immediately, she was sent to the Intensive Care Unit in the Queen Mary Hospital where the doctors tried their best to save her. Unfortunately, their efforts were in vain. She had been too feeble to survive.

The nurses had not told us of her demise, for they feared we would be scared to have our operations. Only when her parents walked into our ward to collect her belongings did we become alarmed. We knew the worst when we noticed her mother was crying.

I had enjoyed some true friendships among my wardmates. We had come through grief and gaiety together and then had gone our separate ways. They will dwell in my memory always.

Bright Spells

During these nine months, I remember some jolly occasions that encouraged us to forget the painful times we were enduring.

Just after I had been fitted with the halo-pelvic traction, there was a farewell party in Ward 8 for a group of patients who were about to be discharged. A few of their wardmates organised the party and they invited the doctors and nurses to join in. The girls prepared food: a large cream cake, biscuits, sandwiches, chicken wings, chocolates and orange squash. They also bought some presents for the departing girls. Each doctor sang a song and some of the nurses sang and danced. One of the departing girls delivered a "thank you" speech to the doctors and nurses — I was very impressed and gathered that hospital life was not going be so bad after all.

Although the girls were looking forward to going home after more than a year in hospital, the farewell party was an emotional time for them. They must have felt a sense of relief that they had come through their treatment successfully and would now lead a life without deformity. Tears flowed as they said farewell, for despite the physical and mental trauma they had experienced during their treatment, they would take home some happy memories of their hospital stay.

I soon learned that hospital life was brightened not only by the celebration of the festivals held in accordance with the Chinese calendar but also by Western festivals. The first celebration I remember was for the Mid-Autumn Festival, also known as the Mooncake festival. It is combined with the Lantern Festival and is held on the fifteenth day of the eighth month of the lunar calendar.

The moon is considered to be at its brightest at this time, and young and old alike climb mountains and hills or go to open spaces to gaze at its beauty.

Children carry glowing lanterns of all shapes and sizes tied on the ends of long sticks. They are colourfully embellished with traditional motifs such as butterflies, carp, dragons and rabbits, all having their own place in mythology.

Sweet, full-moon shaped cakes filled with ground lotus seeds and often whole duck-egg yolks are presented to relatives and friends. The pastry casings of these very sweet cakes are usually stamped with the images of Chang Ho, or the Jade Hare. Both are characters in Chinese mythology believed to reside in the moon.

Chang Ho was the wife of a legendary archer during the Hsia dynasty. She is believed to have flown to the moon after swallowing a pill containing the Elixir of Immortality, which she stole from her husband. He had been given the Elixir by the Goddess of Heaven to make him immortal so that he could defend the Emperor of the time, without fear of dying.

The Jade Hare, it is said, keeps himself occupied on the moon either by pounding the drugs that make up the Elixir of Immortality, or by chopping wood for Chang Ho.

No one knows when the custom of eating moon cakes actually began, but one story is they became popular after they were used to distribute secret messages during the fourteenth century revolution in China, which established the Ming Dynasty.

During the evening of this festival, we were taken into the hospital garden and hoped there would be a cloudless sky so we could appreciate the beauty of the moon. Each of us carried a lantern that we had made under the supervision of an occupational therapist. Cartons containing moon cakes, taro, peanuts and fruit were distributed to us, a sumptuous meal which had been donated by a philanthropist.

As soon as the eating was over, we lit candles and put them inside our lanterns. It was a beautiful scene. Excited children were rushing here and there, holding their glowing lanterns, chattering, laughing and playing games. The wheelchair patients, meanwhile, quietly displayed their lanterns and watched the merriment.

When Christmas drew near, we eagerly looked forward to taking part in these festivities, too. Seasonal decorations were hung in our wards and piles of brightly wrapped gifts stood at the foot of a glistening Christmas tree.

On Christmas Eve, a Midnight Mass was celebrated by a Catholic priest in the Outpatients Department Hall. The patients were invited to attend together with the staff. Even Christians living in the district joined us. We sang Christmas carols and listened to the good news of the Nativity. After the Mass, we enjoyed a special supper.

On Christmas Day, we were served lunch by the doctors, all dressed up in colourful paper hats and aprons. Each patient was given a delectable meal: bacon, roast goose leg, Chinese mushrooms in oyster sauce, chicken, shrimp, eggs, vegetables, fried rice, soup, ice cream, fruit and a cold drink. We could hardly eat such a feast! After the meal, excitement grew as the whole ward prepared for Santa Claus to arrive to give us presents.

The next festival we celebrated was the Chinese New Year of 1972. Without a doubt, we all wished we could have been at home to celebrate this most important festival of the lunar year. This is the occasion when families hold reunions and visit old friends to wish each other *"Kung Hei Fat Choi,"* meaning "Wishing You To Prosper." Children are given *lai see* and employees receive a bonus. Debts are settled and if it has been a prosperous year, the three gods of wealth are thanked and whether it has been a good year or not, they are asked to bless the coming year with good fortune. Homes and work places are adorned with red scrolls inscribed with characters signifying good health, wealth and happiness, and flowers abound. Peach blossoms, kumquat bushes in fruit, narcissus and gladioli, are usually purchased at flower markets, specially set up for the festival.

A week before New Year's Day, it is believed Tsoa Kwan, the kitchen god, leaves his household and goes to heaven to report on the vices and virtues of each family. A picture of him, or an inscription of his name, hangs in the kitchen, usually above the stove. Before he departs, he is worshipped and thanked for watching over the kitchen during the past year. Candy is smeared on his lips, or offered to him so that he will utter only sweet, favourable news in his report. If he has bad news to impart, hopefully his lips would be stuck so fast that he would not be able to speak. The family also burns offerings of paper clothes, money and other necessities for his journey.

During his absence, the home is given a thorough clean. Only members who help with the chores will remain in his favour. A special meal is prepared to welcome him back when the home is ready. After a new picture or an inscription is hung and the old one burned, he is honoured by special food offerings. This should secure his goodwill towards the household throughout the coming year.

On New Year's Eve everyone endeavours to be at their parents' home — the husband's parents' home in the case of a married woman — for the family feast and to welcome the New Year at midnight.

Lai see is given on New Year's Day and ancestors are honoured. There will be a special midday meal that excludes meat if the family is Buddhist. A tray of food is placed on the table to ensure a plentiful supply of food during the coming year and no one must sweep the floor because this symbolises sweeping away the family's wealth.

On the second day, after an early lunch to signify that the New Year has begun, the family visits relatives to wish them *Kung Hei Fat Choi*. They will take with them boxes of cakes and candies and married people will give red envelopes of Lucky Money to children and the unmarried.

Very few people were keen to visit us during the Chinese New Year Festival, for it is a superstition that any contact with a hospital at this time brings bad luck in the coming year. Actually, mobile patients could go home but those in halo-pelvic traction stayed in the hospital. The hospital staff tried their best to help those still hospitalised celebrate the New Year. We received *lai see* from the Matron and the kitchen staff prepared traditional dishes: a black, hair-like vegetable called fat choi; abalone with dried mushrooms; fried chicken and prawn crackers. We watched television throughout the night, nibbling melon seeds, sweets and cakes. Though the atmosphere was not as joyful as at Christmas and we were missing our families, we were content.

Becalmed

During the last stage of my stay in hospital, the pins embedded in my pelvis and skull became loose. I could not sleep at all because of the excruciating pain. Even sedatives and pain-killing tablets were of no use. I could no longer bear the agony and longed to be set free.

Doctor O'Brien had gone to England to get married and I could not possibly wait until he returned to Hong Kong to release me from my torment. Fortunately, another surgeon in the team, Doctor Hsu, took pity on me and agreed that the traction should be removed as soon as possible.

I was released from halo-pelvic traction on February 26, 1972. It was such a relief — I will never forget the day. To be rid of that awful cage felt wonderful. I relished every unrestricted, pain-free movement, but alas, only for a very short time.

While I stayed in bed for about a week, waiting for the pinholes to heal, I found myself cocooned in a plaster jacket from my neck down to my hips. Although not painful, the jacket felt heavy and cumbersome and I found doing things for myself very difficult again.

At last, in March, I was permitted to go home, though the jacket would not be removed for another six months. The weather was beginning to become warm and humid, not the best weather to be in a plaster jacket. Furthermore, our tiny apartment in Aberdeen faced to the west, so the sun shone brightly through the window. Even though I always sat under our ceiling fan, as the temperature rose and the mosquitoes began to roam, I became increasingly more sticky, itchy and uncomfortable. I could not bathe to soothe my body, either. I spent many an hour inserting a knitting needle inside the plaster cast in an attempt to relieve the irritation on my skin.

My family worked, including Choi Ha, who had left school by now, so I spent my days mostly on my own, seldom escaping the stifling confines of our tiny flat except to walk along the corridor outside.

Day after day I read Braille books and listened to the radio and television. The days were monotonous and uneventful except for the day when my mother took me to a Cantonese opera. A friend had given my father two tickets; he was not keen to go, so my mother took me.

The opera was staged in the open near the Aberdeen Tin Wan Pier. From my seat I could only vaguely see the stage but it did not matter. As long as I could hear the singers very clearly, I was happy. The performance was fascinating and I became totally engrossed until near the end of the closing scene. A thunderstorm loomed and my mother was becoming anxious.

On the way to the bus stop the heavens opened. It was impossible for me to hurry in my heavy plaster jacket, of course. As we made our way along the road in the driving rain, my mother, fearing my plaster jacket would soon be ruined, worked herself up into a panic. She protected me with her umbrella but she was soaked through to the skin by the time we boarded the bus for home.

Floating on Air

I had been to the Duchess of Kent Hospital for a check up after six weeks and after another six, it was time to go again. I packed a large bag with the things I might need if my cast needed to be changed, as this would require a few nights' stay.

My father took me to the hospital by taxi and then waited while I joined the queue for consultations.

My turn soon came and I was sent to be X-rayed. I could hardly believe my ears when the doctor announced: "Judging by your X-rays, you may be in for a special treat. Dr. O'Brien might let you out of the plaster cast after only three months instead of six."

I had to wait half an hour before I could see Dr. O'Brien, so, spilling over with excitement, I wandered off to see a few friends who were still in Ward 8. They were pleased to see me and wondered why I looked so flushed.

I could stifle the good news no longer. "Wah, the doctor in the X-ray department says that Dr. O'Brien will probably release me from my jacket today — three months early!" I blurted out so the whole ward could hear.

Sure enough, after he had seen my X-rays, Dr. O'Brien announced that my plaster cast could be removed. My relief was immense but apprehension remained — had my spine remained straight?

As a nurse led me away to the plaster room, my heart beat loudly in anticipation of what would be revealed after the removal of the cast.

I held my breath as the nurse cut away the jacket with an electric saw and hoped that she was very skilful at her job. In a few minutes, it was all over. I began to relax as she gently wiped my reeking body with an antiseptic lotion. My skin could breathe again. It felt wonderful.

I carefully got down from the bed. The sensation was quite unnerving and I felt rather unsteady on my feet. It was as though there was no gravity and I was floating on air.

I breezed into Dr. O'Brien's consulting room and braced myself for his comments as he examined my spine — suddenly he exclaimed: "It's wonderful! It's a miracle!"

This was all Dr. O'Brien could say, over and over again. As for me, I was so full of emotion that I was completely lost for any words at all.

I left the consulting room and then with great pride floated into Ward 8 to show my friends the "miracle." They were so pleased for me and the ones in halo-pelvic traction were very encouraged to see there could be a good result after so much suffering.

I sensed that my father, who would have normally moaned at having had to wait for so long, was overcome when he saw me walking towards him but he did not say much — except that I looked wonderful.

He was not so overcome that he would treat me to another taxi ride. It was the end of May and quite hot, so I did not relish the thought of trudging up such a long, steep hill to Pok Fu Lam Road where we would catch the bus home.

Although the road must have been almost a kilometre long, I managed the uphill drag with more ease than my father — though I was carrying the heavy bag!

The first thing I wanted when I got home was to give myself a good wash. This was no easy task. We had neither a shower nor bathtub, nor even an adequate-sized washbasin. So I had to do the best I could with a small bowl and three buckets of cold water.

It was heaven to be clean again. I lay resting on my bare, wooden bed, wallowing in the tingling freshness of my body and pondering over how much my life would change now that I was free of my deformity.

My mother, sister and brothers were overjoyed with the successful outcome of my treatment and they congratulated me on my new appearance.

Unfortunately, we could not share our joy with Father Edward. He was still in Vietnam and was not due back for another seven or eight months. We corresponded from time to time and now I was anxious to inform him that our prayers had been answered. I longed for his return so I could show him that I was now five inches taller and could walk swiftly with a straight back and my head held high.

I rejoiced in that I was no longer deformed. My dream had come true. I thanked God and blessed the doctors whose skill had rid me of my ugly, humped back. Now I could face life with confidence; but I would still have to contend with being called a "Blind Ghost."

4

Beyond My Depth

After being relieved of my plaster in May 1972, I rested a while before I began to think about my return to school. In June, I received a telephone call from the headmistress of the Blind School. She wanted to discuss the preparation I needed to complete before resuming my studies at the St. Francis' College in the following September. To my horror, she concluded our conversation by warning me that the headmistress of the college was considering not readmitting me. This was because of my poor marks in my last examinations and also of my age, which was now twenty-two years. This revelation came as a shock to me since I had been told that I could return after my treatment.

I desperately wanted to continue my studies at the college. The alternatives were bleak. I could not afford to hire a private tutor and it was very unlikely I would be able to find a job. I feared I would lead a boring, useless existence and be a burden on my family if I could not return to school.

Just as I was beginning to despair, once again dear Father Edward came to my rescue. He had returned from Vietnam for his summer vacation and he came to visit me. He was delighted at the success of my surgery and he envisaged a bright future for me now I could face the world no longer deformed.

I must admit that I should have been more honest with him. He had not known what a struggle it had been for me to compete with sighted students and how miserably I had failed. I had been ashamed to tell him the truth.

So term after wretched term I had said nothing to him and carried the heavy burden of failure alone.

So now, unaware of all the problems I had faced, he intervened again on my behalf and as a result of his persuasion, the headmistress agreed to allow me to resume my studies.

I was very relieved when I heard the news. At the same time, though, I felt quite sick inside, for I realised some people would continue to assume that I must be a very clever student to be attending such a famous school, especially as I was blind. In truth, I was nothing but a fraud.

I tried hard to put all these worries behind me and with the usual pang of dread, I set about spending the rest of the summer vacation attending the Blind School to repeat the boring and arduous task of transcribing the Chinese textbooks into Braille.

I remember being so proud of my straightened back when I entered Form 4 of the college on the first day of term in September 1972.

Though some of my classmates and two of the teachers had been kind enough to visit me in hospital, to my amazement, no one at school made any comment about my new appearance. Nothing had changed where my academic performance was concerned, either. The college syllabus still proved to be too difficult for me. I had not been so naive as to think that my life would drastically change for the better just because of the way I looked. Nonetheless, I had expected at least some improvement. This was not to be. Nothing had changed. I was still an impoverished, blind Tanka girl failing to compete in a sighted world.

There was one consolation that gave me hope. I continued to do well in English. My new English teacher was a tall, slim, elegant English lady who spoke several languages. Not only did she teach us many new words but she was able to explain their roots as well.

I was gratified when I achieved the best marks in the class in my oral examination. Maybe this was due to the fact that when I had been in hospital, I had ample opportunity to speak with the Australian doctor who had treated me. Unfortunately, I could not do so well in the other subjects.

Distant Horizon

Where should I put the blame for my failure to succeed? On looking back over the years I had struggled to win a place in the college, I wondered if I had made the right decision in taking on the challenge.

I had always admired the blind girls who had gained entrance to the college and had always assumed that studying with sighted students was not a difficult situation to cope with. But when it came to my turn, my illusion was shattered. I was dismayed to find that it was an immense struggle, way beyond my imagination.

The main hindrance to my studies was the unreliable supply of Braille books. This caused me to panic on many occasions. I have mentioned before that the American Women's Association provided the funds for textbooks to be transcribed into Braille.

Transcribers were hard to find, unfortunately, so Braille textbooks were always in short supply.

Rarely did a blind student attain a standard higher than Form 3. Two of my blind friends who had made it to Form 5 were experiencing the same difficulties as I was and they feared they would not pass the Public Certificate Examination at the end of their school year. Unfortunately, their fears were realised. During my last years at the college my blind friends and I were filled with despondency. It seemed that to imagine we could ever succeed in the world of the sighted was just a forlorn hope. I felt that surely our failure was not entirely our own fault. After all, how could we succeed when the school system had not given us the support we needed to cope with our studies?

Sadly, at the end of the school year I gave up my struggle. I left the St. Francis' Canossian College with an acute sense of failure and feeling thoroughly disillusioned. I would do my best to continue my studies at home.

However, I will be eternally grateful to Father Edward. He, too, had not imagined the difficulties I would encounter in a school geared for the sighted. He was still away at this time and all I could tell him on his return was that I had tried my utmost to succeed, but had failed.

In an attempt to console myself, I made myself believe that God had other plans for me. He had already mapped out my journey in this world, I told myself.

Silver Linings

My two blind friends, Magdalene and Yvonne, who were in one class above me and both about seventeen years old, shared with me the same experiences and frustrations while studying in the college.

Magdalene, a rather plump young lady, wore her dark, shiny hair in two long plaits. When she was very young she was abandoned by her parents and placed in the Honeyville Convent. Several years later, the headmistress of our Blind School asked her teachers to look for Magdalene's parents. After some time searching, they located them across the harbour in Kowloon at Cheung Sha Wan and she was happily reunited with her family.

I found I could not get really close to her to offer her any kind of help or firm friendship, as sometimes she excluded me, especially from intimate talk with our mutual friends.

Magdalene was not keen on studying at all; she would rather spend her time knitting. Luckily, she could usually just scrape through her exams.

Yvonne had a round face framed by short, dark hair. She was intelligent, liked to help others and especially enjoyed delving into their affairs. Not only was she generous to all and sundry but also she would forgive those who had wronged her. I was impressed by her big-hearted nature and wished I could be like her.

She was very sensitive to other's opinion of herself and went to great lengths to become more popular. Despite this, she had very few close friends. Though she did not always confide in me, I believed that I was one of her close friends. In fact, she came to see me a few times when I was in hospital and it seemed she felt deeply for me in my suffering.

She was a diligent student and excelled in Chinese Literature. She was also a very talented Chinese Opera singer. In recent years, she has performed on television and won awards.

Both Magdalene and Yvonne eventually married visually impaired telephone operators and both now have two children.

Unfortunately, Yvonne and Magdalene frequently quarrelled over trifles. Although I was often a witness to these upsets, I did not take sides and usually ended up as peacemaker.

Whenever we had spare time or during the school holidays the three of us went out together. Both Magdalene and Yvonne were totally blind. Because I could see a little with one eye, I was their guide.

We could not rely on our families to take us around, so we had to explore on our own. We went to Victoria Park, Kowloon Park, City Hall and ate at restaurants. I held their hands as we walked along and did my best to guide them carefully, but sometimes, in our excitement, we would charge along like horses. I wore floppy, rubber shoes that clopped as I ran. This prompted my friends to give me the nickname, *"Ma Gerk"* meaning "Horse Feet." On a visit to Victoria Harbour, our enthusiasm nearly landed us in trouble. I was not familiar with the area and as the three of us dashed along the quayside, suddenly we heard a man's voice shouting, "If you run any further you will fall into the sea. You blind girls must be careful!"

I did not realise this area of the harbour was a shelter for fishing boats, so the water would have been very deep and dirty. Aiyahh, we could have drowned! Fortunately, though a little disconcerted, my friends were not cross with me for guiding them carelessly. Instead, they were relieved at having had such a lucky escape and we ended up laughing.

Some of my blind girlfriends were interested in finding boyfriends, and Yvonne and Magdalene were no exception. I was forever guiding them over to Kowloon to the Blind Centre where they hoped to meet some suitable young men. There was a young man there who was very keen on Magdalene but she was not interested in him. However, she did not mind him taking the three of us out to dinner now and again. The poor young man was really taken advantage of.

Once Yvonne decided she would play matchmaker between her blind ex-boyfriend and Magdalene. So one Saturday during lunchtime, I guided both Magdalene and Yvonne to a rendezvous with the young man outside the Macau Ferry Pier in Central District. But how can the blind recognise the blind?

We thought that this time we would have no problem, as this young man had always insisted he was only partially blind and he could see well enough. So we waited for him to approach us. After a while, I managed to distinguish a figure wandering around nearby with my limited sight. He appeared to have his arms outstretched in front of him, trying to grope for someone with his hands. On realising that this person was probably looking for us, I called out to him.

When he approached we became alarmed. He started to feel us all over! We screamed and tried to recoil from his groping, and Yvonne was shouting: "Who are you? Who are you?"

Aiyahh! It was obvious that this young man could not see at all! The whole performance was very embarrassing. We created such a commotion that the passing public must have wondered what on earth was going on.

It turned out that he was not interested in forming a relationship with Magdalene after all because she was totally blind. He was looking for a sighted or partially-sighted young lady.

Six months later, this young man changed his mind about Magdalene. He tried to woo her with perfume and a souvenir he had brought from England, but it was too late. She was not interested in him; she had found a more suitable young man.

Man of the Sea

During my final term at school in 1973, my grandfather Chan Ying Ho died of a stroke at the age of eighty-five.

A few months before we had moved into our new home, his second wife Ah Mei had moved from her floating home to a small flat also in Aberdeen at Tin Wan and my grandfather went to live with her and their three daughters. He used to visit us every Sunday but did not mention anything of his life with his second family. However, to our dismay, some of his neighbours told us that they frequently heard quarrels coming from his flat, so we gathered that all was not well. My parents were afraid to ask questions in case he suggested that he live with us again. For a long time, he had moved from boat to boat to live with his children and their families. We all now felt that it was his duty to live with his second wife and daughters for a change, especially as she now had a flat.

Grandfather had married his second wife Ah Mei, a widow from Guangdong Province, during the last World War. She had previously married at sixteen but ten years later, her husband was killed in the war with the Japanese. She was left with a young daughter and no livelihood.

Soon, finding herself and her child destitute and near starvation she rowed her small boat along the coast to seek help from her parents. Her mother gave her three-hundred notes of Japanese army money. Ah Mei used this to buy towels and underwear. Then under cover of darkness, she rowed down to the coast of Hong Kong and sold them. With the money she bought taro, sweet potatoes and pumpkins. She then rowed them back to the mainland to feed her daughter and other family members who were desperately hungry. Grandmother's journey down to Hong Kong somehow became known to the Japanese. She was arrested together with her nephew who had helped her organise the trip and they were accused of smuggling.

At the time, my grandfather happened to be a business friend of her nephew and he went to great lengths to persuade the Japanese that they were innocent. Soon they were set free. Their lives had been saved by my grandfather; they would have surely been beheaded if they had been found guilty.

First grandmother Leung Chuen Ho was sick at the time grandfather had saved Ah Mei. This, coupled with the fact that Ah Mei and her child were in dire need of food and lodging, prompted grandfather to offer her a home on his boat in exchange for her looking after his wife.

The young woman gladly accepted the offer. She worked hard for my grandparents and within a few months she and my grandfather became more than good friends — he wanted to take her as his second wife.

To win approval for this marriage from his wife and children, grandfather explained that a fortune-teller had predicted years before that he would have to take a second wife to look after his first wife because she would become sick. By doing this, his first wife would live ten years longer. Believing his story, my grandmother did not object to her husband taking a second wife to look after her. She knew it was no good opposing him anyway because he was a very determined man.

Ah Mei, being grateful to grandfather for saving her life, was more than willing to marry him. They were married in a simple ceremony and then she spent three months carefully nursing my grandmother till she regained her health.

After Ah Mei had given birth to grandfather's daughter the following year, he found he was having difficulty in supporting his second family. There was also resentment among his sons towards his new, young wife, resulting in a great amount of continuous, unbearable family discord.

This episode drove Ah Mei and her children away from the family boat. They settled in Macau Harbour on a sampan and my grandfather persuaded some of his friends to help look after her and her children. She found general work in the harbour, mainly transporting firecrackers. To the dismay of his first wife, grandfather visited Ah Mei frequently and she bore him two more daughters.

The latter part of his life, since he had given up fishing, had been disappointing for grandfather. He had often talked of going back to fishing and enjoyed recounting fond memories of his life on the South China Sea.

He had been one of six children — two girls and four boys — born into a family of fisherfolk. Though he was the youngest son, he was the bravest and the most successful of the four. He was a skilful fisherman and more often than not, luck was on his side, too. In fact, he caught so much fish that he could support not only his own family but his brothers' families as well. His relatives and friends were in awe of his skilfulness and good fortune.

Once, he caught a huge shark. He sold it for a very high price and used the money to help his relatives who could not earn their living as successfully as he did. Soon his benevolent reputation spread far and wide. Even rich traders came to hear of his big-heartedness.

Two of these wealthy men, Wong Fat and Kur Lam, decided to help grandfather expand his fishing business by allowing him to sell his catch in their shops. This gave him a reliable outlet for his abundance of fish and his prosperity grew.

It was further good fortune for my grandfather when Kur Lam was kidnapped by gangsters. Luckily, Kur Lam managed to escape and while he was desperately searching for a hiding place he ran into my grandfather. On hearing of Kur Lam's dangerous situation, my grandfather found him a good hiding place and then later negotiated with the gang on Kur Lam's behalf. Eventually, he persuaded them to abandon their plan to hold Kur Lam for ransom. In gratitude, Kur Lam granted my grandfather many favours and forever after, considered him as his great friend.

My grandfather had endeared himself to all but his immediate family. Apparently, he had not shown much affection or concern for them. Therefore, in later years, his children could summon little affection and respect for him.

When they all lived together on the family fishing junk there were frequent quarrels among them. Moreover, there was no co-operation between them, especially where fishing was concerned. The business deteriorated and they failed to work together to devise a way to save it. Instead, they blamed each other for their bad fortune.

Ultimately, none of them wanted to take on the responsibility of pulling the business into good shape, so this resulted in the big family splitting up. By then, grandfather's three sons and four daughters had begun to have their own families, so they went elsewhere to find jobs to support them, leaving him to fish with my father.

When my grandfather gave up fishing and settled in Aberdeen Harbour in 1956, he did not live with my first grandmother. He did not get on well with her, so he lived with each of his three sons on their houseboats in turn, and grandmother lived with one of her daughters on a houseboat close by.

After a while, his second wife, Ah Mei, and three of her four daughters arrived from Macau. Her eldest daughter, the child of her first husband, went to live with relatives in China. The four settled on a houseboat next to ours but rather than join them, grandfather continued to lodge with his sons.

After my first grandmother's death from tuberculosis in the late 1950s, my grandfather found that he was the one to fill her position as servant to his sixth son and his wife. They both worked and my grandfather found himself responsible for the welfare of their small daughter and two sons during the day.

Everyday, he went to their houseboat to cook, clean and take care of the children. The neighbouring boat dwellers sympathised with him when they saw the sweat pour from his brow as he chopped wood for the cooking stove in the heat of summer. He worked from morning till evening without payment and with only salted fish and rice for his meals.

The relationship between him and the couple became a cause to concern for my parents. They had heard local gossip that he was being taken advantage of and was being badly treated by the selfish pair. Apparently, they continually scolded him because they considered that he had not done the housework properly. This was hard for an old man to bear.

Grandfather was living with us at the time and he used to return to our houseboat complaining about the couple's treatment of him. He had done his best, what else could he do he grumbled. He cried bitterly on occasions and my parents would persuade him not to work for the couple but each time he refused to help them any longer, his daughter-in-law's desperate pleas always persuaded him to change his mind.

Eventually, my sixth aunt gave birth to another daughter, quickly followed by another two sons. After her last confinement, much to my grandfather's relief, she decided to give up her job and stay home to look after her children.

I remember that when my grandfather was really old, he resembled a jolly *Fut Jeung*, meaning "Fat Buddha." He was bald, had a fat stomach and wore a complete set of false teeth. Most of the year, his chest was bare and he wore baggy shorts or pyjama trousers. He hated being too warm and refused to put on extra clothes even in the winter.

When resting, he covered himself with a cotton blanket all the year round. We thought this strange, but he said it kept him warm in the winter and cool even in the hottest weather. Fatty meat was his favourite food and he always kept a large bottle of cola at his side to drink when he was hot and bothered. It seemed that a few gulps of this fizzy beverage would cool him down and his temper, too.

During the day he meandered around the typhoon shelter or sometimes made fishing nets for pocket money. His favourite pastime at home was to listen to soap operas and detective stories on the radio.

One evening, when he was comfortably huddled under his blanket, listening to a detective story on the radio, my father suddenly decided that he wanted the radio. This started a heated argument and the air soon became blue.

Their thundering voices could be heard all around the typhoon shelter. They cursed and hurled abuse at each other till they became so enraged that the situation became a cause for concern. My father threatened to throw my grandfather overboard and my grandfather threatened to kill my father with a big knife! Mother and I did not know what to do.

Luckily, our neighbours rushed over and eventually calmed them down and incredibly, within half an hour, the hotheads were friends again and carried on as though nothing had happened. Though they soon forgot their quarrels, I was left very disturbed and did not forget them so easily. Not only did father and son have similar temperaments, but both were big boasters. They always made sure that everyone knew when they had done someone a favour. They also indulged in the same unpleasant habit — heavy smoking. Father smoked in the conventional way but grandfather used a large piece of bamboo about two to three inches in diameter and about three feet long. There was a hole in the bamboo where the tobacco and incense were inserted. Much to our disgust, the pipe was old and dirty and the odour it exuded was foul.

Although I was not very close to my grandfather, he always treated me well. I cannot remember him scolding any of his grandchildren. He always had a smiling face for us.

After his death, I regret to say, family arguments concerning him continued.

It was my mother's suggestion that my sixth aunt and uncle organise their father's funeral arrangements. When my first grandmother died, my parents had organised her funeral and they felt it was only fair for sixth aunt and uncle to do their duty this time and organise grandfather's funeral.

My aunt, for whom my grandfather had worked so hard, was not very happy with my mother's suggestion, but finally, after a great deal of argument, she reluctantly agreed to make the funeral arrangements.

It was decided that the mourning ceremony and the paying of respects to our ancestors should be held in her flat which happened to be on the fifth floor of our block. This sent her into a panic over all the organising she had to do. Now she knew how my mother had felt when no one had offered to help with my grandmother's funeral.

I attended the simple funeral ceremony at the Queen Mary Mortuary Funeral Parlour but did not go with the rest of the family to his burial in the New Territories.

Changing Course

In September 1973, three months after I had left the college, I enrolled for a six-month course at an evening school in Western District. I studied a total of seven subjects for two hours, five evenings a week. I revised at home during the day and twice a week I travelled to the Maryknoll School in Happy Valley where a sixteen-year-old girl student helped me with English composition after school. As for the other subjects, I had to rely on myself.

That year, the system of the public examinations changed. The new syllabus included many "multiple choice" exercises that I found very difficult because I had no Braille library books to help me. Before the change, students were required to answer questions by just filling in the blank spaces. This was much easier than the answers required now.

At the end of the six-month course, I took the Public Certificate Examinations. After all the hard work and the struggle to get to and from the night school on the bus for all those months, I did not do at all well. I failed all the examinations except English. I was distraught. I had tried so hard but I still could not compete in a sighted world. I knew it was time for me to stop deluding myself. It was pointless carrying on with the struggle. So feeling thoroughly dejected, I made the heartbreaking decision to give up studying altogether.

Almost immediately, I set about trying to find a job. For months I wandered everywhere, prepared to accept anything my sightlessness would allow. Alas, as I had feared, employment eluded me.

Job-hunting had turned out to be a severe test of patience and endurance as far as I was concerned. Daily, I could feel my ardour diminishing and I became increasingly more frustrated and annoyed by my bad luck.

Between times, I kept house while my parents, sister and second brother were at work, and sometimes I had a lady visitor.

During that summer a young lady, a member of a Catholic sodality, had begun to visit me regularly. One day, when we were discussing religion, she suggested that since I had the time I should prepare for my baptism. I agreed. So with her help I began to learn the catechism.

Years before, when I was twelve years old, Father Edward had broached the subject of my baptism with the headmistress of the Blind School but she had replied: "She is too lazy to pray, so she is not ready to become a Christian."

Father Edward did not show his disappointment or mention her criticism to me. In fact, some time later, when she was scolding me for some misdeed, it was the headmistress herself who told me what she had said to him. He had just encouraged me to pray more fervently and ask for God's grace.

On looking back, he had probably found it hard to believe the headmistress's criticism of me because I had always given him a good impression of my behaviour during our brief encounters at school.

So it took another twelve years for my baptism to be considered again. At the age of twenty-four, I was now diligently revising my religious studies, but before my baptism date could be fixed I had to receive religious instruction.

Father Edward had returned from Vietnam earlier in the year, so he obliged and brought my religious knowledge up to the standard required. Finally, my parish priest gave me a test and became satisfied that I was now ready to be received into the Roman Catholic Church.

The ceremony took place at St. Peter's Church, Aberdeen, during the afternoon of Sunday, December 21, 1974. Father Edward baptised me and only the parish priest and a witness were present.

Father Edward was very pleased to see me become a member of the Church at last but my family did not really understand the significance of the ceremony.

Nevertheless, my mother knew it was a special day for me so she invited Father Edward to dine with us at our flat on the Sunday evening. Since we had been friends for many years and he had done so much for me, it was a chance, in a small way, for us to show him our gratitude.

I remember my mother, sister and brother being very excited and nervous on this occasion, for this was the first time they had entertained a Westerner in their home. For some reason, which I cannot remember, my father was not present at this happy occasion.

Keeping Watch

About two months after my Baptism, while I was still plagued by bouts of frustration and depression over job-hunting, a great adventure lifted my spirits. I went to Guangzhou, formerly known as Canton, with Joanna, a friend from my Blind School days.

After she had left school, she had taken lodgings in the Blind Centre Hostel in Kowloon and I often went across the harbour to see her.

She was quite a plump young lady and very robust. Unfortunately, she was strong in her opinions, too — she was very outspoken and blunt. However, she was kind hearted and sympathetic and sometimes invited me to join in the Blind Hostel's social activities and outings; she even paid for my tickets if they were required. On this outing, though, she wanted me to be of service to her.

Two young men from the hostel were also going on the trip to Guangzhou with us and one of them, only partially blind, wanted to court Joanna. Aware of this, she was a little apprehensive and asked me to accompany her on the trip as a chaperone. At the time, I had nothing much else to do, so I promised to go along with her. The four of us took the early morning train from Kowloon to Lo Wu, near the border with China, on the third day of the Chinese New Year. When we arrived, we got off the train and walked across the border into Chinese territory. Here, we were to catch another train to Guangzhou.

It was very difficult for us to find our way around, as we had to plough through hordes of travellers who were heavily laden with New Year gifts for their relatives and friends on the mainland. It was cold and wet, so we stopped at a restaurant for a hot lunch before we joined the queue for Immigration and Customs.

Fortified and warmed by our meal, we shuffled through Customs. The formalities were complex and troublesome. Silly me had stuffed my belongings into just a flimsy plastic carrier bag and to my dismay it was wrenched apart by the rough searching of the officials. I remember cringing with embarrassment as my underwear spilt out onto the floor.

Frantically, I hunted around for another bag until someone in the queue, sympathising with my predicament, shoved a plastic bag into my hands. Then, hoping the display of my underwear had not evoked undue interest, I self-consciously stuffed my belongings inside.

On boarding the train, we pushed hard to get seats and then struggled to make ourselves comfortable among the jumble of people and baggage. Eventually, packed together like fish in a can, we were on our way.

It was already 6 p.m. when we arrived at Guangzhou, so we had to hurry to find lodgings before nightfall. Most of the inns were full, but at last, after a search becoming more frantic by the minute, we found a place with vacancies and could relax.

Two sighted young men, who were friends of one of our male companions and had come into the city from their village in Guangdong Province, helped us in the search. They were very eager to assist us and show us around. Joanna and I were in a small bedroom with camp beds and our four escorts slept in a larger room somewhere in the same building. We could not sleep at all well that night because the inn was so dirty. It smelt strongly of urine and was extremely overcrowded. We looked for another inn the next day. This time, we were lucky to find a good place to stay. Joanna and I shared a room, this time with a bathroom, and the four men shared a larger room along the corridor.

The whole time, Joanna and I were alert to her admirer's behaviour. It was vital for us to be aware of his every move. Joanna was worried that he had a dubious reputation and was not a decent young man, so we concluded that we should be on our guard. Moreover, we imagined that he was not happy with my presence, as he would find it difficult to approach or show his affection for Joanna with me sticking to her like glue.

"You must be wary of him, Joanna," I warned.

"I agree with you, Ma-lai. So don't leave me alone. His bold behaviour frightens me."

"Don't be scared," I replied. "I will always be at your side. I shall keep my eye on him. He will not dare do anything to hurt you. We must pray for God's protection. I'm sure He won't let us fall into a trap."

After hearing these words, she felt less afraid.

Each night, the two of us were very conscientious in looking after ourselves. Few doors had locks in China, but God was on our side — we found one on our door!

During the next couple of days we were on our guard. Much to our surprise, the young man did not attempt to accost either of us. Instead, he was friendly and kind. He took us around the scenic spots in Guangzhou and twice treated us to meals.

Normally, we kept to an agreement to share the cost of food among the six of us, but this young man was very generous; believing we were short of money, he insisted on paying. On realising that he was not so bad after all, we relaxed and enjoyed his company. What a ridiculous joke!

Under Weigh

While I was becoming more and more depressed over my unsuccessful attempts at securing a job for myself, a hopeful announcement from the Society for the Blind came to my attention. The Society was to hold a telephone operator's training course and those who wanted to apply were required to fill in an application form. I sent in an application and after two weeks I was informed that I could take the three written entrance examinations on a specified day. I waited eagerly for that day to dawn.

Finally, after what seemed like ages, the big day arrived. On that morning I woke up very early, bathed and after donning my prettiest dress I carefully combed my hair, which had been permed the day before especially for the occasion. Then, confident that I looked my best, I set off for the bus stop.

The examinations were held at the premises of the Society for the Blind. First, I sat for a General Knowledge test in English with about twenty other applicants. It was not difficult. Then came the Chinese Language test. It was not too daunting and I felt that I had answered the questions correctly.

After lunch provided by the Society, we had a short rest before we took the last test — General Knowledge in Chinese. I tried my best, but found it difficult compared to the previous tests.

Even though I could not answer all the questions, I felt quite confident that the ones I had answered I had answered correctly.

Before I left for home, I asked some of the other applicants, girls who I had known at the Blind School, for their opinion of the tests. They said they had also found the final test the most difficult, an admission that put my mind at rest a little. Some girls were not sure they had done well enough to obtain a place on the course but others were quite confident. We all knew of course, even if we had all done well, that a number of us would end up being disappointed, as places on the course were limited.

About a month later, I was interviewed by the instruction supervisors, the mobility teacher — who taught the blind to move around in strange surroundings, the telephone course teacher, the English teacher and the psychologist.

I had no difficulty in finding my way around, and I could answer all the questions in fluent English. I felt that my other two interviews had gone well, too, so there was no question in my mind that I would qualify for the course.

Soon the names of the successful applicants were announced and I learned that my name was not among them. I was aghast. I could not believe that I had failed.

I wondered why some of the candidates had passed the tests, for they had not even completed their secondary schooling to the public examination level as I had.

I was very upset and angry with what I considered to be unfair judgment of me, so I went to see the person in charge of the Society for the Blind, an English pastor. Still, I could not find out why I had failed. I was so bewildered.

I began to think that prejudice had reared its ugly head once again. Although I no longer had a humped back, my stature was very small and my cataracts made my eyes look very unpleasant. I learned later that Father Edward had been told the reason I was not accepted for the course. Apparently, because I was not completely blind, my sense of touch would be impaired. That meant I would not make an accurate telephone operator. I was disappointed, it was true, but I had to admit that I did not really want to be a telephone operator. At that time, it was considered a prize job for the blind because there was only the remotest chance a blind person could find satisfactory employment elsewhere. In other words, there was not much choice. Bearing this in mind, I felt that I should do my utmost to get accepted for the course.

Several months later, with the assistance of a social worker, I found employment in a factory in Quarry Bay on Hong Kong Island. The factory manufactured doll's garments for export. There were more than fifty staff working in the factory but it was not large compared with the other factories in the area.

My home in Aberdeen was a long way from Shau Kei Wan. So to shorten the travelling distance, I took lodgings at my friend Agnes's home. It was located in an area familiar to me, almost next door to the Blind School in St. Francis Street, Wan Chai. Agnes lived in an old, typically Chinese building that had six floors and no lift. Everyday, after work, I struggled up the very steep St. Francis Street from the bus stop and then climbed several flights of steep stairs to her small room on the fourth floor. This was exhausting and I always arrived at her door hot and gasping for breath.

The room was part of a large flat that was divided into four rooms by thin wooden partitions. The flat was owned by a married couple with no children. They lived in one room, and the other two were let to three families.

Agnes, her friend Rose and I shared the very small room. Agnes slept on the top bunk of a bunk bed and Rose and I shared the bottom bunk. Although the room was rather cramped and noises could be heard through the thin walls, we managed to live quite comfortably.

Agnes was a blind, middle-aged lady who had remained single. We had met in the Blind School where she had taught me Braille. She was now employed as a telephone operator. She was easy-going and moved very slowly, just like a snail. I could not bear the slow way she did her housework but when I tried to help her tidy up, I felt she did not entirely trust me. I was sure she thought that I might steal from her or deceive her in some way. Apparently, in the past, a partially blind girl like me had deceived her. I did not know this at the time, so I wondered why she seemed not to trust me.

All who knew Agnes were impressed by her friendliness and the hospitality she offered at her humble home. My stay with her was certainly very pleasant.

I had also met Rose, our other roommate, years ago at the Blind School. A fair-skinned, well-built girl with short, dark hair, she was about two years younger and still studying at the St. Francis' Canossian College nearby.

In contrast to Agnes, she acted on impulse and would do things very quickly, without hesitating for a moment. She was also very quick thinking, which helped a great deal in her studies. She was not very successful at making anything with her hands, though, mainly because she lacked co-ordination. I remember one thing she did well: selecting and cooking Chinese herbs to make remedies for headaches and other minor health problems that occurred from time to time.

Rose was blessed with some fine attributes. She was sensible, extremely polite and treated her friends well. On the other hand, sometimes she could be sarcastic out of envy and rather cynical. It was Rose who once remarked that sighted students helped us with our studies at the college only because they pitied us.

Despite being totally blind, Rose loved going to the movies. When Agnes realised I was guiding Rose to the cinema, she wanted to come, too. I used to enjoy taking them both but it was not always easy. We used to go in the evening when it was dark and I could not see either so we used to stumble and fall and giggle on our way, praying we would arrive there safely.

One evening I remember the ticket sales girl laughing and asking, "What is the point of you blind girls coming to watch a film?"

I replied with the question: "Why not?"

After all, we were not deaf as well — we could understand the whole story by just listening to the dialogue.

I remember taking Rose to her home in Sheung Shui in the New Territories on quite a few occasions. The very first time I met her parents, I was impressed by their loving care for her. They loved her so dearly that I believe she was rather spoiled.

We experienced some good times together, Rose and I, but because of our different interests and eventual living locations, our friendship did not endure.

I used to wake up at 7 a.m., and leave for the factory at about 7:30 a.m. I would then take a bus or tram to Shau Kei Wan, a journey that caused no problem for me as I usually caught the correct tram or bus because most of them went to my destination.

I could easily recognise where I had to alight going to work but coming home was a different matter. While waiting at the bus stop near the factory, I had to find someone to tell me the number of the approaching bus, so that I did not board the wrong one. Then, once on the correct bus, I had to make sure I alighted at the bus stop near St. Francis Street.

So often, having missed this bus stop, I found myself walking a long way back to where I lived. It was very difficult for me to negotiate such a long, busy route and then have to suffer the drag up the hill to my lodgings. On occasions such as these, I became very frustrated and cursed my blindness.

Nevertheless, six days a week, I found my way to and from the factory, mostly without too much incident.

My job was to snap together pairs of metal fasteners on the dolls' clothes that were to be packaged into sets. It was a most difficult task for me to do, as I found I could not snap the fasteners together successfully with my fingers. I resorted to using my teeth to bite them shut. This, of course, was not hygienic at all and it did not do my teeth any good, either. It was not surprising that before long, I received a complaint about my method of working and I was transferred to another type of work — folding the clothes for packaging.

Soon it came to light that none of the other employees who were assigned to my first job could join the fasteners with their fingers, either. The supervisors now understood why I had such a problem. They could not say that I was incompetent or say anything else to hurt my feelings.

Storm Brewing

I had only been working for about two months when I noticed numbness in my toes. Gradually, it spread to my feet. A few weeks later, I began to lose control over my legs from my knees downwards and I walked as though I was drunk. Sometimes, I fell to the ground when my legs collapsed under me and I was so worried I might fall in front of traffic when I crossed the roads.

I could not understand what was robbing my legs of their sensation and strength, and panic began to take hold of me. Soon, I could hardly walk and it was impossible for me to go to the factory and negotiate the stairs to my lodgings. So in the space of a few days, I resigned from my job, said goodbye to my roommates and took a taxi to my home in Aberdeen, lamenting that once again my health had caused another setback in my life. I had grown accustomed to a life assailed by disappointments but I did not envisage that my working days were over, even though I sensed there was something seriously wrong with me.

I was terribly upset that my one and only job had been so brief, but I was grateful that I had benefited from the experience. Being out in society had helped widen my experience of life and I had found working with a large group of people from different living environments fascinating. I studied their behaviour and characteristics carefully and learned to evaluate them well.

Being handicapped, it is always important for me to observe people attentively so that I can form a careful judgment of their characters and assess their attitude towards me.

Beached

After resting at home for a while, my condition showed no sign of improvement, so I decided to seek acupuncture treatment in the Western District. This was applied by a small, middle-aged lady who spoke Cantonese with a Mandarin accent. As I ascended to her flat in the lift, it was with immense fear that I contemplated the next few hours.

I told her my problem and she concluded I was suffering from a disorder of my nerves. She said acupuncture would stimulate these nerves and improve my condition. After she disclosed her fee, which was not too exorbitant, I summoned all my courage and surrendered my body to her needles.

At each session, I lay face down on a small bed, bracing myself while she inserted her needles into various locations on my back. It seemed like ages before the needles were removed but I think it must have been well within half an hour.

I endured session after session in the hope of some improvement, but the acupuncture did not help my weakened legs. Instead, after about five or six treatments, my lower body began to feel as though it was on fire inside and the numbness in my legs grew more intense.

I used to take a taxi to and from the clinic on my own. Each time I got out I would tense with fear as I tried to walk. I knew I was likely to fall onto the pavement and would have to suffer embarrassment when passers-by helped me up onto my feet. Some even accused me of being drunk!

Deep down, I knew I was gradually becoming paralysed. I also knew that it was no good discussing my dilemma with my family. They did not understand that something very serious was happening to me and they would have had no idea of what I should do anyway. So it was up to me to seek medical help on my own.

It was now April 1976 and I had been going to the Duchess of Kent Hospital Outpatients Department for yearly checkups since the straightening of my spine in 1971. I therefore made an urgent appointment. After an examination I was admitted to the hospital — the third time in my twenty-six years.

I underwent two weeks of examinations and then I was discharged. I went home in a cloud of gloom, still not knowing what was wrong with me. I had to wait for the outcome of the doctors' conference concerning my case, which was scheduled to take place after the Easter holiday.

While I was waiting, I experienced something even more disconcerting than the numbness. I became convinced that the sensation in my lower limbs was diminishing. Day by day my worries grew more intolerable until desperation engulfed me and I could keep my fears to myself no longer. I was trapped in a nightmare and there was only one person who would understand, comfort me and hopefully suggest a way out.

I do not know how I managed the journey in my distressed and unsteady state but I went to see Father Edward. At that time, he was staying in a house in Robinson Road, about a fifteen-minute taxi ride away from my home.

I could not prevent the tears falling down my face and I was hardly coherent through my sobs as I told him of the worsening numbness in my limbs. I could still walk, but not very well and when he saw how unsteady I was on my feet, he was alarmed and terribly upset.

Neither of us could understand why the doctors had not diagnosed the cause of my illness after the extensive preliminary examinations they had given me. He understood the unbearable anxiety I was going through and the very best he could do to comfort me and help alleviate my fear was to pray for me. "Only God can give us the strength to deal with illness," he explained in his soft, reassuring voice.

To my horror, two weeks later, the numbness escalated, so much so that I panicked and telephoned the hospital. Immediately, I was readmitted.

5

Whirlpool

The doctors still could not discover what was wrong with me. At first they thought the cause of the numbness might be a vertebra putting pressure on my nerves.

In May, my spine was injected with a radio-opaque fluid and then X-rayed.

Later, a young trainee doctor drew a sample of cerebro-spinal fluid from my spine with a long syringe to test for neurological damage and disease. I remember scolding him, for not only was the procedure very painful but I was convinced he was taking the sample from the wrong place.

A month passed. Then I underwent an operation called a decompression, performed by Dr. Yau who had been a surgeon on the team which had straightened my spine in 1971. During this, the fragments of bone, which were thought to be trapping my nerves, were removed.

After this operation, to my consternation, I could feel no sensation in my lower body at all and I could no longer pass urine easily. One of the nurses, a very kind nun, Sister Joan, came to my rescue and helped me put pressure on my abdomen to force out the urine. Happily, ten days later, most of the sensation in the area returned and I was able to pass urine normally again. However, the numbness remained.

I was transferred to Ward 2 and after six months, despite all the treatment and regular physiotherapy, there was no improvement. Panic gripped me; numbness slowly crept up my legs to my lower body.

Every week, when the day came for my doctor, Dr. Hsu, to visit me on his ward rounds, I awoke so sick with fear anticipating what he might report that I could not eat my lunch. Dr. Hsu became more and more disappointed but said nothing.

In January 1977, after I was told that a mass on my spine had shown up on an X-ray, Dr. Hsu informed me: "You are going to be chopped up!" He meant, of course, that I was to have an operation on my spine.

After the operation, Dr. Hsu came to see me in the Intensive Care ward and asked: "How are you feeling now, Ma-lai?" I felt very poorly but I forced a smile and replied, "I am afraid the coffin lid is gradually closing above me."

"Don't worry Ma-lai. You are not going to die yet," he laughed.

The doctors told me that after a couple of months my condition would improve and I would be able to walk again.

A nurse told me later that a benign tumour had been discovered and it could not be removed because veins and nerves ran through it. Then when a physiotherapist told me that my paralysis was caused by a shock to my spine during surgery, I did not know who to believe and to this day I still do not know what caused my back problems — no doctor told me or my parents. I wondered if the doctors, nurse and physiotherapist thought they were being kind by trying to protect me from the truth.

I waited and waited but to my deep dismay, the only thing that happened was that the numbness increased. So much so that the sensation in my lower body up to my navel disappeared completely and I was confined to a wheelchair.

I felt the whole world was against me. I even imagined there was a change in the attitude of some of the staff towards me because I was becoming more troublesome to them the less I was able to do things for myself. Worst of all, I felt that my wardmates shied away from me. This compounded my loneliness and misery. I did not think that maybe they were embarrassed by my misfortune and could not find the words to comfort me.

I sank into loneliness and despair. It seemed that only Sister Joan was willing to help me and I clung to her tender words as she tried hard to comfort me.

Chinese New Year was about a week after the operation and Father Edward came to see me on New Year's Day.

He gave me a red envelope containing HK$100 Lucky Money, the largest amount I had ever received, but alas, I was in the lowest spirits of my life. At first, I thought God had played a joke on me or perhaps it was all a bad dream, but finally, I had to face up to reality — my paralysis was permanent. I was filled with terror.

Now that I had become severely handicapped, I anticipated alienation to an even greater extent from everyone, including my family now that I would be more of a burden on them. My heart was heavy and I did not know what to do or where to turn for consolation.

After my surgery in 1971, Father Edward had been delighted to see my new appearance. He had touched my straightened back and exclaimed, "What a new look! So smart and pretty." Then he shook hands with me heartily.

After this great relief and happiness, was it now my destiny to lose something so precious?

One morning, the hospital social worker appeared at my bedside and said the doctors had agreed I could go home.

I had feared I would be in hospital forever, so the thought of going home filled me with relief. This was quickly followed by apprehension. How could I go home? Our flat was far too small to accommodate me in a wheelchair. Furthermore, my family would have difficulty in coping with the demanding task of caring for me. None of them could stay at home with me — they all needed to go out to work; but all was not lost.

A few days later, the social worker told me that my family would be allocated another flat and said they should start looking for one of suitable size and convenient location immediately. This they began to do with the assistance of our faithful friend, Father Edward.

Now, I looked forward to being home again. I could hardly wait for the day and my spirits soared. Then, my luck changed once more.

A pressure sore was beginning to appear on my left buttock and it would require months of treatment. My going home was postponed indefinitely.

It was now May 1977, and for approximately the next eight years the Duchess of Kent Children's Hospital was to replace my home.

Ploughing the Deep

Nineteen seventy-eight was the most terrible year of my life. Soon after I became paralysed, pressure sores began to appear on my skin. These are caused by the pressure of continuous contact on the skin, beginning as a painful red patch. If not treated, they can develop into open, ulcer-like sores which can become infected and take months to heal. In my case, due to my paraplegia, I could not feel the sores developing in my lower regions, so I had to rely on the medical staff to spot them.

The first one that appeared was the one on my left buttock — the one that had prevented me from going home. This was noticed at the end of May and by September, I had developed a raging fever as the sore grew deeper.

After the infected tissue had been removed from the sore, my doctor, Dr. Hsu, an orthopaedic surgeon, feared that he could not repair the very deep sore himself, so he asked another surgeon, Dr. Leung, to close it. Tissue was removed from my thigh to fill the cavity and during the closure a small tube was inserted to drain it. The tube was removed after two weeks and the small hole it left soon healed.

By the end of the year another pressure sore had appeared, this time on my right hip. In January 1978, Dr. Leung performed the closure but after a while, it reappeared. Thereafter, nothing was done to treat it except to clean and dress it daily. The sore was a nuisance, to say the least, but something even more disconcerting was bothering me.

In April of that year, I had felt pain in my upper back and had complained about my discomfort to the nurses but they had taken no heed. As time went on, the pain became so severe that I could not sleep nor eat.

At the beginning of May, I mentioned my pain to the physiotherapist. She soon discovered that I could not carry out certain movements without pain. So she discussed my problem with the doctors who prescribed some strong medication to relieve the pain, but it did not give me much relief.

I was X-rayed to find out what was causing the pain. It was discovered there was an infection in my back that affected my spinal cord. The doctors decided to perform spinal surgery on me as soon as possible. Although I had experienced many operations before, this time I was really scared.

On the ninth of May, when I was taken to the operating theatre, I cried bitterly. I had a terrible feeling of foreboding.

My fears materialised.

The surgeons had made a hole in the side of my back to drain blood from the surgery and now it appeared that urine was seeping through as well. The problem was discovered by a very efficient nurse in the Intensive Care Unit.

My doctor was informed immediately and within minutes, I was given an X-ray. The X-ray confirmed there were two small holes in my ureter.

Almost immediately, I was sent to Queen Mary Hospital to be examined by another medical team. Surprisingly, they could not find any sign that my ureter was damaged. So I was sent back to the Duchess of Kent Hospital. It was not long before I developed a very high fever. So once again, I was admitted to the Queen Mary Hospital.

I was being shuttled between hospitals like a football being kicked here and there. I was thoroughly disillusioned by the treatment meted out to me and becoming more and more despondent.

While I was in this deep depression, my good friend Father Edward came to visit me. Now, seven years after the straightening of my spine, he looked at my tear-blotched face and then down at my paralysed limbs and said: "Maybe I was wrong in advising you to see a specialist about your curved spine. If I ever imagined that this might be the result, I would not have suggested it. Do you regret the decision you made?"

"No, I definitely have no regrets," I replied emphatically. "I could not miss the chance to change my fate — the chance I had always dreamed of. I was proud of my straightened back. If I am suffering the consequences, it's not your fault. It was my decision and you should not blame yourself."

He sighed, and then patting my hand he said: "Well, you are a brave girl to endure so much suffering. I am amazed at your courage."

Stemming the Torrent

My mother did not stop caring for me. She visited me regularly, no matter what kind of weather prevailed. She usually came on her own on Sunday afternoons.

Naturally, I was depressed at this time, so I looked forward to her visits and the comfort she brought me. She travelled quite a long way on the bus, always carrying with her a flask of hot soup, cooked food, fruit and my usual daily needs, such as toilet paper. She would stay for an hour or more and do what she could to cheer me up and make me more comfortable.

My brothers and sister came to see me from time to time but I sensed they found my plight not only depressing but also very tiresome. They held out no hope for me. My mother, however, had not lost hope of seeing my recovery.

Now that I was in another serious condition with a damaged ureter, my mother could not just stand by and do nothing. If earthly beings could not save me, maybe the spirits could, she told me. She rushed all over Hong Kong visiting temples. In each holy place, she would lay out offerings and burn joss sticks for the deities and beg for their mercy and guidance.

In order to receive an answer to a petition from a god, a worshipper kneels before an altar in prayer, holding with both hands a beaker of 100 numbered bamboo sticks. While in bowing motion, this is shaken up and down until one of the sticks falls to the ground. The number on the stick corresponds with a note on a rack. The worshipper must then collect the note and give it to the resident soothsayer. On being told the nature of the petition, for a small fee, the soothsayer will interpret the message from the deity the worshipper has petitioned. This method of consulting the gods that my mother used is called *chim*.

In my mother's case, a soothsayer interpreted the message as a spell that would cure my afflictions. She wrote it down and gave it to my mother, rather as a doctor gives a prescription.

Mother took the spell home, burnt it, mixed it the ashes with water, and brought the awful concoction to the hospital for me to drink. Though I was doubtful of the effects of this "medicine," I had to carry out her wishes because I knew she had put her trust in the gods and she was really doing what she thought was the best for me.

The only other significant message interpreted by another of these soothsayers was: "Ma-lai has incurred the wrath of the gods, for she came into this world at the wrong minute, during the wrong hour and on the wrong day."

Of course, this message did not help either of us. In spite of swallowing the spell, my condition did not show any signs of improvement. Day by day, I was becoming weaker and my mother could not bear looking at my sallow and gaunt appearance any longer. In desperation, she decided there was one last thing she could do — take the advice of my fifth aunt and seek counsel from the spirits of my deceased brothers and sisters.

For a long time my aunt had been urging my mother to consult a medium who lived in Macau. This medium had acquired a big following.

My aunt was a regular visitor to Macau as she still maintained a small home there. She had sought counsel from the dead through this medium many times and had great confidence in her powers. Now, at last, she had persuaded my mother to consult the woman.

Only my aunt knew the whereabouts of the medium's house and only she could understand her dialect. So she agreed to accompany my mother, and together with my sister Choi Ha, they took the ferry to Macau.

It looked a very ordinary house but inside there was a candlelit room that resembled a temple. In a thick fog of burning joss sticks and incense, there was a long table laden with religious images and a few offerings of fruit.

The medium, a small, rather ancient lady, greeted her clients and introduced them to her equally ancient husband who was her assistant.

My mother, believing she had exhausted all other possibilities desperately wanted to believe in the medium's powers. "Please help me," she implored the old lady while my aunt interpreted. "Many of my children have died. Please can you contact their spirits? Perhaps they can tell me why my family has such terrible problems."

"Madam Leung," said the medium, "how many of your children have left this world, and can you remember their dates of birth?"

Mother could not recall the dates but she had a piece of red cloth in her handbag on which were recorded the dates of birth of two girls and three boys.

The medium was satisfied with this information and for an initial small payment she agreed to reach into the world of the dead to summon their spirits.

While my mother, aunt and sister sat nervously in front of the table, the medium closed her eyes and fell into a trance.

Soon it seemed that a spirit had entered the old lady. It began to speak Cantonese in a distant, quavering voice, gradually becoming stronger in volume. "*Amah!*" meaning Mama, the voice wailed, "I have ascended from the underworld where I, my two brothers and two sisters are suffering greatly. We died at sea and the sea will not relinquish us. Our feet are still dangling in the water. We are cold, wet and hungry, but we have neither clothes to wear, nor food to sustain us. Please, we beg you, save us from this torment!"

The spirit went on to talk about certain events that had happened in our family's past and my mother was convinced that she was hearing the voice of one of her sons who had died in infancy.

This was truly an emotional experience, and both my mother and Choi Ha could no longer contain their feelings. As tears rolled down their cheeks my mother choked: "Have any of you dead children been playing pranks on your earth-bound family? Your poor sister Ma-lai has been living a life of torment. What can we do to help her escape the serious illnesses which have stalked her for so long?"

"Ma-lai's destiny was preordained in her previous life," the spirit replied. "Nothing can change it, but do not despair. There will be many kind hearts along the way to help her."

There was a pause. Then the spirit reassured her: "Ma-lai will recover from her present illness. It is only temporary. There is no need to seek further counsel regarding her blindness and paralysis because it is decreed that she will never be cured. Nevertheless, you must continue to pray to the gods and appease us Hungry Ghosts, for this will ease her suffering."

Of course, mother was bitterly disappointed by the prediction that my blindness and paralysis would remain with me. However, she was overwhelmed with relief that I would not die from the illness, which had driven her to undertake this desperate mission.

Mother had another big worry on her mind, which to a Chinese parent is a major catastrophe. So she took this opportunity to ask the spirit: "Please can you tell me why your brother Chan Lai Yan has not yet married? He is already almost forty years old and I am losing hope that he will ever find a wife."

At this, the voice became louder and began to scold my mother: "For a long time you refused to heed my aunt when she recommended this medium because you did not believe she had the powers to evoke the spirits of the dead. Therefore, we played a prank on our living brother by not giving him an opportunity to marry. Now that you have come, we will not be angry with you anymore. If you grant our requests, your wish for Chan Lai Yan to marry will soon be fulfilled."

Mother was heartened by this and asked: "What is it that you require of me?"

"To remind you to pay homage to us and keep our memory, place images of us in your ancestral altar and you must send us spouses because we all desire to marry."

After mother had promised to meet these demands, the spirit's voice became softer as it addressed my sister: "Choi Ha, you must be a good daughter." Then as the voice faded away: "Please Choi Ha, take good care of our mother."

My poor mother was thoroughly shaken by all this. She believed the reason her children had not been able to enter heaven was due to her neglect. She had failed, mainly because of her toilsome and impoverished lifestyle, to perform the ceremonies to ensure their contentment in the afterlife.

It is believed that if ancestors are not revered in the proper way their souls will wander as Hungry Ghosts and bestow evil upon their living kindred. So if our family wanted no more pranks played on them, my mother must appease the lost souls of her offspring.

My mother realised that it is impossible to live in happiness in the world of the spirits without the articles of necessity and luxury that earthly beings require for comfort and happiness. The medium therefore, recommended the ritual in which paper replicas of these articles would be burned. The items would pass through the smoke into the spirit world. This would cost HK$1,000, a very large sum of money at that time, especially for my mother.

In order to establish an auspicious day for the ceremony, the medium consulted an almanac called Tung Sing. By coincidence, according to the birth dates of the dead children, the most auspicious day would be exactly a week later. The medium would supply everything. All mother was required to do was to pay the fee and bring some clothes belonging to my brother Chan Lai Yan and me.

The following week my aunt and my sister accompanied my mother to the ceremony. This was conducted in the same darkened room. This time the table was laden with an array of traditional funeral offerings: roast pork, steamed chicken, roast duck, a roast goose, a bowl of rice and a selection of fruit.

After greetings were exchanged, the medium circled the table followed by the three in procession. She was holding the clothes she had required —

mine and my second brother's — in one hand and a live cock by the feet in the other, swinging them around above her head through clouds of incense. The old lady chanted and the three following behind muttered incantations.

At last, the medium's husband beckoned them all to join him at the main door to witness the burning of the offerings.

Just outside on the pavement stood a large tin box. In this he burnt a set of brightly coloured-paper replicas for each of the five children.

Each set contained a Fairy Bridge of Gold and Silver to enable the soul to cross safely over the Inevitable River, which is full of rapids, whirlpools and snakes. A paper house, furniture, household goods and a complete wardrobe of garments also went up in smoke, together with the most important of all, imitation paper money and as the spirit had requested spouses, three paper girl dolls and two paper boy dolls were also reduced to ashes.

The three left with one last prayer, recited by my aunt, imploring the spirits of the children to forevermore leave our family in peace.

This story was related to me by Choi Ha, who was twenty-three years old when she attended the seance. Mother has always been very reluctant to talk about the experience; she just makes inarticulate mumblings whenever the subject is broached.

My poor mother has remained very disgruntled over the affair, for in spite of her expensive offerings I was not fully cured. Though I had escaped death, she had expected more.

My brother did in fact find a wife six months after the seance. Later, when a grandson arrived, my mother attributed this good fortune to the appeasement of her dead children. Nevertheless, to this day, she is firmly convinced that the medium was a charlatan and that she was cheated out of her hard-earned money.

While these dramatic events were taking place, I waited in Queen Mary Hospital while the doctors tried to diagnose my illness. I had to suffer another I.V.P. — intravenous pyelography — injection, which caused me far more discomfort than the last one. Some male patients, who had also received the injection, could not bear the pain and burning sensation it gave them. They complained loudly to the nurses who replied, " You silly fools! You are all such big men, yet you cannot tolerate a little pain!"

Finally, after more tests, the exact location of the holes was determined and the specialist decided I should have surgery to repair my ureter as soon as possible.

As it happened, I had to wait a long time for the operation because the surgeon was so busy. Meanwhile, a tube was inserted into a hole in my back to drain the urine. On one occasion, the tube came out of the hole. Then, because my urine could not drain away, I developed a high fever and my health deteriorated yet again.

Eventually, on the afternoon of July 29, 1978, while I was being prepared yet again for the operation, I was assured that this time it would go ahead.

I remember my heart thumping loudly as a haze of moving, masked faces loomed above me. However, the theatre staff relaxed me by telling jokes while the anaesthetist put me under. At last my surgery was under way.

Five hours later, I was awakened. Then, with tubes emerging from several parts of my body, I was transferred to the Intensive Care Unit.

The next day, after the doctor had checked my condition, I was admitted to the Surgical Ward. Within the next week, the tubes were removed and I began to feel much better.

In the middle of August, I returned to Ward 2 in the Duchess of Kent Children's Hospital.

When Dr. Hsu and his medical team appeared at my bedside on his ward round, he exclaimed: "Ma-lai, you look so thin!"

"It's not only me that's thin. I have a new ten-inch scar which is thin as well!" I said cheekily.

The surgery to repair the holes in my ureter had been successful, but my suffering continued. I had an infection in my ureter and I was still troubled by the original pressure sore on my right hip — it just refused to heal. Apparently, the sore had been very deep and had infected my hip bone. This underlying infection had caused the sore to gradually reappear after Dr. Leung had closed it in the previous January.

Over the months, it became steadily worse and in December, two surgeons from two different hospitals got together to try to close it again. Even this attempt was unsuccessful. So by March the following year, it was in a really serious condition. Day by day my appearance was becoming more gaunt and my fever was rising. I felt really ill. In the end, it was my doctor, Dr. Hsu himself, who eventually closed the sore and to my relief it did not recur.

The infection in my ureter took quite a long time to clear. I had to wear a catheter and a plastic bag to collect my urine, just as my neighbour in the next bed, Su Ying, had done since childhood.

The nurses continually reminded me to drink pints of water to help clear the infection and I took medication that turned my urine a pretty rose colour. This delighted one of the old *amahs* in our ward; when she noticed the beautiful colour, she wanted to collect it! She lived in a squatter hut very near the hospital and she wanted my urine to fertilise her vegetable garden.

I wondered why she was especially interested in my urine and asked, "Ah Yin, why don't you collect Su Ying's urine as well?"

"Well, your urine is an attractive colour, just like Mui Kwai Lo wine. Please drink as much fluid as you can, for your urine will be especially beneficial to my vegetables. I shall come every morning to collect it."

"Ah Yin," I laughed, "my urine will be harmful to your crops because of the medicine I am taking. Please don't use it!"

She pondered for a moment and then replied, "You are talking nonsense. Your urine looks fine to me. It will make my crops flourish. Don't be concerned — just keep on supplying me with plenty of your rose-coloured urine."

"Aiyahh!" I thought to myself. "I hope she does not sell the vegetables. It's very likely they would be poisonous."

Every morning thereafter, she crept into my ward and emptied my urine bag into a container. "What a ridiculous joke!" I used to think.

She was quite disappointed when after about a month, I stopped taking the medication and my urine returned to its normal colour.

In the Suds

I have fond memories of the many kind and considerate staff members in my ward who did their utmost to make life more pleasant and comfortable for the patients entrusted to their care. Regrettably, there were a few staff members who took great satisfaction in scolding the long-term patients in my ward. On occasions, I was one of their victims.

I suffered from recurring pressure sores which needed to be dressed a few times a day and because of this troublesome extra work, a few of the nurses would grumble and make sour faces as they tended me. This upset me and I would almost burst with frustration when I wanted to scold them but dared not.

When I was confined to bed after surgery or through serious pressures sores, I required the services of both nurses and *amahs* and it was sometimes a major task for them to make me feel comfortable. In bed, I needed four pillows to raise my paralysed feet because of my poor circulation and a pillow at either side of me to prevent pressure sores.

Each morning after breakfast, the nurses would give a bed bath to the patients who required it. I always worried over which nurse would bathe me.

If the nurse approaching me was one that would not bathe me properly, I would insist I could manage by myself if she supplied me with a towel and sufficient water. I always used to get the bed rather wet and there were usually complaints when my sheets had to be changed and the floor mopped. Nevertheless, I would rather put up with a scolding than end up not feeling clean.

I preferred the times when there were not too many patients to bed bath because two nurses would bathe me. I used to look forward to these occasions because they would share their gossip as they washed me.

I was sometimes bathed by a very talkative nurse who was nicknamed Crazy Chong by her colleagues. When she was in a good mood, she liked to sing in a high-pitched tone — so shrill that it used to jar our ears — as she worked. She did not seem to understand why her singing always attracted so many derogatory comments.

When my health improved and I was no longer bed bound, I used to bathe myself morning and evening. I used to get up around 6 a.m. to try to occupy the bathroom before Su Ying, who was still in the next bed. She took ages to bathe because of her severe disability.

After I once scalded myself by lowering myself into very hot water, which of course I was unable to feel, I devised a safer method. First, I lifted my legs over the side of the bath and rested my feet on a wooden bench that was placed in the bath lengthways. Then I would edge myself from my wheelchair seat to the rim of the bath and then lower my feet from the bench into a bowl placed directly under the taps. This way I could wash my lower body thoroughly and safely.

Usually, my bath took about an hour and I took the opportunity to wash my clothes. I used to hang them on a rattan chair outside on the verandah or on a rail attached to my locker. In the evening after dinner, I went through the whole performance again.

I hated using the hospital wheelchairs when mine was being repaired. I remember once quarrelling with a nurse who refused to let me keep one beside me during the night in case I wanted to go to the toilet. I protested very strongly and she finally relented. She did not realise how important it was for me to be mobile and independent.

An unfortunate thing happened to me when I was using an old hospital wheelchair one morning when the *amahs* were giving our ward a thorough clean. To keep out of the way, I decided to go for a "walk."

I am only a tiny person and the wheelchair was far too big for me. My feet had not been securely placed on the footrests and as I rolled down a sloping path in the hospital garden in the rickety chair my feet dragged on the tarmac. I could not feel the friction, so I paid no heed until a passing member of staff noticed my dragging feet. Aiyahh!

The attention of the man in charge of mending my wheelchair was called to my torn, bleeding feet. He immediately ensured that the repairs to my own wheelchair would be carried out without delay. Within a couple of hours, I was relieved to be back in the security of my own, snug-fitting wheelchair again.

6

Keeping on Course

The years 1979 to 1985 were the busiest and happiest years of my hospital life. Not only did my English improve significantly, but I also learned to be skilful at handicrafts. Under the tuition of the play therapists and an English lady, Jan Ford, I learned to knit soldiers, Santas and rabbits in vibrant colours. They were sold at the hospital annual bazaar to raise funds for the hospital.

Though I was able to communicate with English-speaking foreigners, I was not fluent. My pronunciation was not perfect and sometimes I could not understand when people spoke quickly or with an accent. Therefore, I seldom told anyone that I had been educated to Form 4 level in a school which taught in the English medium because they would expect me to speak English of that standard. For years no one in the hospital knew that I could speak any English. Some of the nurses had been curious and had asked me about my education, but I avoided details because I felt that they would not believe me.

In 1979, the hospital employed a play therapist whose responsibility was to teach the patients to make handicrafts and generally keep us occupied. This was Helen Spinks, an attractive English lady, with long, brown hair and a fringe. I had the impression that she was about thirty years old, but she looked a lot younger.

One morning, when I was confined to bed in a poor condition, she walked into my ward. She approached me and spoke to me in English.

Helen came from Yorkshire in northern England and she spoke quickly with a slight accent. At first I had difficulty in understanding her if she spoke too quickly, but after a few conversations I was able to understand her very well. I began to interpret for her to the other patients who had no knowledge of English.

Helen had been a Home Economics teacher in England and had come to Hong Kong with her husband who was an assistant lecturer in psychology at the University of Hong Kong.

She was a very enthusiastic therapist and did her utmost to make the lives of the patients more interesting by organising various activities such as play groups, parties and outings. She taught me how to crochet shawls, which I made for gifts or to sell at the hospital bazaar.

One day, she held a barbecue especially for me on the verandah of my ward. It was the first time in my life that I had invited my friends to my very own party. I had not even dreamed this would ever happen to me, so I was very excited. The barbecue turned out to be a big success.

When Helen became pregnant in 1980 and decided to return to England for her confinement, there was to be a replacement for her while she was away and when she returned they would share the job. Our new play therapist would be an English lady in her late thirties named Gill — pronounced "Jill."

It was a Hospital Open Day when Helen introduced me to her. For about five years, she had been a volunteer in the Occupational Therapy Department, helping to run play groups for the younger patients. She and her three children had come to live in Hong Kong in 1975 when her husband, a civil engineer, had come to work in his company's Hong Kong office.

Over the next few months we became very good friends. Through her constant attention, my English steadily improved and I learned a great deal about English customs and the English way of life. Everyday she used to spend at least an hour reading to me. She was always very surprised when I had remembered the spellings and meanings of all the words the next day.

Day after day Gill taught me, and after a while, she thought I was ready to learn a few words of slang that I would be likely to come across one day. So she read me a book called *The Outsiders*, which was about American teenagers, and then a book about gangsters in the 1930s. She was very amused when I "christened" one of the unpopular nurses in my ward "Sarcastic Broad." We still refer to her by that name today. Another book she read to me was *The Thorn Birds* and when it was serialised on television, she recorded it and took me home one Sunday afternoon to watch it.

Soon, many volunteers were found to read to me and give me a hand in other ways. These very kind expatriate women were Frances Rasmussen, an American; Felicity Wilkes, an Australian; Marlene Brune and Liza Collins, both Germans and Mrs Collins, an elderly English lady. By conversing with all these ladies I found myself being able to understand English with a variety of accents.

Among the foreigners, Gill was my best friend. I had soon given her the nickname "Heung Jiu" (because Jiu sounds like Jill), which is a type of banana literally translated as Sweet Banana. We got on so well together and held the same point of view on many matters. Very often she listened to my problems and helped me solve them.

Since my English had improved significantly, Heung Jiu began to encourage me to listen to English radio programmes on tape. First, she explained the roles in a serial called *The Archers*, which she recorded for me every week. I listened attentively and gradually I could distinguish between the voices and begin to understand most of the colloquial expressions.

Every week, Heung Jiu discussed the unfolding events in the programmes and I looked forward to listening to the next tape. Unfortunately, I cannot listen to *The Archers* any more. It is broadcast on the British Forces Network, which has reduced its power and can now only be heard in a few areas of Hong Kong.

Besides working to improve my English I helped Helen and Heung Jiu make handicrafts for the hospital's annual bazaar, held every November. Usually, I organised a group of girls to knit and sew in the Play Therapy Room. My speciality was knitting long, colourfully-striped snakes out of scraps of wool. We appreciated having an electric kettle in the Play Room to boil water to make our own noodle breakfast, and were happy to share our food while chatting and working together.

Sometimes, we were allowed to use the kitchen in the Occupational Therapy Department to prepare some of our meals. We could use the cooking utensils and crockery if we cleared up the kitchen when we had finished. The department *amah*, Ah Yung, was a cheerful, kindly lady who encouraged us handicapped patients to do some of our own cooking, even though she knew that it would probably give her extra work.

I went on a few boat trips to the outlying islands during my long stay in the hospital. The boat was a huge sailing junk called the Adventure Ship. It was run by a charitable organisation and was offered to our hospital free of charge to take patients for day trips.

Usually, staff from the Occupational Therapy Department, a few nurses and *amahs*, and a few Western women volunteers used to accompany about twelve patients on the trips. The hospital bus used to take us to the junk, which was moored in Aberdeen Harbour. A few patients were in wheelchairs and plaster casts, but with the help of the crew and the marine police we were always safely hauled aboard.

On one trip, despite using its engine rather than sail-power, I remember the junk seeming very majestic as it moved towards Lantau Island. And while sounds and the motion of this hour-long voyage stirred up memories of my early childhood, the other patients amused themselves by singing songs, playing board games and admiring the scenery as we passed by various other islands.

We disembarked at a pier on Chi Ma Wan, a southern peninsula of Lantau Island. Here, we went to the garden of a detention centre located near the beach.

Once the train of invalids had made it along the jetty, then over the beach into the garden, we settled down under the trees to enjoy our hospital-made picnic lunch.

Milling around nearby were four or five detainees. I wondered what these young men thought of us, all twisted and deformed, hobbling along or having to rely on people to push us around.

I knew there was a drug rehabilitation centre on one of the islands.

If any of them had been drug addicts, I hoped the sight of us had encouraged them to value the healthy body and freedom God had given them.

The next junk trip was also to Chi Ma Wan about a year later. On approaching the island a foul smell wafted towards us. As we sailed closer we were surprised to see that the beach near the jetty looked and smelled extremely polluted.

After we came ashore, we were approached by policemen who directed us towards a path. This led away from the beach along the side of what we suddenly realised was the high barbed-wire fence of a Vietnamese refugee camp.

We felt very uncomfortable as the refugees — men, women and children — just stood and stared at our sorry band of physically handicapped young people struggling by. They were extremely curious and probably wondering where on earth we had come from. We in turn, stared back, not believing what we were seeing, either. The poor bedraggled people, mostly dressed in T-shirts and shorts, were just standing around in the compound looking bored and dejected and some children were clinging to the fence.

We sat down on a small lawn outside the camp to have our picnic, but we could still smell the sewage that flowed onto the beach. The weather was not favourable, so as soon as we could we made our way back to the junk and set sail for Hong Kong Island.

Usually, we liked to take photographs of our adventures outside the hospital but on this occasion we found there were notices warning the public not to take photographs. For those of us who experienced the stench and the pitiful sight of those forlorn, unfortunate people behind the high wire fence, the memory will never be erased. Really, this time the junk outing was no fun.

A Motley Crew

For most of my ten years in the Duchess of Kent Children's Hospital, I occupied a bed in Ward 2, a single-storey building housing twenty-four beds. There were five long-term patients, including me, at the far end of the ward furthest away from the nurses' office. I suppose you could have called our end of the ward the "Not Much Hope Section." We could not be cured, there was no other place to go, and nothing else could be done for us except to look after our daily needs and keep our bodies and souls together.

My four companions were in a more unfortunate state than I. Su Ying was a Spina Bifida case; Mei Mei was severely brain damaged; Choi Mei Ling had a malignant tumour on her spinal cord and Lai Kit, the only boy, had a tiny brain and was almost a vegetable. There was no way their families could possibly look after these severely handicapped young people at home, and as for me, I could not go home because my family's flat was not large enough to accommodate me in my wheelchair. So we did our best to exist side by side and make what we could of our lives.

In contrast to the very noisy patients, there were four very silent patients with us in the "Hopeless Section." They were aged between about seven and seventeen and all were hydrocephalics. This condition, a collection of fluid on the brain, had severely damaged their brains and rendered them helpless. Their heads were gradually growing larger and they were slowly dying. It seemed that nothing could be done for them other than nurse them tenderly and feed them with a tube. I prayed for these poor young people; they were suffering so much. I felt that when they left this world they would surely find happiness in the next.

All at Sea

Some strange happenings occurred in Ward 2, especially between the years 1981 to 1984.

Opposite our ward in Sandy Bay Road was a mortuary, and a little further up stood the "Dead Man's Hotel." Here, rooms were rented to keep corpses indefinitely, or they were just waiting for their relatives to return from abroad to give them proper burial rites. Beyond was the huge Pok Fu Lam Christian Cemetery, which stretched up a steep hillside to Pok Fu Lam Road. Even taxi drivers sometimes refused to drive down Sandy Bay Road at night because they feared they would encounter wandering ghosts.

For months at night, it seemed to Su Ying and I that somebody was walking on the verandah outside our ward. It sounded like someone wearing callipers was dragging himself along with crutches. He "walked" every night unceasingly to and fro along the verandah from 11 p.m. to 3 a.m. Even on rainy nights he was out there walking. The sound grew louder as he dragged himself nearer to our end of the ward. Then we heard a creaking like the phantom was sitting down on the rattan chair on the verandah. Su Ying and I, terrified, used to gasp and tremble in our beds.

One of the nurses suggested that the sound could be that of a patrolling policeman doing his rounds on Sandy Bay Road. She told us not to worry. I did not believe her explanation, and continued to spend sleepless nights listening to the eerie sound and praying.

Eventually, after what seemed like months, the nocturnal wanderings suddenly ceased and Su Ying and I could relax. The ghost or policeman had probably changed his shift! What a ridiculous joke!

Another supernatural event occurred after the death of my good friend Choi Mei Ling. Since the July she died, we believed that her spirit was still occupying our ward in the form of a butterfly. Day after day, this beautiful creature would fly around and eventually settle on Choi Mei Ling's bedpan, still stored in the bathroom.

The following Christmas Eve, I was in this bathroom, opposite my bed, when I heard her voice calling: "Ma-lai?. . . Ma-lai?"

When she was alive, she would usually call out to me when I was in the bathroom at night to ask if I was all right.

I thought, this must be the night-duty nurse calling and I replied, "Nurse Jong, I'm all right. I have finished and I am coming now!"

The girls in the ward were puzzled and I heard a voice shouting, "Ma-lai, why are you talking to yourself? Have you gone crazy?"

"Wasn't that Nurse Jong who was calling me?"

"No," they replied, "No one was calling you. It must have been your imagination."

I did not believe them, so I asked Nurse Jong if she had called me. She said she had been busy attending to another patient. I believe that it must have been Choi Mei Ling's voice. I thought that she had not meant any harm — she had only been having fun with me on Christmas Eve.

From time to time I continued to hear her voice calling me, especially when I wheeled my chair down the sloping path to the table tennis area in the playground. Maybe she remembered when I tore my feet and was trying to remind me to be careful.

An *amah* in our ward believed she had actually seen Choi Mei Ling's ghost. Late one evening, this *amah* had been dozing on a sofa in the lobby at the entrance to our ward. In her dozy state, she heard the laughter of children playing near the entrance. At first, she thought they were the resident staff's children, staying up late. But when she roused herself, she saw a young lady dressed in Chinese-style pyjamas enter the lobby. She was leading a group of small children who were jumping around in excitement. At once, the *amah* recognised the young lady as being Choi Mei Ling! The *amah* was so alarmed that she ran out of the lobby without her shoes.

Very strange events connected with Choi Mei Ling also happened to my English friend, Heung Jiu, when she was working at the hospital as a play therapist. At beginning of July 1981, a few weeks before Choi Mei Ling died, Heung Jiu went home to England for a four-week holiday. The wedding of Prince Charles and Diana took place during her stay there and she thought that Su Ying, Choi Mei Ling and I would like a memento of the occasion. So at the airport, while waiting for her return flight to Hong Kong with her family, she bought three tins of biscuits with pictures of the royal couple on the lids.

When she arrived back home in Hong Kong, she opened her hand-luggage and to her dismay there were only two tins inside. When she entered our ward, after greeting Su Ying and me, she asked where Choi Mei Ling was. I broke the sad news that Choi Mei Ling had died. Heung Jiu was upset. She had just begun to teach Choi Mei Ling a few English phrases and they looked forward to their little chat everyday.

After Heung Jiu had explained about the disappearance of the gift on the flight, we all agreed that if heaven is up in the sky, then maybe Choi Mei Ling had received her souvenir after all — anyway, we hoped she had.

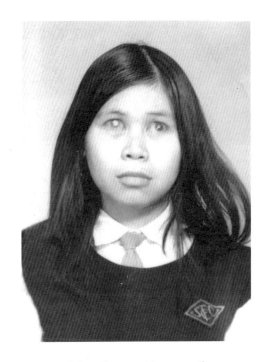

Mary Chan, age 13, as a pupil
at St. Francis' Canossian College, Wan Chai.

Mary Chan's paternal grandparents: Chan Ying Ho and his first wife Leung Cheung Ho.

Photo credit: Mr W. Gibson
A junk in Aberdeen Harbour very similar to the Chan family houseboat of the early 1960s.
The first family flat at Ap Lei Chau is in the block to the top right of the photo.

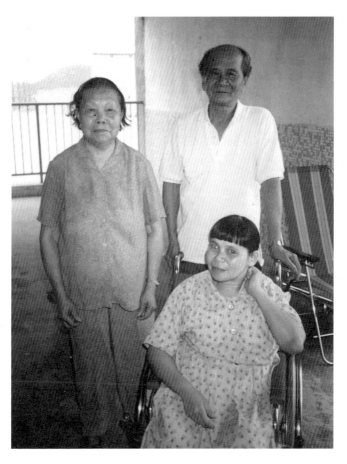

Mary and her parents in the corridor of their Ap Lei Chau flat
in the early 1980s.

Tanka woman on a sampan similar to the one Mrs Chan had in Macau
when Mary was a baby in the early 1950s.

Father Edward with Mary at the Sandy Bay promenade near the Duchess of Kent hospital in the early 1980s.

Mary with Father John (left) and Father Edward (right) at the Palace Restaurant in Wan Chai in 1992 to celebrate Mrs Chan's 80th birthday.

Mary and her good friend Heung Jiu in the 1980s.

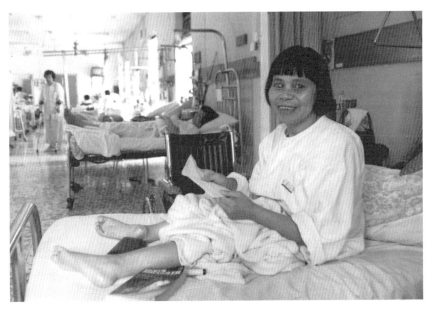

Mary in 1987, recovering from surgery at the Duchess of Kent Hospital.

Photo credit: Origin unknown

Staunton Creek, Aberdeen, in the 1950s. Mary's family boat was probably moored at the right hand side of the photo. The South China Regional Seminary, later known as The Holy Spirit Seminary, where Father Edward lived, is just visible on the right hand side. Father Edward would walk down the slope and through the boats to see Mary and her family.

Heung Jiu lived very close to the hospital and for more than a month after she had returned from England, she sensed a presence in her kitchen. She often turned round to speak to her husband or children and found there was no one there. Sometimes, she heard someone trying to open the kitchen door. Assuming it was one of her children struggling to get through the door with their hands full, she would open the door and find no one there. She made sure she always left the kitchen door wide open but she kept finding it shut.

When she mentioned the odd affair to me, I suggested that maybe it was Choi Mei Ling; after all, August is the month of the "Hungry Ghosts" when the spirits of the unappeased departed wander the earth seeking consolation. They are usually pacified by offerings of food, so that would explain why the spirit was hovering in the kitchen.

After about six weeks, the presence was no longer felt and the strange happenings ceased.

Cruising Along

During our long years enduring the hospital routine, occasionally something happened to attract our interest. Although Su Ying and I had been troublesome to the nurses and *amahs*, some of them sympathised with us because we were severely incapacitated and we were the longest resident patients in the hospital. So on some occasions when Sister was on night duty, she, together with two *amahs*, would prepare a middle-of-the-night supper for us, usually congee or chicken soup. We never complained about being awakened at 2 a.m. to eat. During the day, they sometimes provided us with special dishes, too.

We had three meals a day: breakfast at seven, lunch at eleven-thirty, dinner at four-thirty and a snack at eight in the evening. The food was quite varied but the same menu was usually served on the same day every week. It was a standing joke for the staff to ask me if I could guess what was going to be served on that day and my guess would always be right. So as far as I was concerned, any break from hospital food was very welcome.

In the late evenings during the long intervals between our treats provided by kindly members of staff, Su Ying and I usually suffered hunger pangs. The snack at eight, milk and biscuits, was not enough to sustain us throughout the night, so we used to reserve some food for the late hours.

On the days my mother had brought me hot food, rather than eat all the rice at once, I used to keep some to make rice with diced, tinned pork luncheon meat. We did not mind cold meat but we hated cold rice.

We used to surreptitiously wheel ourselves into the bathroom where the only containers were an old mop bucket and row of bedpans, and we could hardly steep our aluminium flask of rice in those! So I would fill the bath with about six inches of hot water. Then I would bend over from my wheelchair and struggle to place the flask very carefully in the water while Su Ying looked on anxiously. This did not always work, however. More often than not it would tip over and the water would seep in through the lid. The result was a soggy mess. But on the days our plan was successful, we enjoyed a tasty, though rather lukewarm snack.

One of the nurses, who also provided us with a break from hospital food, we called Lo Chui. *Lo* means "old" in Cantonese, but I thought that she was no more than forty. However, for some reason, she thought she was old and the nickname stuck. Bespectacled and with a small, neat figure, she carried out her duties in a quick and efficient manner and demonstrated a sympathetic attitude towards all the patients, especially those in a critical or hopeless condition.

When she was appointed to work in our ward, I think at first she formed an unfavourable impression of Su Ying and me. She had obviously heard other staff complaining that we were very troublesome, due to the work involved in continually changing our dressings. Later, when she got to know us better, we became close friends and she began to confide in us.

She complimented me by asking: "You are very good at speaking English. Can you teach me?"

I was surprised and flattered by her request and replied: "Really, I should learn from you, instead. I wish I could express myself as well as you in Cantonese. You have the knack of criticising unpleasant people without causing them offence."

Through this exchange of compliments we had endeared ourselves to each other and from then onwards we conversed quite often.

Several times we secretly ate hotpot in her apartment in the nurses' quarters and we contributed only a small amount of money towards the cost.

Lo Chui was also extremely kind to two little patients in our ward. One was a boy who had a huge tumour under his chin that restricted his throat. The nurses had fought to keep him alive since he was a baby by feeding him with a tube. But when he was about four years old, he choked to death on a sweet during a short visit to his home.

The other was a bright girl whose story had a happier ending. Her parents had abandoned her and she had been kept in hospital since birth rather than an orphanage because she was expected to die in infancy of a liver ailment. She was adopted by a very loving American family when she was four years old. Since then, she has been living in America and is now a thriving, beautiful and very intelligent teenager.

There was another nurse who was very friendly towards Su Ying and me. She was a pretty, young lady, gentle and diligent in her duties. She broke the monotony of our evenings one summer when she organised a barbecue for Su Ying and me on the beach near the hospital.

About five-thirty, the nurse led us in our wheelchairs towards the beach, which was only about 200 yards from the hospital. The nurse gathered rocks for the fireplace and lit the coals.

It was a warm evening and I could hear the sea gently lapping the shore. I could distinguish the lights of passing ships and hear the "pop pop" sound of the motorised sampans.

Soon the coals were glowing brightly in the darkness. We impaled fishballs, meatballs and dried cuttlefish on the end of long barbecue forks and cooked them. The food was delicious.

When we had finished eating, the nurse helped us wheel our way back along the bumpy, overgrown path towards Sandy Bay Road. I remember I could distinguish neither stars nor the moon. There were no earthly lights, either. The stillness was eerie. There was nobody around, only the three of us cautiously manoeuvring the two wheelchairs along the rough path.

Having seldom been out at night in my wheelchair before, I worried we would never find our way in the darkness. Our nurse allayed our fears and returned us to our ward safe and sound.

Although we were very excited by our evening out, it remained our secret. We did not dare tell anyone, for we feared our nurse might face a reprimand.

The play therapists had also brightened up our lives in many ways. Wannie took over from the two part-time English therapists when they left the hospital in 1985. She had a pleasant appearance and disposition and was always friendly and understanding.

On several occasions, she cooked dinner for Su Ying and me. After Wannie had prepared the meal in the kitchen in her hospital quarters, she would bring the food downstairs to the Play Therapy room on the ground floor.

Su Ying and I had to wheel ourselves as quietly as we could out of our ward so no one would notice us leaving. The *amahs* would object to Su Ying's extra consumption of food because she easily developed diarrhoea, which caused them a lot of unpleasant extra work.

I enjoyed these meals because they reminded me of the ones I used to have during my last few years at home: soup, steamed fish, flattened duck and fried chicken with vegetables. For Su Ying, they were a special treat. She had been hospitalised all her life, so she had rarely tasted real, home-style cooking.

The Moon Festival was always a happy event. Every year in Mid-Autumn the hospital provided festive food for all the wards to celebrate. But one year, our ward was the envy of the other wards when the male patients from Ward 1,which was attached to our ward, supplied the money to purchase some additional food from an outside restaurant. Then they organised a moon cake party outside the rear entrance of the hospital where there was a vast open space used as a car park.

Some patients helped to light lanterns of assorted shapes and colours, which were placed along the slope of a hill at the back of the open space. The children were holding their lanterns and the ones who were mobile were laughing and jumping everywhere. Everyone was excited and enjoying themselves, even the staff. They sat at a long table chattering among themselves — all the while admiring the beauty of the moon.

There was an abundance of festive food on the long table: pomelo (a large citrus fruit), bananas, peanuts, pork steaks, chicken wings, and of course, moon cakes. But because the food was not divided into separate portions and some patients were not able — or were too shy — to make a grab for the food, it was a free-for-all, which I thought was unfair to the weaker and timid patients who could not help themselves to much party food.

Luckily, for the patients in Wards 1 and 2 who were bedridden, helpings of the food was served to them by the staff on duty that evening.

Both patients and staff looked forward to the most exciting day of the hospital year — the bazaar, a fund-raising event held every November in the hospital gardens since 1981.

Our stall, manned by at least six stallholders, was piled high with colourful toys and useful things we patients had made. And among the items which sold like hot cakes were my knitted snakes! In fact, of all the stalls that first year, ours happened to make the most money.

I remember the exciting carnival atmosphere of the first fair particularly.

While music and announcements were provided by Commercial Radio, we mobile patients, assisted by volunteers and members of hospital staff, mingled with the crowds, milling around the stalls and attractions which skirted the garden's pathways.

There were food stalls galore, many operated by the ladies of the Consular Corp, and in one of the garden's quadrangles a beer garden where thirsty dads could relax while the rest of the family went hunting for bargains among the handicraft, white elephant, book, cake and plant stalls. The most popular stalls of all, though, were those that sold mounds of clothes and toys donated by local factories. I could not get anywhere near those particular stalls for the crowds!

Other attractions were rides for the children, side-shows, lucky draws, a marching brass band, and a wheelchair dance performed by a group of our patients. And then there was face painting organised by staff of the Occupational Therapy Department. This produced hilarious masterpieces that sent children away whooping with glee.

Among the highlights of the day, Eaon Jackson, alias Jacko the Jester, a long-time friend of the hospital, entertained the children with his magic show. This was followed by a colourful parade of children dressed in their national costumes and then a Lion Dance performed by an energetic group of young men from the Junior Police Corps.

Friends pushed Su Ying and me around the fair with great enthusiasm. But first, before we watched any of the performances or attempted to buy any of the articles on sale, we insisted we made straight for the food stalls. The barbecued chicken wings were my favourite.

My mother and sister came to this first fair and have turned up at most of the fairs since. They always stay late to look for bargains when the prices are reduced to clear the stalls. And I have attended the fair every year since I was discharged from the hospital, usually with friends who can drive me there. Each time, I make sure I spend at least half an hour in Ward 2 chatting to my long-time hospital friend, Mei Mei.

Sudden Squalls

I have mentioned briefly that there were male patients in our hospital. Small boys shared my ward, Ward 2, and the older males were in Ward 1, which was at right angles to ours. Older male patients had been admitted to our hospital since the mid-eighties. With many childhood diseases on the decline there were fewer children being admitted to the hospital, so there was room to accept older patients from overcrowded hospitals such as the Queen Mary.

There happened to be a very pleasant nurse who worked in Ward 1 and 2 named Nurse Mui. Her nickname was "Queen of Western Market." I never knew why. She was hard working and everyone liked her. She was such a diligent and obliging nurse that she was often taken advantage of and ended up doing the jobs that none of the other nurses wanted to do. She was always willing to help me when my catheter leaked and she changed my dressings with no complaint.

Being a registered nurse, she used to take charge when Sister was off duty. Since she was lenient with us patients, some of the male patients played pranks on her.

Some of these young men were quite rough. Several of them were suffering from injuries as a result of gang-related violence, such as chopper wounds. At every opportunity they would use foul language and make sexual innuendoes. They refused to dress decently and delighted in showing off their bodies to the embarrassment of the nurses. Consequently, some of the nurses avoided caring for them. Nurse Miu ignored their indecent behaviour and treated them no differently from the other patients.

Smoking was not permitted in the wards, but these young men always broke the rule. When the medical director discharged a couple of them one day for being abusive to a doctor when he caught them smoking, Nurse Miu was very upset. She had been in charge of the ward at the time and felt she had failed in her responsibility to keep good order. Some of her colleagues sympathised with her because it was difficult to control these wilful young men, but others thought it was her leniency that had contributed to the problem.

Most patients who passed through Ward 1 were decent, well-mannered young men, of course. One such was a bachelor suffering from tuberculosis who required oxygen to help him breathe. Some of the nurses were wary of nursing him because of his infectious illness, but not Nurse Miu — she gave him injections and tended to him willingly.

Regrettably, after a while she began to feel poorly and it was suspected that she had something wrong with her lungs. She was examined and it was confirmed that she had contracted tuberculosis. I felt really upset for her, for she had paid a price for being a very good nurse. Needless to say, she did not complain and was quite happy to take a rest and build up her strength. After a few months, she was back attending to us again and was just as willing as ever.

Another male patient she did not discriminate against was a poor, uneducated man in his thirties who had been transferred from Queen Mary Hospital. Both patients and staff alike were horrified when they discovered he was suffering from leprosy. Petrified of catching the disease, no one would go near him, except for Nurse Miu.

The staff complained to Matron and begged her to get rid of him. Poor Matron, she was a lovely lady who was very westernised in her ideas, but being Chinese, she understood the attitude of her staff. There was still prejudice against lepers in this part of the world, as most people did not understand the disease.

I agreed he should not have been in our hospital, for I was ignorant of the disease and believed we could catch his affliction.

In the end, with both her staff and patients protesting, Matron had no alternative but to agree to have him sent back to the Queen Mary Hospital.

As for the poor man, he adamantly refused to be sent away, and to the dismay of everyone in Wards 1 and 2, he proceeded to cause pandemonium. But his protest was of no use. The ward Sister called the police. Total alarm and confusion followed, with the paramedics and the police chasing him around the ward.

Finally, in his desperation, he produced a knife and threatened to commit suicide. But while he stood brandishing his weapon, warning that he would attack anyone who would dare to approach him, someone managed to distract him. The police pounced, and we all gasped with relief when they led the poor man away.

7

Casting Nets

In the spring of 1984, during a conversation with Heung Jiu, I mentioned that I no longer needed medical attention and if my family's flat was larger I could be discharged from hospital to live at home again.

Having seen the flat, Heung Jiu fully understood the problems that would beset me living there. She agreed the place was far too small to accommodate me and remembered she and a friend had had to carry me up two flights of stairs and then return for my wheelchair because the lift only stopped at every third floor, missing ours.

Heung Jiu, knowing that I was always rather timid in approaching anyone in authority about anything, agreed to see the social worker on my behalf to enquire if my family could be allocated a larger and more convenient flat.

To my surprise and delight, a few months later, my mother and sister were called to the social worker's office where they were given the good news that the Housing Authority had agreed the family could look for a new flat.

My mother was still worried whether she could cope with me at home. My sister and father worked and my mother, now retired, wanted to stay near my married brother Chan Lai Yan. He lived at Ap Lei Chau — an island joined by a bridge to Hong Kong Island at Aberdeen. If we lived nearby he would be able to give us his support and his wife could assist us if there were any problems during the day when he was at work.

By June, my family had been allocated a flat near my brother. My mother was so overjoyed that you would have thought she had found a pot of gold!

Before the end of July, they had moved in. Now we were waiting for the Housing Department to provide the funds for alterations to the flat to accommodate my wheelchair and I. I waited patiently for all these arrangements to be completed, anticipating it would take a long time.

Months went by before I had yet another exciting event to look forward to. One afternoon towards the end of November that year, my old friend Father Edward came to see me. We were chatting away when suddenly he asked, almost jokingly, "Mary, if you had the opportunity to go on a pilgrimage to Lourdes next year, would you like to go?"

I was quite taken aback and not sure if he was serious, but I had no hesitation in replying that I would love to go. Truthfully, I did not know what "going on a pilgrimage" really involved. Some time ago, I had heard that invalids from Hong Kong had made a pilgrimage to this famous shrine in search of a cure and I had mentioned this to Father Edward and said I wished I could go one day. Since then, unknown to me, he had submitted my name for a place on prospective pilgrimages quite a few times, but to no avail.

With me eagerly listening, Father Edward continued: "A friend of mine from England has come to work in Hong Kong and he intends to ask for donations from the big companies here to finance the sending of two handicapped people on a pilgrimage to Lourdes. I have warned him that it is not an easy task. For this is a place with little religious sentiment and the population will not be keen to contribute, especially to a Christian project. I have nevertheless asked that your name be put on the top of the list of prospective pilgrims. So keep on praying and keep your fingers crossed that the funds can be raised."

From that moment the prospect of going on a pilgrimage to a foreign land filled me with excitement. Secretly, I wondered if I dare hope for a miraculous cure for both my afflictions. Night after night, while I drowsed, I imagined what it would be like to see clearly and walk again.

If I was not worthy of a complete cure, I would really appreciate it if God would at least grant me the return of enough sensation in the relevant parts of my anatomy to enable me to know when the call of nature was imminent. Aiyahh, finding myself, usually on waking up, in a mess of faeces and urine had not only caused me extreme frustration and embarrassment, but had often brought the wrath of the ward *amahs* upon my head when they had to clean me up and change my bedding. I could pray to the Blessed Virgin at the shrine for help for my sick wardmates, too.

The next time Heung Jiu came to see me, I told her the good news I had received from Father Edward. She was delighted and proceeded to tell me as much as she knew about Lourdes.

Although one of her aunts was reputed to have been cured there decades before, she warned me that not every sick person who sought help there was restored to good health. "Nonetheless, if it is not God's will that you be cured physically, the pilgrimage will certainly be of great benefit spiritually. So we must hope and pray that the funds will be raised."

Two anxious months dragged by before Father Edward appeared at my bedside bearing discouraging news. He found it hard to say that he had heard nothing from his friend, which meant that he was not having great luck in raising the funds. My heart sank. Was the whole affair just too much for me to hope for after all?

Father Edward's friend was an Irishman named Rory. He was a member of the Order of Malta Volunteers who, as part of their charity programme, organised pilgrimages to Lourdes. He was finding fund raising in Southeast Asia was not as easy as in Britain, even though he had tried his luck in the Philippines, a predominantly Catholic country. This was the first time he had failed in his quest; he now understood what Father Edward had meant.

I discussed my disappointment with Heung Jiu and that same day, she spoke to a very distressed Father Edward on the phone and ended by assuring him she would do her best to find a way to raise the funds. She suggested she should start by asking for donations from my friends. This raised enough money to pay for my air ticket, but I would need the money for other expenses and the expenses of a travelling companion, too! "Never mind. Don't worry," advised Heung Jiu. "We will find the rest of the money from somewhere."

Unfortunately for me, in 1985, Heung Jiu's husband was being transferred by his company to Taiwan in a few week's time and she was worried she might not raise the required amount of money before she left. So she decided to tell the whole story to Gillian Petersen, a volunteer in the hospital's Fund Raising Department and a member of the Hospital Committee. Gillian and Hilary Prior, who ran the department, were very keen to help raise the rest of the money and the whole affair seemed to escalate from there. Finally, Heung Jiu left Hong Kong fully confident adequate funds would be raised and that my dream would come true.

It was thought the best way to raise donations was to get some publicity. It happened that an English student had come to Hong Kong for the summer to gain work experience as a reporter for the *South China Morning Post*, an English-language newspaper, and he was keen to report my story. His name was Martin.

He interviewed Father Edward, then came to see me. Of course, this was the first time I had been interviewed by the press. I was very nervous. To make me feel at ease, the young man proceeded to joke and teach me some English slang and soon I was enjoying a friendly chat with him.

He was a very enthusiastic young man keen to learn about Chinese culture, the language and as much as he could about our way of life. I learned, too, that he was especially fond of sampling the delicacies offered on the cooked food stalls in the streets and markets and he could already communicate quite well with the local people in colloquial slang.

A few days after the interview, the newspaper photographer arrived. I had donned my prettiest dress and a cluster of friends had helped me look my best for the occasion. Rather self-consciously, I posed for the shots sitting in my wheelchair on the verandah outside my ward.

The following Friday morning, a voice exclaimed: "Mary, you're in the newspaper!" It was Gillian Petersen who had rushed into my ward and there was a flurry of excitement as she began to read the article to me.

I must have been grinning like a Cheshire cat as I listened very attentively to her voice. The report went a bit over the top in saying that I could knit very fast; it said I could knit two or three knitted items a day! Gillian was amused by this, too. The rest of the article gave a resume of my life and the details of my intended pilgrimage. It was accompanied by a large photograph of me. Aiyahh!

Many readers were moved by my story and sent cheques ranging from tens to thousands of dollars. Among the donors were The Shanghai Sodality, St. Teresa's Church and the Catholic Woman's League. Cathay Pacific Airways kindly donated my air ticket. I was overwhelmed by such generosity. How lucky I was!

Another good thing happened as a result of the newspaper article. My long-lost former classmate, Louise Da Rosario, my faithful helper in the St.Francis' College years ago, was surprised to see my story and photograph in the newspaper. As soon as she was able, she came to see me and we had a long chat about old times and her career as a journalist. She had contacted two of our mutual school friends and they had come to see me a few days earlier. All were surprised to hear about the traumatic events I had experienced since I had left the college and wished me well on my great adventure.

It took three weeks for Father Edward to find the ideal person to be my companion. I was so pleased to hear that it was Sister Justine, a Missionary Sister, who I already knew. As a member of the Missionary Sisters of St. Columban, she had worked in the orthopaedic unit and operating theatre of the Duchess of Kent Children's Hospital from 1964, when it was known as the Sandy Bay Convalescent Home, until the Sisters ceased to run it in 1977.

Sister Justine, a bespectacled, gracious, middle-aged Irish lady, had been held in high regard by both patients and ward staff. She loved children and while off duty she enjoyed playing with the patients, especially the ones who were the most feeble.

When the hospital was extended in 1971, the year I was admitted for the straightening of my spine, she became the sister in charge of the new operating theatre unit. I was in no doubt that Father Edward had found the best companion in the world for me and I could rest assured that I would be in capable and caring hands.

One Sunday afternoon, Sister Justine came to talk about our trip and to be briefed on my health. At that time, I needed to be constantly fitted with a catheter and urine bag, so she asked my ward Sister to prepare all the medical items I would need to take on our journey.

In the two weeks, we were to travel to England and then overland to France, which would surely be a hectic and exhausting journey, therefore we needed to anticipate and be prepared for any medical problems that may arise.

During the excitement of the preparations, no one had thought to ask me what type of travel document I held. Everyone had assumed that I held a Hong Kong British Passport, but I only held a Certificate of Identity, which did not even guarantee entry to the UK. With this document I would need a visa to enter the countries on my itinerary.

First of all, my mother was urged to bring my Identity Card to me urgently. My mother had borrowed the card, which all Hong Kong residents are required to carry, to help negotiate with the Housing Authority for our new flat. The card was taken to the Immigration Department, together with the relevant forms duly completed and my Certificate of Identity. At the eleventh hour, my British visa was secured. It had been a nerve-racking experience for all concerned.

Journey of Hope

My spirits were high and my friends were as excited as I was. As I prepared for my trip, a stream of visitors appeared at my bedside, inundating me with things I might need for my journey. Soon, I could hardly move because packages and plastic carrier bags surrounded my bed.

My luggage was packed and checked over and over again until I was satisfied everything was in order for my departure. All I had to do now was to wait patiently for the dawning of the day I had long awaited — July 24, 1985.

In the late afternoon, feeling excited, yet a little apprehensive, I took a bath and then put on a pink dress embroidered with golden flowers that my sister had bought for me. Then I watched television at the end of my ward while I waited for Hilary Prior to arrive to drive me to Kai Tak airport on the Kowloon side of the harbour.

At 7:30 p.m., Hilary appeared. A nurse handed her my passport, air tickets and pocket money, which Matron had prepared before she went off duty. An *amah* carried my luggage to the car and another helped me into the front seat. Then to the sounds of enthusiastic farewells from both staff and patients, we set off with my heart pounding with excitement.

As we approached the Central District, I could see on both sides of the road a myriad of colourful lights, some dancing, some still. I had not seen such a wonderful sight for a long time.

Hilary and I chatted away and it seemed that in no time we reached the airport. Hilary helped me out of the car and into my wheelchair. She then had to drive the car to the car park, so she left me in my chair and assured me that she would return soon with my suitcase. Before driving off, she cautioned me to grasp my hand luggage as tightly as possible for fear that someone, noticing my blindness, might steal it.

It was the first time I had been to the airport. While anxiously hanging on to my baggage with all my strength, I peered around to see what I could distinguish.

After a few minutes, I heard Father Edward's voice and I relaxed. No sooner had we struck up a conversation than Hilary appeared with my suitcase. We proceeded to the departure hall where we were greeted by Sister Justine, Rory, Martin and a few other journalists.

An airline attendant arrived to transfer me to an airline wheelchair and my own was checked in with our luggage. Dizzy with all the attention, I posed for photographs with some of my friends who had also turned up to see me off.

Eventually, feeling deeply touched by everyone's concern and good wishes, Sister and I proceeded through the entrance to Immigration, leaving behind a chorus of fond farewells. Once in the departure lounge, we had an hour to recover from the whirl of excitement before boarding.

It was 10 p.m. when we heard our flight announced and I was the first passenger to board the Cathay Pacific jumbo jet. I remember being pushed by an attendant, with Sister Justine following, along a long tunnel. I did not realise we were on board until I felt a cushioned seat under me and recognised a row of seats.

I usually suffer from travel sickness when I am in a bus or a car but fortunately, though I felt rather nervous during takeoff, I was fine and I had no problem for the rest of the flight — much to the relief of Sister Justine.

Luckily, there was a vacant seat next to ours, so as soon as the safety-belt sign was switched off, Sister lifted the armrest and made me very comfortable on the two seats. Despite that, I could not sleep due to the drone of the engines and the noise from passengers who would not settle down.

The delivery of meals disturbed me, too. It seemed that we were expected to consume meals all the time. I tried but I could not eat so many meals.

I was thankful for the hush when the lights went out for the film. Perhaps people would settle down now and there will be no more meals, I thought. I listened to the dialogue on the headphones and this kept me entertained for a long while.

Sister and I talked a lot throughout the flight and gradually we felt at ease with each other. She looked after my every need and from time to time went to the toilet to empty my urine bag. I was so grateful to her for the way she handled my embarrassing situation. Poor Sister could not rest much and I felt very guilty for causing her so much trouble.

In the middle of the night the plane landed at Bahrain to refuel and for a crew change; a few passengers disembarked. Patiently, we waited the hour till we took off again. The pilot announced that it would be another eight hours before we reached London.

At last, we began our descent to London Gatwick Airport. I was nervous and brimming over with expectation; I was looking forward to my first glimpse of England.

We landed smoothly and I waited impatiently for our turn to disembark. Finally, after the other passengers had filed out of the cabins, a strong man scooped me up into his arms and carried me out of the plane. Then he carefully carried me down the steps and across the tarmac to an airport entrance. According to a flight attendant, this tall, gallant, uniformed man happened to be John — the pilot!

My first breath of English air was exhilarating, and though it was only about 6 a.m. I had the feeling the day was going to be dry and sunny. The day I had left behind had been very humid, with a temperature of more than 30° Celsius. Here in England, the air was fresh, cool and comfortable — just like the air in Hong Kong during November. I was going to love the English summer, I decided.

Just inside the entrance, I was astonished to find myself being placed on what felt like an ordinary chair with no armrest. I became extremely alarmed when I was pulled backwards along the corridor to the Immigration Hall. I did not realise at the time that I was in fact strapped into a special transfer chair/stretcher used to transport the disabled along stairways and narrow corridors.

Terrified I might fall, I held onto the back of the chair with all my might. Aiyahh, what a strange, primitive and undignified way to make my first entry into Europe!

After we had passed through Immigration, my own wheelchair arrived with the priority baggage. Then, once I had been transferred into my own snug chair, we waited patiently for our luggage to arrive.

The movement of the luggage as it slowly trundled by on the carousel fascinated me. "Worhh! Just like dogs chasing a rabbit," I chortled. I eyed and listened to everything going on around me with wonderment, as a village girl would when going to town for the first time.

Soon, Sister grabbed our suitcases and put them on a trolley. Then we made our way through the Customs to the arrival hall. Here, to meet us as promised, were three friendly young ladies from the Knights of Malta Volunteers.

After cheery introductions all round, they escorted us on the few minutes walk to the railway platform in the airport where tickets were bought for the journey to London.

A female station attendant laid down a gangplank for me to be wheeled onto the train. She was cheerful and friendly and willingly assisted me on board.

To my surprise, during my first hour on British soil, I had been treated far more courteously than I had ever been in my homeland.

It was my opinion that most of Hong Kong's population was indifferent to the plight of their disabled. It was very difficult for us to venture even a short distance from our homes without feeling that we were a nuisance to people. Disregarding the transfer chair episode at Gatwick, I had left the plane and boarded the train with considerable ease and had not felt a nuisance to anyone.

As we sped along through the green countryside, I caught glimpses of strange shapes — houses and farmsteads, I presumed. The landscape was such a contrast to the high-rise apartment blocks and the congested, hilly terrain of Hong Kong Island.

With my nose glued to the window, I stared at everything we passed, not wanting to miss anything, all the while listening to the conversation between the young ladies and Sister Justine.

After about an hour, we arrived at Victoria Station and the young ladies then took us to their car. From here we were driven to Camden Town where Sister and I were to stay two nights in a hostel which was cared for by an Irish pastor. Unfortunately, I became car sick on the way. I soon recovered, however, by taking a deep breath of fresh, cool air when we alighted at the hostel entrance.

We were welcomed by the pastor, who led us to a suite of rooms on the ground floor. It comprised of a living room, a bedroom and a bathroom — simply furnished and neat.

In the living room we found a sofa, a television set, a small table and a chest of drawers — a group of religious ornaments stood on its polished surface. The bedroom was adequately furnished with two single beds, a bedside chest and a wardrobe. At first glance the smallness of the bathroom worried me but on experimenting I found there was room enough for me to turn my wheelchair.

After this cursory look around, in rather a dazed state, we unpacked a few of our things, then settled down for an afternoon nap.

Late in the afternoon, Sister Justine went out to telephone her Columba Sisters in Hong Kong and to collect a meal for us from a Chinese restaurant.

During this short time alone, I reflected on the events that had happened to me during the last two months. Was I really in England? I could not believe it. I had been blessed with a miracle already — Chan Ma-lai, the impoverished Tanka girl, in a foreign land! Would it be too greedy of me to pray for another miracle? I wondered.

My meditation was interrupted by Sister Justine returning with the meal — hot Chinese noodles!

The next morning, Sister Justine's priest brother, Father Michael, arrived from Scotland. It was a short visit to meet us both before we set off for Lourdes. He was a rotund, grey-haired gentleman, his rosy face jolly and round. In fact, he reminded me of Santa Claus.

"If you ever go to Hong Kong at Christmas time, I'm sure a department store will employ you as a Santa Claus," I said. "Chinese children would love your jolly appearance."

At hearing this, he burst into hearty laughter. "I would not be able to stand the heat in Hong Kong," he said.

"It's not hot in the winter. Better yet, go in the autumn when the weather is like an English summer without the rain. I'm sure my Jesuit friend, Father Edward, would be pleased to show you around," I said.

"That sounds like a good idea," he said.

After this light-hearted conversation, to my surprise, he complimented me on my English. He said that I was more fluent than a Chinese girl he was sponsoring in her studies who had been in Scotland for more than a year.

A coach tour of London had been arranged for Sister and I in the afternoon. Fortunately, we were lodging near the coach terminal, so Sister could wheel me there quite easily.

On our arrival, the cheerful driver lifted me up onto a seat and stowed my wheelchair in the luggage compartment. His patience and consideration left a deep impression on me — I would have been astonished if I came across these virtues in a driver at home.

As we slowly passed the sights, our driver gave a commentary. I listened intently and peered through the window while Sister Justine took photographs for me. Among the sights, Buckingham Palace and the Tower of London thrilled me the most.

Later the same evening, Father Michael returned and presented me with a box of chocolates and a ten-pound note. The gesture was so kind of him.

On the third morning, after breakfast prepared by Sister Justine, we were to go to the pilgrimage gathering point at the entrance of a church.

We boarded the taxi with our luggage and to my surprise I found it was much bigger than a Hong Kong taxi. I liked the interior very much; it was spacious and there was plenty of room even for my wheelchair.

However, the exterior was horrid — black and ugly just like a hearse! I thought if they were painted a nice, deep scarlet and exported to Hong Kong, they would be very popular, especially with the wheelchair-bound.

We arrived at the church rather early, so as we had time to spare, Sister Justine wheeled me around the beautiful old church, all the while describing it to me in detail. I was initially struck by its vastness and then on pausing to pray, by the calmness and solemnity of its atmosphere.

I had heard that on visiting a church for the first time, if one made three petitions, eventually they would be granted. So when I found myself before the main altar, I followed that advice. First, I prayed for my benefactors to be blessed with good health, good luck and a long life. Second, I begged God to shower His grace upon my family, friends and relatives and grant them health, happiness and a smooth life. Finally, I asked God to bestow a special blessing upon me and guide me to a more promising future.

Outside, more pilgrims were arriving. They were suffering from a vast range of disabilities. Some were in wheelchairs; they were either paralysed like me, very sick or struck down by cerebral palsy, and others, less disabled, hobbled around on crutches. The chronically sick were on stretchers and some were in such serious conditions that they were equipped with oxygen tanks.

Finally, forty infirm and well over one hundred able-bodied volunteers were assembled. We were divided into several teams, which then boarded about six coaches in turn. Then, to a medley of farewells, the coaches proceeded through the cacophony of London's traffic. Once out of London, we were heading southeast for the English Channel port of Dover to board the ferry for Calais, France.

I sat in the window seat of the first row, with Sister Justine beside me enjoying the ride. We sang songs, munched potato crisps and sipped orange juice on the way. The coach arrived at the ferry in just under two hours.

It took ages for all of us to alight, but finally, the handicapped were safely matched to the jumble of crutches and wheelchairs and then in procession, we boarded the double-decked ferry.

This huge vessel appeared to be twice the size of a Hong Kong ferry and proved to be rather more comfortable, the seats being cushioned rather than just bare, wooden slats.

I was the only Chinese girl in the group and I turned out to be a curiosity. Once it had been recognised that I could speak English, I attracted a crowd who wanted to know all about me. Though some spoke with heavy regional accents new to me, I could understand them and could reply to their questions spontaneously.

I told my audience a few facts about China and Hong Kong and my life. They in turn, told me about themselves and their homelands.

The crossing turned out to be thoroughly enjoyable.

The ferry docked and slowly, one behind the other, we disembarked. Safely ashore, we made our way to the train station to catch the 6 p.m. train for Lourdes.

Luckily, there were an adequate number of strong volunteers to lift us swiftly and the train pulled out of the station on schedule.

Members of our group who were mobile were allocated a top bunk bed and the severely disabled the lower ones.

After passing quite some time being organised satisfactorily, we were ready to settle down to eat our supper. Each of us was given a drink and a box containing meat, a huge piece of bread, a packet of potato crisps and some sweets.

Unfortunately, due to the excitement and strain of the long journey, I was too exhausted to summon an appetite. So I occupied myself by gazing through the compartment window at the blur of the French countryside flashing by. Eventually, I managed to sleep for a few hours and by the time breakfast arrived I was as hungry as a wolf.

On being greeted by Sister Justine that morning, I learned she had hardly slept. The compartment she had been assigned to with other volunteers had no bunks; there were only seats, which were not comfortable enough to sleep on.

During the rest of the journey the pilgrims in my carriage were entertained by my neighbour in the upper bunk, a thirteen-year-old girl who suffered from a mental illness. She chattered constantly and loved to flirt with the boys. Her attempts at kissing them would send them fleeing in embarrassment and when some were not quick enough to escape her advances, cries of alarm and hoots of laughter would almost rock the train.

The train continued its journey towards the Massabielle Grotto at Lourdes where the young St. Bernadette had seen apparitions of the Virgin Mary in 1858.

The ninth apparition happened to be the most significant. During Bernadette's trance the lady told her to drink at the spring but Bernadette, not knowing of a spring, went to drink at the river. She stopped in her tracks when the lady pointed to a patch of muddy earth on the riverbank. Bernadette plunged her hand into the mud and clear water flowed. This was the miraculous spring.

Since the apparitions, the spring water worked countless miracles recognised by the Roman Catholic Church, and pilgrims have been flocking to Lourdes in the thousands from all over the world in hope of cures.

Now I, a lowly Tanka girl from the Orient, together with fellow pilgrims, soul mates struck down by illness, trauma and catastrophe, were on the same long journey of hope.

The pilgrimage was proving to be more than a spiritual exercise for me; it was also an exciting first adventure into the outside world. New surroundings, new sensations and meeting new people from all countries and all walks of life could only help broaden my mind and satisfy my appetite for knowledge. I absorbed every sight, sound and smell — and thanked God for every moment.

Haven of Hope

Our train arrived at the nearest station to Lourdes on a bright, sunny Sunday morning. After being warned of thieves, pick pockets and touts, we disembarked and then piled into coaches for the journey to the little town of Mary on the South. We sang hymns and recited the Rosary along the way; we finally arrived at the hospital around lunchtime.

Once again, I made my entrance in style. Frantically, I grasped the seat of what I mistook to be a conventional chair, as I was transported backwards on a special transfer chair from the hospital lobby to the canteen. "Yet another nerve-racking performance," I sighed. "Aiyahh, what's wrong with these Europeans!"

Sister Justine knew I was never at ease being parted from my wheelchair for long, so while I waited crumpled and shaken, she hurried back to the coach to retrieve it.

In the huge dining hall the clattering of cutlery and the clinking of crockery, coupled with the hubbub from the multitude of diners, made up the medley of sounds that greeted us.

Our group sat at very long tables and was served by waitresses flitting around in bright yellow uniforms. The severely handicapped were fed by volunteers who exercised great care and patience in their task.

I remember the food well: macaroni soup, bread, potatoes, beef and a vegetable that resembled a Chinese preserved vegetable — I wondered what it was.

I was hungry after the long journey, as was the rest of my group who were keen to eat as fast as they could and have second helpings; but my struggle to use a knife and fork left me way behind in the race. I did manage to have a second helping of the first course, the delicious macaroni soup, which I found easy to eat with a spoon.

After the meal, we invalids were taken up to the bedrooms in a lift. I was assigned to a bed in a ten-bed ward on the third floor. Sister Justine helped me unpack and then wheeled me around the interior of the building to ensure that I knew my own floor and could recognise my ward and the position of my bed.

At 3 p.m., our group, with the other recent arrivals, attended a Mass in the hospital hall. The priest was very eloquent and I left the hall instilled with a greater confidence not only in Jesus but also in His Holy Mother.

Later in the afternoon, our group crossed the bridge, explored the Esplanade of the sanctuaries and then strolled along the riverside as far as the grotto.

Our chatting ceased as we approached the famous shrine. We stopped and enveloped in an atmosphere of reverence and quietude, I gazed up. A feeling of profound wonderment overwhelmed me as my eye fell upon the white statue of Our Lady, appearing heavenly against the dark grey of the rock. My eye then moved down to a pyramid of candles glowing in the foreground. Indeed, this was the moment I had longed for. Enraptured, I raised my eye to Our Lady once more and prayed with all my heart.

We returned to the hospital for supper and before retiring, we spent an hour chatting and getting to know our fellow pilgrims and the volunteers. There were some interesting and moving exchanges, I remember.

One of the volunteers told us of a lady who had brought her crippled son to the shrine. She had firmly believed that if she prayed to Our Lady of Lourdes her son would be cured. Alas, she left very disappointed, as there had been no improvement in her son's condition. On her homeward journey, she confessed to her fellow pilgrims that her faith in God was beginning to wane and in an outburst of despair she implored the Virgin Mary to tell her why her son was unworthy of a cure. Almost in an instant, she noticed that her son was no longer infirm. Joy overwhelmed her and in floods of tears she renewed her faith in God.

Another lady told me her story. Years before, she had suffered from liver cancer and on being told it was incurable she sank into deep despair. So taking the advice of a friend, she joined a pilgrimage and made a dedicated effort to believe in the power of God and Our Lady. She did not experience a cure after the first pilgrimage, but afterwards she felt better physically and stronger spiritually. So she went on many subsequent tours.

After one tour, she went for a medical check-up and the doctors found that her cancer had miraculously disappeared. Since then, she has made the trip every year as a volunteer, in gratitude for her cure. She advised me: "Be good, and try your best to pray fervently, especially to Our Lady, then maybe one day you will be cured." I took her advice and prayed almost continually for my humble petitions to be heard and for Our Lady to put in a good word for me with her Son.

Katie was a nurse and a volunteer in our group. She owned a vast farm in Australia. She said one of her two sons was murdered by a man who accused him of stealing his girlfriend. The tragedy had sent her plunging into the depths of depression and bitterness. She could not find peace in her heart until she took part in a pilgrimage as a helper. By and by, she found peace and happiness again. There was no doubt, she said, that her faith had helped her overcome her weakness and sorrow.

Luke, aged nine, and Benjamin, aged eight, were the youngest on our tour and they certainly made their presence felt. They were a lively pair and Benjamin especially took great delight in playing pranks. His lower limbs had been stricken with paralysis since an accident on a family picnic and his mother, being deeply religious, hoped this pilgrimage would improve his condition.

Despite being lame, Luke, the less vocal of the two, was very independent. He was a sensible boy, giving the impression he was virtuous and that he regularly kept in touch with God, whereas Benjamin took no heed when he was scolded and seemed not to take the religious aspect of the tour seriously. Nevertheless, his boyish antics and light-heartedness provided us with light relief throughout our tour.

The most serious case in our group was a twelve-year-old orphan boy who was blind and dumb. His ear-piercing screams and explosions of excitement whenever he heard music often annoyed the less tolerant among us. Months after the pilgrimage, I heard that the poor boy had died. I believed he had won a victory in a way — he had been released from his torment.

On Monday morning we were awakened at 6 a.m. The volunteers had arrived from their lodgings nearby to help us rise, bathe and eat breakfast. They also cleaned the wards and bathrooms and made the beds. I was impressed by their efficiency and the way they carried out these humble and tiresome jobs in such good humour.

This was the morning for us invalids to bathe in the holy spring. A volunteer wheeled me along past the grotto to join a queue at one of a long line of bathhouses.

When it came to my turn, I was placed supine on a trolley by two male helpers and then wheeled to the entrance of a bathhouse. Two French women took me inside and then through some curtains into a small room. Then they proceeded to remove all my clothes!

The next thing I remember was being carefully lowered into a long, narrow tub of ice-cold water and while I lay shocked and shivering, the women bathed my whole body and then my eyes, praying in French throughout. At the end of the ritual they held a statue of the Virgin Mary before my lips for me to kiss.

I had been too dumbfounded to pray or think about a cure during the bathing but on the way back to the hospital I dared to expect a difference in my condition. Alas, I was disappointed.

With the afternoon came a coach visit to the Parish Church, which stood on a nearby hill. The volunteers, expending a great deal of energy, carried the wheelchair-bound from the coach and then up the steep, narrow steps that led to the church's main entrance.

The church was in darkness except for the light of a few candles. Then I noticed the glow of a stained glass window looming bright with the light of the day outside. I gazed entranced at the spectacle as we huddled together to take part in the Mass and I prayed, remembering my three petitions.

That evening, two pleasant young men and an enthusiastic young lady came to escort me to the Candlelight Ceremony. Thousands of pilgrims thronged the Esplanade, each holding a glowing candle. It was a magical sight: the candles and glistening lights from the surrounding buildings and stars in the sky.

In procession, we circled the Esplanade. As the pilgrims sang hymns, strange languages intrigued me. My escorts explained that some hymns were sung in French and some in Italian.

The ceremony lasted for more than an hour. I was in awe to see these thousands of souls from all over the world coming together to honour Our Lady, in a spirit of joy and hope.

After prayers that evening, I went to bed with the "Ave Maria" and the sweet tinkling of bells ringing in my ears, dreaming of a miraculous cure by the morning but it was not to be.

I decided not to despair. Instead, I vowed not to abandon hope of a cure, or of at least some improvement in my condition. Perhaps the cool water would prevent the reoccurrence of the dreaded pressure sores, I told myself. So I would continue to take the bath every morning of my stay and pray more than ever.

I awoke to an overcast day Tuesday and after breakfast, I bathed in the holy spring once more. Later, I joined a congregation of thousands for Mass in the huge underground Basilica of Saint Pius X.

When it came to the Holy Communion, the celebrant, assisted by other priests, distributed the "Body of Christ" while the congregation sang hymns. The uplifting, joyous voices of souls from the far corners of the earth filled me with joy and hope. I was convinced that this time God would certainly hear my three petitions. They would rise up with the glorious singing, and make their way towards heaven.

At about 10.a.m. that morning, we embarked on a long excursion to the Chapel of Saint Bernadette, high on a mountainside. A convoy of coaches carrying us pilgrims groaned its way up the long, narrow, winding roads of the southwest Pyrenees. I wondered how anyone could live in such a lonely place, with no shops or markets nearby. The Hong Kong Chinese people would hate to live in such isolation. We would prefer to live in or near the hustle and bustle of a town where everything is at hand.

We arrived at our destination within an hour and after the usual muddle of matching us to our wheelchairs and crutches, we struggled up a slope to the chapel, assisted by the volunteers. The chapel, a lofty structure, was simply furnished with rows of ancient pews. There was also an ancient organ which one of our members played while we sang the litany of the Mass, celebrated by two priests robed in shiny white vestments decorated with glistening embroidery.

After an hour of worship we bumped and hobbled down the rough hillside path to the centre of the small town. Trailing in convoy, we browsed in the shops stretching along the long, narrow alleys. Many of the souvenirs on sale, I was surprised to learn, were imported from Hong Kong and Taiwan.

It was chilly, so we stopped for a cup of tea to warm ourselves before we explored any further. By noon, we had come across a tavern where we stopped to order lunch. Sitting at tables in the open, we found we were in a good location to observe the activity of the local population. This will broaden our knowledge of life in the Pyrenees, I thought, and a Chinese saying came to mind: "Instead of reading books, take a million-mile walk on distant roads."

The highlight of this mountain trip for me happened at this tavern table. Three inquisitive donkeys suddenly appeared right next to me, so close that I could distinguish that they had long ears, bulky noses and enormous round eyes.

At the time, I was eating potato crisps and the donkeys were very interested. They kept nuzzling up to me, making it obvious they were keen to share my snack. So I nervously held out some crisps for them. As soon as I felt a wet mouth take them, I snatched my hand away swiftly, fearing big white teeth might gobble up my fingers as well.

It happened that these cheeky beasts were not satisfied with just a few crisps and they continued to nuzzle towards my hands. In the end, they persuaded me to part with two more packets of crisps, to the amusement of the people watching.

On returning to our accommodation, I took a rest, and then just before supper that evening, Sister Justine and I explored the local souvenir shops. I bought a silver crucifix and a copper necklace, but before buying them I ensured they were really French products.

Later, on the last evening of our stay, our group held a farewell party in a local restaurant.

Our group of about sixty was seated at ten round tables. Solicitous waiters brought each of us a glass of fruit juice and a selection of savouries. This was followed by bowls of delicious oxtail soup, which I ate with chunks of crusty bread. My first taste of French wine was disappointing, though; it was sour and I did not care for its heaviness.

The next course was beef steak, colourfully accompanied by golden French fries, green celery and slices of bright red tomato. Then Neapolitan ice cream, topped with red strawberries, was served. That evening meal was a treat to remember.

Once the tables were cleared, we remained seated for entertainment performed by about twenty able-bodied members of our group. Some played guitars and violins, while others, dressed in national costumes, performed folk dances and sang songs in their mother tongue. This was followed by a very emotive play entitled "The Life of an Orphan in an Orphanage."

Finally, after a recital of poems, both joyful and sad, the evening ended with comic mimicry. This had us roaring with laughter and sent us home to the hospital in very high spirits.

Before retiring on my last night, I attended the usual evening prayers and at 10 p.m. rolled into bed. As I lay reflecting on the last three days, for the

first time in my life, I felt real hope for my future. After all, I could see —
though only a little — and my hands and brain still functioned well. I was
also blessed with a loving mother and many good friends who supported me.
Compared with some of the other pilgrims, I was very fortunate.

Sister Justine and I had decided to leave Lourdes during the afternoon of
Thursday, August 1. Rather than return overland to London we would fly
to Ireland to see her relatives. Earlier, her family in Ireland had kindly
telephoned and offered to pay for our flights to Dublin and thence to
London, and also the hotel at Gatwick Airport, so that we could visit them
before our return flight to Hong Kong. We were delighted with this
generous proposal, so immediately all was arranged for us to take the Lady
Goulding's special pilgrimage flight to Dublin, together with a group of
Irish children. Lady Goulding, a very gracious lady, is well known for her
love and care of spastic children internationally. She was then the president
of the Spastic Association of Ireland.

In the morning, we took part in the "Stations of the Cross for the Sick,"
which was held along the stretch of path beyond the grotto. Members of our
group re-enacted the last hours of Jesus. A young man carried a heavy cross on
his shoulders along the route and we pilgrims followed, stopping and praying
at each of the fourteen stations of Jesus' tortuous walk to his crucifixion at
Calvary. It was a gloomy, damp day — quite fitting for the occasion.

Immediately after lunch, several volunteers arrived in my ward to take
my luggage and help me to a coach waiting at the hospital entrance. As I
waited to board the coach with Sister, I blushed when a barrage of kisses
were pecked at my cheeks! Aiyahh! I was trapped in my wheelchair — there
was no escape for me.

We Chinese do not show each other this kind of open affection and over
those last three days I would shrink away from the kisses, which the
boyfriend of a young lady in our group frequently planted on my cheek.
This apart, I appreciated the affection these well-meaning temporary friends
had shown me and I will not forget their kindness, ever.

Still filled with emotion, I was whisked up into the coach by a strong
young man and placed on the first window seat. Then Sister Justine settled
down beside me and a group of about ten Irish children sat behind us, and
we were away.

My attention was soon taken by some of the children who came along
the bus to speak to me. They told me they were from a boarding school in
Ireland. Some of them were disabled and together they had spent part of
their summer holiday in Lourdes accompanied by three teachers. The
children were very inquisitive and I answered their questions enthusiastically

until they asked how old I was. I thought they would not have believed me if I told them my age because of my small stature, so I just smiled and changed the subject.

We arrived at the airport within half an hour and we were led to a small departure area, furnished with only a few rows of seats. Consequently, there were crowds of people standing around, obscuring the long queues of travellers waiting to check in.

Eventually, strong arms carried me onto the Aer Lingus aircraft and sat me down in a row of light-green seats. I noticed the stewardesses' uniforms were green, too.

While I listened to the flight safety instructions, I began to feel chilled. So a blanket I had stowed in my hand luggage was urgently retrieved by Sister and snugly wrapped around me. Just after takeoff, cold drinks were offered and a while later, a chicken leg was placed in front of me but I had lost my appetite and could only gaze at it in a cloud of gloom. "What a ridiculous joke!" I thought. "It is my favourite food and I cannot possibly eat it."

Midway through the flight there was an emergency when a sick pilgrim became seriously ill. Fortunately, there was a doctor on board and while he treated the poor man, a passenger led us in a prayer for the pilgrim's recovery. I, too, began to feel unwell; spells of shivering had taken hold of me and I began to fear a fever was creeping up on me.

Emerald Isle

In contrast to the bright weather above the clouds, on our arrival at Dublin, Ireland's capital, the evening appeared to be a damp and dismal one.

As I was carried down the steps from the aircraft, I wondered if I was going to arrive in the usual style this time. It was with great relief that I found my wheelchair waiting for me on the tarmac below.

We passed smoothly through Immigration and collected our luggage. Then I waited patiently while Sister Justine rang her relatives from a telephone booth. She informed her brother-in-law Bill that we had arrived and he told her he was coming to collect us. Within fifteen minutes, he had arrived.

We greeted each other gladly and proceeded in the rain, which was now falling heavily, to Bill's car in the car park. So with haste and much effort, we were helped into the car and Bill proceeded to drive us to his home on the south side of the city. I remember his name because he was the first of the many relatives of Sister Justine I met. The names of other relatives have since escaped me.

During the fifteen-minute drive, I could not see much through the rain splattered window, but I formed the impression that the houses along the way were luxurious. The people who live here must lead a very sophisticated life-style and must be very well-off, I remember thinking.

The first sound that greeted us when we spluttered to a halt outside the house was the barking of a dog and I filled with alarm when, as I wheeled towards the house, the large brown, sodden creature jumped up at me. Bill could see I was scared and he rushed to control the dog, but the dog was excited and the effort was in vain.

Once inside and safely away from the monster, Sister Justine introduced me to her sister and then to her niece, a young lady in her twenties. The first thing they asked was whether I could speak English and I could sense their relief when I replied in their tongue.

Sister Justine's sister, alarmed at my pallor, disappeared into the kitchen to fetch me a glass of hot water and a dish of hot noodles, but I had to apologise — I could not eat because I felt so poorly.

Though it was summer, it was a cold evening and despite the central heating being on, I felt cold. So my hosts insisted that I sit near an electric heater. From here, I surveyed the living room while Sister chatted with her relatives, telling them my history and all about our trip. I pondered and came to the conclusion that the room appeared to be the size of an average government resettlement estate apartment in Hong Kong.

Soon their conversation turned to the latest news of the family and Sister Justine passed me photographs of a recent wedding. As I peered my way through them, my hosts played a recording of the Nuptial Mass. It was beautiful. I wished Sister Justine and I could have arrived early enough to have been present at the ceremony.

As the evening grew later, I grew more poorly. Eventually, Sister laid me on the living room sofa but I became so restless that she began to be very concerned about me. She assured me that a bed was being prepared for me and I would be able to sleep soon. I had assumed that the bed was in this house but I was wrong. Strangely, it happened to be in a house about twenty minutes away — the family summer house in the Dublin mountains, which her brothers and sisters jointly owned. Two brothers were on vacation there at the time — one a doctor practicing in Dublin and the other a priest visiting from Florida.

Soon I could not bear my condition any longer; my head had begun to pound and I became so desperate to lie in a comfortable bed and sleep that impatience took hold of me. Using a sharp tone, I urged Sister Justine to let me lie down in a bed at once. What a pity I could not contain myself — I hated my rudeness, but the family understood and, as soon as they could, took me to the other house.

I could not remember the journey clearly because I was drifting in a half-conscious state. In no time I found myself under two thick quilts on a comfortable bed. Apparently, Sister Justine had ensured that two mattresses were used to bring the bed to the same height as the seat of my wheelchair, so I could transfer easily.

Despite the bed being so cosy, I was restless and could not sleep. Concerned, Sister took my temperature — it was 102° Fahrenheit. She gave me two tablets to swallow and gradually my fever subsided. More comfortable now, I drifted into sleep. But after an hour, I was awakened by voices in the next room. Thereafter, my attempts to sleep were futile; I tossed and turned for the rest of the night.

My bedroom was on the ground floor and Sister came downstairs from her room to check on me at intervals throughout the night, bringing me endless glasses of warm water. When morning came we were both too tired to get up for breakfast.

About midday, I roused myself when Sister appeared beside me, bearing a dish of macaroni. My mouth tasted very bitter and I did not feel like eating but she persuaded me to eat a little; otherwise, I would have no strength, she said. I remained in bed for the rest of the day in the care of her brother, the doctor.

I met the next morning feeling much better and in higher spirits. Now, I discovered that my warm, cosy room was actually the laundry. There were no other spare rooms downstairs and this room was considered convenient for me because there was a shower, a toilet large enough for my wheelchair, and no carpet to hinder my wheels or become soiled should an accident occur with my urine bag. Moreover, I had easy access to the garden, kitchenette and the dining and living rooms. I did not mind in the least being in the laundry; I could wheel around safely there and with all the facilities it provided I could be independent. All this made me very happy.

After exploring the room with great interest, I washed and dressed, and then wheeled to the kitchen for breakfast. During the meal, on asking what was in store for the rest of the day, I learned that Sister Justine and I had been invited out to lunch. Our hosts were to be a Chinese family, named Lee, who were eager to entertain us at a restaurant they owned in town.

I had been confined to the house since I had arrived and so this morning, feeling chirpy, I was anxious to take a look at my surroundings. When I was wheeled out into the front garden, I was charmed. Bright hues met my eye and delicate scents danced by on the fresh, cool breeze. Lofty trees stood out against the sky and clusters of cottage-garden flowers were in profusion. My eye was particularly drawn to clumps of fragrant lavender and tall white daises dominating a flowerbed under a window and peering across the vast, vibrant green, sweeping lawn. I also spied the view of Dublin Harbour.

The doctor was soon ready to drive us to the restaurant. On arrival, Mary Lee met us on the pavement outside and the doctor helped me out of the vehicle. Then he left to go to the horse races, and dropped his priest brother in town on the way.

The restaurant happened to be on the second floor, so three strong people carried me up the steep, narrow wooden stairs. I was surprised as I thought such staircases only existed in the tenements of Hong Kong.

Mrs Lee made us very welcome and introduced me to her nephews who helped run the business. She explained that her parents had left Hong Kong in the 1960s and were now the proprietors of this restaurant and one other Chinese restaurant in Dublin.

While we chatted away with our hosts, Sister and I received solicitous attention from the waiters. They served the most delicious meal; heaped dishes were supplied in plenty, along with endless cups of tea.

Finding it difficult to tear ourselves away from such genial hospitality, we thanked the family profusely and took our leave to go shopping in the town.

The streets appeared to be wide and clean; not too crowded with shoppers like Hong Kong. It was relatively easy for Sister Justine to wheel me from shop to shop. We browsed around a huge department store where I was fascinated with the goods on sale; even more so with the items in another store nearby which were clothes and articles Religious Orders might require. Sister Justine bought several garments there for herself and also a selection for her brothers in the clergy.

After a couple of hours exploring the streets and admiring the Georgian character of the city, we joined Sister's priest brother at the designated spot where we were to be picked up by the doctor.

During the drive back to the house, Trinity College, St. Patrick's Cathedral and various other landmarks and scenic spots were pointed out to me. We had almost arrived at the house when the priest presented me with a lovely necklace in a very attractive box. I was touched by his thoughtfulness. Had he left us to go shopping especially to buy the gift for me? I wondered.

On the Saturday morning, we went on another shopping jaunt and in the afternoon, my hosts, determined I should see as much as possible, took me to scenic spots and places of interest in the city and its environs.

Sunday, however, was more memorable for me. I woke up earlier than usual, pulled my wheels from their resting place, washed and then tried to make myself as neat as possible in my best suit. Then spruced up and happy, I emerged from my room and wheeled into a small room which had been converted into a chapel.

Here, Sister and I, together with her eldest brother who had just called in, awaited the arrival of the priest brother who was to celebrate Mass. He soon appeared in his vestments and began to say Mass, assisted by the doctor. There were only five of us present — so few felt very strange. Nevertheless, it was a lovely, intimate service and I remember the sermon well — how we should treat others with fairness and justice. I received Holy Communion and besides praying for my three petitions, I prayed with all my heart for this family who had been so kind to me and had made me feel so welcome in their home.

After Mass, feeling cheerful and at ease in the company of the two brothers, I sat at the dining table with them for Sunday lunch, prepared by Sister Justine. Similar in appearance, of stocky stature with ruddy faces topped by greying hair, both were blessed with a terrific sense of humour. In their Irish brogue, they regaled me with jokes, anecdotes and blarney while we ate the most delicious meal: roast beef, roast potatoes, a variety of vegetables and plain rice, too. I admired Sister Justine, for not only was she a good nurse and could remain calm and patient when dealing with complicated issues, but she was a good cook as well.

I relaxed the whole afternoon and watched television for the first time in Europe. I remember being totally absorbed by an old black-and-white film with a story reminiscent of a Chinese soap opera. I watched till the evening meal arrived and once more found the food delicious: oxtail soup, roast chicken and crispy potatoes. In delightful company, I raised my glass — of cola rather than beer or wine — to toast my hosts and made a speech in appreciation of their hospitality.

A host of Sister Justine's relatives arrived in the evening, many of them from other regions of Ireland. They crammed into the parlour where she offered them tea and cakes and the young nephews and nieces tucked into ice cream.

One of the boys, a tall, thin twelve year old, was curious and came across to talk to me. His lilting voice already had a manly tone and he appeared to be very confident in his abilities. He was doing well at school and loved to play all types of sport. All this and his involvement in church activities kept him very busy, he informed me. I was very impressed by this young man's approach to life and wished him well.

The newly married couple came to the reunion and also a couple with a baby boy. Everyone made a tremendous fuss of him and judging by the chuckles I could hear, he was enjoying every moment. I stared at him, fascinated because to me he looked bald. Perhaps he was — often European babies are born hairless, I reminded myself. Finally, overwhelmed by the attention, he became restless, so he was settled into his pram and encouraged to sleep. I paid special attention to the pram; to me it was a novelty because I had never come across one before.

I went to bed at about 10:30 p.m., but could not settle down because of the noise emanating from the guests in the next room. Sister and I were leaving the next morning, so I thought I would abandon trying to sleep and attempt to pack a few things. Many gifts that the guests had so kindly showered upon me were scattered around the room — an assortment of toiletries among them. Apparently, Sister Justine had told them that these items needed to be replenished for the rest of my journey.

In the morning, I took a bath and put on my most colourful dress, for today Sister Justine and I were to say farewell to everyone, pose for photos, then catch an Aer Lingus flight to London, the first leg of our journey back to Hong Kong.

The eldest brother arrived with his wife and while she and Sister Justine finished my packing, the brother presented me with a box of miniature bottles of perfume. Previously, I had told Sister Justine that I wanted to buy these perfumes to give as presents back home. The brother would not let me reimburse him even though I intended to give them away. Sister Justine did advise me to reserve them only for those who were close to me or had shown me special concern.

After a quick lunch, we were ready to pile into the two cars that were waiting outside in the driveway. Confusion had plagued me throughout my stay over who was who — amongst the multitude of Sister's brothers and sisters, brothers-in-law and sisters-in-law — I had met. So I will say: two ladies and two gentlemen accompanied us to the airport. While we were checking in, I was taken by surprise when one of the airport officials — a friend of the family — heartily greeted me and placed a box of sweets and a large tin of talcum powder on my lap. What a lovely gesture! Everyone had been so kind to me in Ireland.

While we were waiting for our flight to be called, Sister Justine engaged in last minute conversation with her relatives and I reflected on my very enjoyable four-night stay in Dublin. The only thing that had marred our stay was my fever during the first two days. I was so sorry that I had been so much trouble to Sister Justine and my hosts. I did not know at the time that my fever was a sign of something more sinister, which was to manifest itself months later.

Finally, it was time to board and after emotional hugs and kisses, especially where Sister was concerned, two airport staff took us down in a lift to an ambulance that ferried us to the plane.

Two hours later, the approach to Gatwick London Airport at dusk was unforgettable. The red glow of sunset and the sparkling of the lights on the ground below enthralled me. I imagined the hustle and bustle of traffic, people making their way home from work or going out for an evening of entertainment and families watching television after their evening meal.

We disembarked smoothly and when a jolly young male ground attendant jauntily wheeled me to an airport lift, I burst into giggles. Sister Justine could not detect the reason for my amusement and seeing that the young man looked embarrassed, she whispered in my ear: "Mary, control yourself. What's wrong with you? Why are you laughing at this young man?"

"As soon as he spoke, he reminded me of Eddie Grundy in *The Archers*," I explained in a hushed voice. "He has the same accent! Worhh, it could be him!"

At this, Sister chuckled and then told the puzzled young man the reason for my giggles. He chuckled, too, and I could sense his relief that my amusement had not been roused by something more embarrassing. He must have thought: how on earth does a Chinese girl know about Eddie Grundy, of all people! I have mentioned before that I listened to *The Archers*, a long-running British radio serial broadcast on the British Forces Radio Network in Hong Kong for years.

We trundled through the normal arrival formalities, collected our mountain of luggage and then boarded a minibus to the Gatwick Hilton Hotel where we were to stay for one night. Once settled into our twin-bedded room on the second floor, Sister Justine announced: "I am going to find out where we can eat a late meal. You stay here. Don't venture outside the room. I'll be back soon."

This was the first time I had stayed in a high-class hotel and I was anxious to explore. So while on my own, I wheeled around the room, peering at and touching everything I encountered. The room was large, furnished with two single beds made up with fresh white sheets and pillowcases and draped with crimson quilts. I peered into the huge wardrobe and investigated a large desk and bedside chests; then at the window, I lifted the corner of white net curtains only to find no hint of a view.

I was intrigued by the bathroom and while exploring, I suddenly realised Sister Justine had been gone for rather a long time. I was just beginning to worry when she came hurrying through the door. "I'm sorry I was such a long time," she panted, "but I came across some friends and with talking to them, I lost track of time. Anyway, they showed me a restaurant still serving; it's getting late, so we had better go right away."

I remember the restaurant well. I was captivated by the place. I had not been waited on by waiters in black suits and bow ties before and to dine to the accompaniment of a live band and singer was sheer luxury. The food was delicious; being ravenous, I ate my roast chicken swiftly and then demolished two fresh fruit desserts!

The next morning we took a minibus to the airport to catch the Cathay Pacific flight to Hong Kong. After checking in, we breakfasted in the coffee shop and then filed through the passport and hand-baggage check to the Departure Lounge.

On our way through the corridor to board the plane, I became aware of a giant-sized, dark figure ambling towards us, and when he greeted us I realised that it was John the pilot! I was astonished to come across him again. What a coincidence! To the amusement of all, once again he whisked me up in his strong arms and then carried me on board and placed me in my seat.

We expected our flight to take off on time with no hassle, but that was not to be. With all the passengers settled into their seats, the pilot announced: "I'm sorry to inform you there is a problem with an engine and we will have to taxi to a hangar for repair. We anticipate this will not take too long and we apologise for the delay."

While we waited, the air-conditioning did not seem to be working and the cabin became stuffy. I soon noticed my fellow passengers becoming restless as their discomfort grew and some began to grumble as their patience frayed. I heard someone suggest we leave the aircraft but that was not practical with so many passengers. Just as I was beginning to fear that somebody would soon complain to the crew, it was announced that we would soon be on our way. Thank goodness, I thought. I did not want to witness any unpleasantness.

Besides having a bad start to our journey, once in the air, I found the service was not as good as on our outward flight. I did not feel like eating but from time to time, I asked for water. Each time, I became very frustrated when the stewardess forgot to heed my request and in the end Sister Justine had to complain. Maybe a bad start meant a bad flight, I remember thinking.

There was no empty seat next to us this time; it was taken by a very pleasant young businessman who disappeared now and again to smoke in the smoking section. Sister Justine struck up a conversation with him and I was amused by the way she was asking him questions — just like a Chinese mother interviewing her prospective son-in-law, I thought. During one of his absences, I remarked to Sister Justine that I feared I did not have enough presents for the staff in my ward. "Never mind," she said. "If the young man visits the transit lounge in Bahrain, I'll ask him if he wouldn't mind buying some chocolates for you in the duty-free shop." To my relief, he did decide to leave the plane for the hour stopover and he happily agreed to our request.

The hour soon passed and when the young man returned to his seat, he handed me the chocolates. I did not know what to say when he refused to take the money for them. "Och, just give him a kiss," joked Sister Justine, knowing I would be too shy to do such a thing. Instead, I shook hands with him and expressed my thanks and he nodded in acceptance.

The last leg of our journey seemed endless. I could neither sleep nor relax even a little. So it was with a huge sigh of relief that I heard the announcement that we were beginning our descent into Hong Kong.

Once through Customs, we wearily battled through throngs of people, many of them were applauding the victorious return of a large group of disabled athletes who had been on our flight.

Eventually, rather harassed, we met up with Hilary Prior and Father Edward on the fringe of the crowd. Though they could see I looked exhausted, they were relieved that I had coped with my travels and had returned safe and sound.

On the way to the car, I could not wait to give these two special people their gifts — a bottle of wine for Hilary and some packets of Irish tea and coffee for Father Edward. Hilary showered me with hugs and kisses and as she lifted me into her car, Father Edward thanked me for his gift and bade us farewell. Despite my fatigue, my excitement bubbled over and I did not stop talking on our way home. I had so much to tell.

When we stopped to drop Sister Justine at the Ruttonjee Hospital in Wan Chai, where she worked, I could not thank her enough for all she had done for me. I would be forever grateful to her.

With me still chattering away, we arrived at the Duchess of Kent Hospital just after lunch. Hilary, with the help of some *amahs*, unloaded me and the luggage and then returned to her office in the hospital Fund Raising Department.

Matron had thoughtfully asked the kitchen staff to keep me some lunch, but I was too excited to eat. The first thing I wanted was a quick bath.

Having freshened up, I was now anxious to distribute my gifts to my friends and the staff and tell them about my great adventure.

First, I gave Su Ying a large bottle of perfume together with a wooden crucifix and a small plastic statuette of the Virgin Mary containing miraculous spring water. I could hear that Mei Mei had recognised my return; she was shrieking so loudly in her bed. I had bought a statuette for her, too. So I wheeled over to her bed and recited a prayer as I lent over and dropped droplets of the holy water into her mouth.

With Mei Mei more subdued now, I left her bed and then wheeled around the ward, enthusiastically distributing sweets and chocolates to the nurses and *amahs*, in thanks for their much appreciated care of me. My elation suddenly drained from me when I heard that some of the *amahs* had complained that I should have brought them each a more expensive present. They could afford to buy their own sweets and chocolates, they grumbled. They had assumed that the fund-raising campaign had made me rich. What they did not know was that the hospital committee had handled the finances; I had taken only a certain amount of money with me on the trip and had no idea how much was donated. I was terribly upset by their greediness and I considered telling Matron about their remarks but I could not summon the courage.

So it was, on that afternoon of August 7, 1985, after two weeks of floating on clouds with the "angels," that I had been brought back down to earth with a heavy bump.

8

A New Day Dawning

Shortly after I returned from the pilgrimage, I was dismayed to learn that the alterations to our Ap Lei Chau flat had still not been carried out. The doorway to the toilet needed to be widened, the kitchen sink lowered and a step between two rooms replaced by a ramp. As I waited, month after month passed like years and I became increasingly annoyed and frustrated. When concerned folk asked when I was going home, I grew weary of explaining time and again the reason for the delay.

These dreary days were brightened by a series of visitors enquiring about my trip to Europe. First, as he had promised, Rory paid me a visit.

As I was regaling him with the highlights of my adventure, his attention was drawn to Mei Mei in the bed opposite. Deeply moved by her pitiful condition, he was suddenly keen to put her name forward for a pilgrimage to Lourdes. Later, on serious consideration of her case, he gave up the idea, mainly because the journey would have been too gruelling for her in her feeble state.

In late September, a few days after Father Edward had paid me a visit, Heung Jiu walked into my ward. Her arrival took me by surprise because she had not written to say she intended stopping off in Hong Kong on her way back to Taiwan from London.

I remember clearly — I was sitting in my wheelchair talking to Su Ying that afternoon when I heard a voice call "Mary" from the entrance at the far end of the ward. Immediately, I recognised the voice was Heung Jiu's. She has always wondered since how I knew it was her.

Before she reached my bed, I rummaged around for the package that contained a holy water statuette and a bottle of perfume — my gifts to her from Lourdes. I had waited so long for her to visit and I could not wait for her to be seated before I handed over the rather crumpled package. She was delighted, especially with the water from the Miraculous Spring.

When we settled down to chat, I told her about my trip in detail and showed her the photographs. Our conversation then turned to my return home and she commiserated with me over the delay. I went on to confide in her that I was concerned about what I would do at home to keep myself occupied. She suggested: "Why don't you teach students in the neighbourhood who need help with their oral English?"

"I could do that voluntarily," I replied. "But really, I would like to earn some pocket money. Parents would be hesitant to pay for only oral lessons, especially from a non-native speaker. They would want grammar tuition, too."

"Having learned English as a second language, you are able to explain grammar better than I can," replied Heung Jiu. "Many is the time you have explained it to me."

Looking back, although I dismissed the idea at the time, Heung Jiu had sown a seed.

Before she left, she briefly practiced her Cantonese on Su Ying and Mei Mei and then turned to me and said: "Keep up your spirits Mary. Everything will work out OK in the end. I'm sure the flat will be ready soon. I'll visit you there when I'm next passing through. Thanks for the gifts. Bye-bye. I'll write soon." Then she was gone.

It was a Sunday at the beginning of October 1985, just when I was beginning to be assailed by fears that I would have to be content with communal living indefinitely, that my gloom over the delay in the flat alterations gave way to relief and joy.

My sister Choi Ha, whose English name is Irene, had come rushing into my ward and breathlessly announced: "Wah, the flat is ready, you can come home! You had better tell Sister that now you can leave. Ask her to make arrangements as soon as possible."

I was elated. Immediately, I informed Sister Chan and Matron; they were both very pleased for me. "Tell me which day you want to go home, then I can make the arrangements," enthused Sister Chan.

"Saturday would be a good day," I suggested hopefully.

"OK, I will ask the driver if the hospital bus is free," she replied.

In a short while, Sister came back to say that the bus was free. Then, giddy with happiness, I began to plan for my going home.

One afternoon before I was due to leave, Matron, Gillian Ford formerly Petersen, Hilary Prior and Wannie the Play Therapist gave a small farewell party for me in the Play Therapy Room. I invited only Su Ying and two other friends.

While we munched tasty snacks, we reminisced over my hospital years and they all shared in my joy at being reunited with my family.

The gathering concluded with Hilary presenting me with parting gifts, which were beautifully wrapped. Inside were two colourful blouses and a scarf. My heart was full. I would miss my friends and the benevolent members of staff such as these — they had made my long years in hospital more bearable.

On the Friday evening, I packed the chattels I had accumulated during my long years of hospital life and then chatted to my friends till very late. Though I was weary when I retired to spend the last night in my hospital bed, excitement, coupled with a turmoil of fearful thoughts, kept me tossing and turning till dawn.

Reflections had also kept me awake. I had realised that my painful times were relatively few when I remembered the good times I had experienced in the hospital. Moreover, I had become acquainted with many interesting people over the years, not only among my fellow patients, but also among the staff and friends of the hospital. I had made many firm friendships, too, especially among the volunteers. I had also seen how hard the doctors had to work in order to achieve success with their skills. On the other hand, I learned that sometimes they failed many times before they succeeded in treating many of the complex cases they were presented with.

Although I had presented the medical teams with a string of complex illnesses over the years, disregarding my paralysis, they had been able to cure me. So I had been lucky. I would be eternally grateful to them and the nursing staff for the medical treatment and care they gave me.

I had certainly become well versed in medical terms during my stay. I did not anticipate that this would be a boon to me in the future, however. The fact that I had gained a fluency in English, thanks to the English-speaking volunteers, filled me with the hope that I would be able to use the language one day to my advantage.

Despite the restless night, I had no problem rising early for in my joy, I had a pressing urge to leap out of bed to meet the dawning of a new chapter in my life. In the event, of course, I had no alternative but to rise in the usual painstaking way.

At 8:30 a.m., Irene, who had taken a day off work, arrived anxious to take me home. First, I asked her to push me up the slope to the Fund Raising Department since I wanted to say goodbye to Hilary Prior and Gillian Ford, both good friends to me for many of my years in the hospital.

Meanwhile, a washing machine, an electric fan and a toaster that Heung Jiu had given to me were loaded onto the hospital bus. They had been in store in the Fund Raising Department since she had left Hong Kong for Taiwan five months before.

Our farewells over, we returned to the hospital's back entrance where we found that a group of my friends and staff had gathered to see me off.

When the bus was loaded with my luggage, Irene, a nurse and myself, the engine revved, sending my heart into somersaults — I was going home at last!

As the bus pulled away to the sound of fond farewells, I wondered if this would be my last farewell to my surrogate home in the peaceful cove of Sandy Bay.

My sister and I chatted excitedly along the way but as the bus crossed the bridge joining Aberdeen to the island of Ap Lei Chau, I found myself in rather a pensive mood. As had been the case in all the highlights of my life, apprehension still bothered me.

Certain aspects of my homecoming had worried me since it was first discussed. I knew my life would take on a new pattern but would this mean that my days at home would drag on in monotonous routine, more so than they had in hospital?

I wondered how I would keep myself occupied. The prospect of being confined to my new high-rise home, facing day after day fraught with boredom and frustration depressed me.

Furthermore, despite my elation on being reunited with my family, I realised that not everyday would be blissful. I knew we would have to adjust to living together again and the fact that I was now more disabled than when I had lived at home almost nine years before would undoubtedly cause problems.

I was concerned, too, over whether I would be a burden on my family, not only physically, but also financially. I wondered if I would summon the strength and courage to overcome the problems I would face as well. All I could do was cling to the hope that my prayers would help me through.

Regardless, this was a joyous occasion. When my sister announced that the bus had pulled up outside our block, I forced myself not to let my worries curb my enthusiasm.

On alighting, I was anxious to survey my new surroundings. So with Irene bubbling over trying to explain everything, I gazed around. All I could see were drab, grey blocks looming above me. They appeared to be surrounding a cul-de-sac jam-packed with vehicles of all shapes and sizes.

Accompanied by the nurse and the driver, we squashed into the lift with my luggage and electrical appliances and then pressed the button for the twelfth floor of the fifteen-storey block.

It took a concerted effort to extricate everyone and everything from the lift before we found ourselves making our way towards the daylight at the end of a long, dark corridor. Smells of cooking and incense drifted by as we passed the usual iron grills on the apartment doorways with the doors ajar to encourage any hint of breeze wafting along the corridor. Sounds abounded; the familiar sounds of high-rise, resettlement estate living: televisions blaring, tenants bellowing, children whimpering and the clattering of mahjong tiles. Our flat was the last on the right.

My mother rushed through the door to greet me; my father hovered behind. The nurse and the driver kindly helped take the appliances and my luggage inside, then took their leave.

Apart from a few "wahs" and "ahhs" from my mother, my welcome was rather subdued. Nevertheless, I could sense my parents were inwardly exultant and I could detect no hint that they were apprehensive about my homecoming.

Gingerly, I wheeled myself around to inspect our domain, very careful to avoid colliding with door posts and furniture. The first thing that struck me was its size. Over the years I had become accustomed to the vastness of Ward 2; in comparison, the flat was minute. I worried how I was going to cope with normal life again, in such a confined space shared with three other adults.

In all, the flat measured three hundred and ten square feet. It had been partitioned into a living room, enclosed balcony, kitchen, toilet/shower cubicle and a sleeping compartment.

The door from the corridor led directly into the living room. Against the wall dividing the flat from the corridor stood a long, built-in cupboard and drawer unit with shelves above. A wooden sofa and a desk stretched along the left-hand wall as far as the glazed partition, separating the living room from the balcony. A table and a couple of chairs were kept folded away, only brought out into the living area at mealtimes or for visitors.

The enclosed balcony housed the refrigerator, washing machine, wardrobe and our ancestral altar. Bamboo washing poles cantilevered from the balcony window, from where there was a view of Aberdeen Harbour and the mountains beyond. It especially pleased my mother that to the far right of our block down on the shoreline nestled a temple dedicated to Hung Shing, the weather forecaster, a popular deity with the fisherfolk.

The kitchen was located on the right of the balcony. Being very small, it was equipped with only a concrete bench for the gas cooking-ring and a deep, rectangular sink, which, to the annoyance of us all, happened to have faulty plumbing.

On the right of the sitting room, sandwiched between the kitchen and the one and only sleeping compartment, was the toilet cubicle. It was just about wide enough for me in my wheelchair to approach the toilet bowl from the front. The shower protruded from the left-hand wall. When it was used, the whole cubicle, including the toilet bowl, became drenched — a very precarious situation for me.

A tiny hand-basin was the only other facility for washing oneself — it was fixed to a wall in the balcony area just outside the toilet.

Except for the main door, all doorways were curtained, there being insufficient space for opening doors.

The sleeping compartment was divided from the living room by a wooden partition. Mother, Irene and I slept here on wooden beds covered with raffia mats. My father either slept on the wooden sofa in the living room or just outside the flat, depending on the season. Our flat happened to be next to the stairs at the northern end of the building that faced the open sea. Three sides of the landing were open to the elements and there was always a breeze. So during the oppressive heat of summer, my father felt more comfortable sleeping here, or sometimes in the corridor.

On moving in, mother had purchased a wardrobe, a ventilation fan for the kitchen and a few lights. She had also arranged for workmen to enclose the balcony with a window to keep out the elements. An allowance had been given by the Social Welfare Department to purchase a water heater for the shower, especially for me.

Ap Lei Chau is accessible from Aberdeen on Hong Kong Island either by the road bridge, a small ferry or *kaidos,* meaning "water taxis." The island has always been renowned for its boat builders who build all kinds of crafts, including eighty-foot traditional teak junks.

Our block was one of many in a government housing estate on the northwest tip of the island. To the east, we looked down upon a mass of boats anchored in Aberdeen Harbour where we had lived on our houseboat in the early 1950s. On the west side towered a huge power station.

Further to the east of the harbour, Father Edward's former abode, the Holy Spirit Seminary, still stood on its hill but no longer overlooked Staunton Creek as we knew it. Instead, it commanded a view of the Ap Lei Chau Bridge and the factories which had been built on the land reclaimed from the creek in the early 1960s.

Sheltered Cove

It transpired that my home life was not as boring as I had expected. Every morning, I rose early and after the rest of the family had used the shower cubicle, I took more than an hour bathing, a difficult and precarious task.

In the confined space, still sitting in my wheelchair, I used to struggle to reach every part of my body while everything around me became drenched from the shower.

Throughout this procedure and the transferring to and from the toilet bowl, I tensed with fear. I imagined that my chair would slide on the flooded floor, which was slow to drain, or that I would slip off the wet toilet bowl. Being rather deaf, my mother used to hover just outside to make sure she would hear my call if I needed assistance.

During the day, I listened to the radio or watched television while my mother pottered around and made her daily trip to the local market.

I seldom went out because I would not know when I needed to go to the toilet due to the lack of sensation in the relevant regions of my body. Since returning home, I had already suffered acute embarrassment due to a few accidents in that direction. I hated being a nuisance to my family and on occasions such as these, frustration over my paraplegia overwhelmed me. Though my mother was considerate and did not complain, I feared it would take some time for my family to understand and accept the problems caused by my condition.

I could not do much around the house. Cooking was out of the question as the gas ring flames were dangerously fierce, but I could use the electric rice cooker to make myself a simple meal. Washing my clothes was no problem. Daily, after I had bathed, I wedged a bucket of warm water into the toilet bowl, then rinsed a few of my under garments through. My sister washed my outerwear in the washing machine.

With my daily chores completed, I turned to the schedule I had devised to keep myself occupied as much as possible for the remainder of the day.

I read Braille books that were sent through the post by the Hong Kong Society for the Blind and then practised writing the English alphabet with a pen. Writing in English was much easier for me than writing complicated Chinese characters. Between times, I knitted snakes and crocheted shawls for the Duchess of Kent Hospital bazaar, with an abundance of wool supplied by the hospital.

A succession of visitors arrived at my flat, which also helped to fill my days. Sister Justine and Louise Da Rosario and her husband called in and

Marlene Brune, a volunteer at the Duchess of Kent Hospital, came almost every week to teach me French.

I went on a few outings, too. Hilary Prior took me to a folk dancing performance at the City Hall and a rugby match at the British Army Base at Stanley Fort, a fund-raising event for the Duchess of Kent Hospital.

With each passing day, my anxieties dwindled and by June, I had adjusted to my new life. I had been heartened that my family had soon grown accustomed to my being at home and had tried their best to understand my problems. Even my father had been surprisingly sympathetic. Sometimes though, he did not like to keep me company when my mother was out and the rascal would bribe my young nephew Carl to stay with me.

All was going smoothly and now it was time to invite our good friend Father Edward to visit and see me happily settled down with my family.

My second brother Chan Lai Yan and his family lived in the same housing estate. He was working on the Sunday we invited Father Edward, but his wife Ah So came over to prepare lunch. This gave Father Edward the opportunity to meet her children, Cathy aged one, and five-year-old Carl, for the first time.

My mother thought our good friend looked tired, also much thinner than she remembered. This sparked concern that he was not well. "I'm fine. It's the heat of the summer that tires me and makes me thin," he explained.

Nineteen eighty-five was drawing to a close when my sister introduced me to her friend Cammie, her workmate in an electronics factory in Aberdeen. Cammie wanted me to help improve her English. I told her that I had no experience in teaching and would not know where to start. Nevertheless, she wanted to be my first pupil. After a few minutes of persuasion, I agreed to teach her. We agreed to share the cost of a set of English textbooks and a pack of audio tapes.

Luckily, Cammie was considerate and patient with me while I did my best to teach her to write and pronounce English well. She in fact taught me the Cantonese for some English words along the way and since she spoke with a strong Tanka accent, I sometimes corrected her pronunciation of Cantonese. She was punctual and our lessons went smoothly.

Through her hard work, Cammie steadily progressed and her confidence in speaking and writing English increased. So now, my apprehension over whether I could teach or not was beginning to be replaced by rising confidence. Furthermore, I was gratified that my teaching method, now tried and tested, had obtained satisfactory results. Cammie was satisfied with her progress, too, and soon she brought her friend Kitty to learn. My teaching career took off slowly but surely from there.

One of my regular visitors since I had returned home was Frances Rasmussen, a motherly, public spirited, middle-aged American lady from Hawaii who had lived in Hong Kong for many years. A friend of Heung Jiu's, she had been a volunteer in the Duchess of Kent Hospital since early 1970. On one of her visits, she realised I was unable to write to my friends. So being a member of the Hong Kong Chapter of Ikebana International, long time supporters of the Duchess of Kent Hospital, she persuaded them to raise the funds to buy me an electric typewriter. I was thrilled. Now, I could fill some of my hours practicing typing and writing to Felicity Wilkes, an Occupational Therapy volunteer who had returned to Australia and Heung Jiu who was now living in Taiwan.

Before I had left the hospital in October 1985, Matron had introduced me to Judy Carl, another American in her middle years. She often brought Su Ying and I an abundance of tasty snacks, and also spent many hours reading to me. After I went home, she still kept in touch and on one occasion she took me back to the hospital to visit Su Ying. It was Judy who introduced me to a group of ladies who attended the Baptist Church at Repulse Bay, some of whom have remained my staunchest friends to this day.

Many of these ladies were concerned about my disabilities and one day in the July 1986, three of them took me to see a private specialist for yet another opinion on my eyes.

Unfortunately, we were told the same prognosis: nothing could be done and only a miracle would help. However, the specialist, Mr MacRobert, prescribed some ointment for my eyes, instructing me to apply it everyday because the most important source of lubrication for my eyes, my tear ducts, were not functioning. His concern was that the limited visibility in my left eye be maintained. I was charged no fee for the consultation, or for the medication.

Soon I was attending regular Bible studies and other activities connected with the Baptist Church. The ladies were very friendly and in a few weeks, I began telephoning two or three of them to practise my English.

One of these ladies, an English lady named Carolyn Thompson, was very keen to help me improve my English. Besides our conversations on the phone, she came to see me once a week. Sometimes, she would help me mark Cammie's written work; at the same time, I learned too.

I recall with a chuckle, the first impression I formed of Carolyn. It was in the early summer of 1986 that I found myself sitting next to her in a noisy, bustling Chinese restaurant in Wan Chai. About eighteen of us from the Bible Study Group had gathered around a very large circular table to enjoy a farewell lunch for Anita Harlock, an American friend who was about to move to Brussels. Upon our introduction, Carolyn appeared to be rather stern. She carried the air of a very strict schoolteacher, I thought. So feeling rather nervous of her, I did not converse freely.

It was not long before my unfavourable impression of Carolyn changed.

I remember clearly, feeling rather apprehensive one September afternoon, when Anita Harlock, who had first taken me to the Bible Study Group, brought Carolyn to my home. Nervously, I showed Carolyn the photographs of my Pilgrimage and when I explained them in English, she was surprised; she hadn't realised, on our first acquaintance, that I would be able to converse with her so easily. She relaxed and we chatted like old friends.

It came as a great relief that my first impression of her was shattered.

"If you have anything you want to know, or if you need any help, just give me a call. I'll be very happy to talk to you on the phone and to help you with your English, too," she said as she handed me her phone number. From that day, she came to see me regularly.

Carolyn, a slightly built, pretty woman, was in her late thirties when I first met her. Her husband, an English structural engineer, had been based in Hong Kong at that time for about sixteen years. Their eldest daughter, a primary schoolteacher and their son, who was at college, lived in England. Their youngest daughter, a teenager, attended school in Hong Kong.

Both Carolyn and her husband were members of the Baptist Church and took part in Bible Studies and the charitable activities of the Church.

Carolyn taught English voluntarily at the Baptist Church School in Aberdeen for more than a decade. Through her help, my essay writing improved greatly, so much so that at her suggestion, I began to write the essays about my experiences, which have helped in forming this book. Through her constant support, also, I began to teach my students with more confidence.

Besides all this, she frequently invited me to her home and took me on outings. Furthermore, she was always ready to help with any problems I had with my health or other matters.

When Heung Jiu passed through Hong Kong at the end of August 1986 on her way from Taiwan to live in Greece, she was delighted to see me settled in the bosom of my family. She was also delighted to hear that I was persevering with my teaching and that I had Carolyn to support me.

Cammie came over especially to meet Heung Jiu and to practise her English. I was proud of the way Cammie conversed and hoped it was due to my efforts, which, of course, had been backed up by Carolyn.

Fisherfolk Reunion

In January 1987, my mother's youngest brother who lived in Kowloon asked if she would like to accompany him to China to visit their eldest brother's widow.

Mother was very keen to go. She had been unable to venture up to China to see her relatives for more than thirty years, mainly due to the Mainland's travel restrictions, which were not relaxed until the late seventies.

The widow lived in a village about thirty miles from the border with Macau. Though they farmed, they had remained fisherfolk to a certain extent, but fished the rivers rather than the sea.

My mother had always been confused over how many siblings she had. As far as I could make out, some had died in infancy, three brothers had remained in China, one older sister had since died and two brothers had settled in Hong Kong.

One of the Hong Kong brothers, her second youngest, owned two herbal medicine shops in Kwai Chung. His two wives in China had died many years ago and his Hong Kong wife passed away when he was in his late sixties. Unhappy being a widower, he rented out the shops and returned to China. There, to the amazement of all the family, he settled down with a new twenty-five-year-old wife. He returns to Hong Kong now and again to collect the rent.

Mother's family was also of the Tanka people.

During her childhood, her parents' boat was moored in the estuary of the West River near the small town of Sun Wui in Guangdong Province, southern China. She used to help look after her younger siblings, as well as get up early in the morning to work in the fields. She gathered corn for a local farmer, always with a little brother or sister strapped on her back. When her father fished, she operated the sampan that assisted the junk in hauling in the nets and then ferried the catch to the junk.

Her family were very poor and food was scarce. Mostly, they ate fish if their father happened to have a good catch, but sometimes they only ate rice with a sauce made from insects, now preserved, which had lived among the corn. If they had managed to sell an abundance of fish throughout the year, they could put some money aside and then look forward to eating a goose at Chinese New Year.

As in most families, the eldest daughter is very bossy. So it was with mother's eldest sister and they did not get along with each other very well. Her eldest brother, however, treated her very kindly and she could always rely on him for help and advice when she had problems. But if my mother did not sell enough fish at the market or get a good price, then her brother would scold her.

Times were hard in China in those days and some turned to crime to earn a living. One common practice where my mother lived was the abduction of children, especially the daughters of poor peasants and fisherfolk. They were sold as servants.

Night after night, the boats in the harbour were raided. So after hurriedly eating her evening meal, my mother used to meet with the other girls from the local floating community. Frantically, they would run as fast as they could to seek out kind-hearted local women ashore who would hide them in their homes.

Once, her father was kidnapped and held for ransom. The kidnappers asked for children or money in return for his release. If the children had been forfeited, they would never have been seen again. So the eldest brother decided to sell a younger brother and sister to raise the ransom. After her father was released, the whole family had to work very hard to earn the money to buy back the children.

However, the young brother in question had been sold to a family who had no son and was not returned. All contact with him was lost until recently. Some members of mother's family in Hong Kong had received a message from him requesting his long-lost family to travel to China for a reunion.

None of the family was keen to go, except my mother. Having no one to accompany her and not having a clearly defined address for him in China, she feared she may not find him if she went alone.

Now, this pending visit — just before Chinese New Year 1987 — was a different matter. Mother was happy to seek out her relatives, especially as she was to be accompanied by her brother and his wife.

They began their journey by taking a ferry to Macau. Then they took a bus to the border. To complete the rest of the journey, they hired bicycles. After three strenuous hours, the three sexagenarians reached my aunt's house exhausted. Nevertheless, fuelled by their excitement, they summoned the energy to talk late into the night. The family had so much to talk about after three decades of separation.

My aunt had been widowed in the mid-1960s. Her husband had left her and his children to attempt to enter Hong Kong illegally with a younger brother. They were swimming across the Sham Chun River, between China and Hong Kong, when they were spotted by the Hong Kong Marine Police. During the ensuing chase my younger uncle escaped but the elder, being in his sixties and in poor health, drowned.

It was not until about twelve years later that my aunt heard what had happened to him, through relatives visiting from Hong Kong.

The second day, my aunt took my mother to see a medium who evoked the spirit of my maternal grandfather from the spirit world. The first thing he said to my mother was: "You ungrateful daughter. You haven't given me any money to spend. Why are you so mean to me? I'm very angry with you."

"It's your fault," mother chided. "You chose a poor husband for me. I have had a hard life, and I couldn't afford to send you money."

After this rebuke, my grandfather dared not argue but he asked: "Please burn paper money and paper clothes and when you return to your sister-in-law's home, present the ashes at the ancestral altar." An effigy of grandfather stood on the altar at my aunt's home where my mother was staying.

Ancestral shrines in the home are usually handed down from one generation to another. Effigies, or tablets inscribed with family names are placed inside the altar, together with an oil lamp or electric light that is kept alight. Joss sticks are burned and flowers and food are usually offered each day to pacify and nourish the dead.

It is the custom that a married daughter should visit her ancestral shrine every Chinese New Year, or Spring Festival as it is called in China, to present gifts to her dead parents. But because of restricted travel into China, my mother had not done so for decades. It seemed that her neglect had upset my grandfather. Obviously, news that she had obtained permanent residence in Hong Kong and that it was difficult for her to travel to China had not reached him in the spirit world.

According to my mother, my grandfather had been a very mild-natured man when he was alive but after he died, he became very bad tempered. Whenever his progeny evoked his spirit, he scolded them severely in a very stern voice and if they displeased him greatly, he was likely to cause bad things to happen to them.

Conversely, his wife had a very bad temper while she lived but she became very placid in her afterlife. This was fortunate for the family because pacifying my grandfather's angry spirit was difficult and worrying enough for them to contend with.

Troubled Waters

Mother returned from China just in time to celebrate Chinese New Year. I congratulated myself that I had coped very well during her absence, albeit only for three days. Apparently, her father's spirit had told her to return home quickly; he must have known that she had a handicapped daughter to care for.

Cheered by her China visit and the Chinese New Year festivities, mother was happy. Everything was going well for me, too, far better than I had expected. Something was troubling me. I wondered why a fever had been chasing me like the devil ever since I had left Lourdes about eighteen months ago. Then, one day in March, I discovered what my system had been trying to fend off — a pressure sore in my groin. My spirits sank like a stone. "Aiyahh," I remember muttering, "not another spell in hospital!" The last time I went to hospital with a pressure sore, I stayed for four years!

Unfortunately, because of the lack of sensation in my lower body and also my limited sight, by the time I had noticed the sore it was serious. After treatment at a local clinic, it did not improve. In fact, it worsened considerably. Then when my temperature began to soar, Carolyn drove me to the casualty ward at the Queen Mary Hospital. Immediately, I was hospitalised.

Initially, I received treatment for a common pressure sore and a few days passed before the doctors realised my sore was more complex. They recommended that I be sent to the Duchess of Kent Hospital at Sandy Bay where again I met up with my old friends, although I was not assigned to the same ward.

When the surgeon opened the sore, he found it was very deep and near the intestine, so he dared not yet take the risk of closing it. Instead, I was put on a course of antibiotics and the sore was dressed daily. After three long months, it was healthy enough to be closed and I found myself back in the Queen Mary Hospital, awaiting the closure by a more experienced surgeon.

When the attempt was made to close it, however, the surgeon discovered a small hole had developed next to the pressure sore and inside it led into the original hole.

Due to this complication, surgery was abandoned once again. This roused misgivings within me that I would never be cured.

Day by day, I sank deeper into depression. I could not understand why the doctors could not decide on effective treatment for my sore. "Please God, don't let my condition be beyond help; I don't want to spend any more years of my life in hospital," I remember praying.

During the next week, the surgical and orthopaedic teams consulted each other about my case. Then one evening, a lady surgeon, Doctor Lau, appeared at my bedside. She examined my wound and pressed the flesh on my thigh to see if it was suitable to use for a graft. Then she pressed my stomach. "What a big tummy! There's plenty of flesh for us to use here!" she exclaimed.

"That's a good idea," I chuckled. "It will be one way of making it flatter."

Seriously, though, I did not want my tummy to be spoiled, as so far, it was one of the few parts of my anatomy that had escaped the surgeon's knife.

The next morning, Doctor Lau and her surgical team surrounded my bed. After their brief discussion, during which I strained my ears to gather even a whisper of hope, Doctor Lau announced that they would operate. "At last," I sighed, as my despondency changed to relief.

Almost immediately, I was transferred to the surgical ward upstairs, but I still had to wait. The longer I waited the more I was moved from bed to bed, until finally, I ended up in a camp bed due to the shortage of beds. I feared that the next move would be out into the corridor!

Then one evening, with more than two weeks of "musical beds" behind me, I was transferred to the Tung Wah Hospital in the Western District. Here, I was to have my wound closed, and then plastic surgery performed by Doctor Lau.

I had never been to this hospital before. So, immediately on my arrival in a ward on the sixth floor, I took note of the nurses' performance and attitude. If they were not efficient and pleasant to the patients, my stay would not be a happy one.

Within minutes, dismay overcame me. It became evident that some of the nurses had already assumed that I would be troublesome to them because of my disabilities. This was manifested when, feeling hot and sticky after the ambulance journey, I requested a bed bath. My perfectly reasonable request prompted an unpleasant reaction from some of the nurses. They were churlish and impatient with me and did not attend to me willingly. I was given a bed in a hot, dark, airless corner of the ward. Feeling very uncomfortable and deeply troubled, sleep did not come easily to me that night.

The next day, my bed was moved to a brighter, more airy position, and lifting my spirits further — I had my first visitor. She was my German friend Marlene Brune, who had been a good friend to me and Su Ying in the Duchess of Kent Hospital. Besides regularly supplying us with a selection of food, she kept my hair looking tidy by giving it a trim now and again. Touchingly, though she could not do much for her, Marlene had paid special attention to Mei Mei, too.

It was through Marlene that I acquired a new wheel-chair. She had noticed the dilapidated condition of the one I was using and persuaded her husband's company to donate a new one. Her visit this time was not a happy occasion. She had come to say goodbye. In a week's time, she was leaving Hong Kong and returning to Germany.

Thereafter, from time to time, some of my other expatriate friends came to visit: Frances Rasmussen, Carolyn Thompson and a new couple from the Baptist Bible Study Group — Nancy and Harvey Willis.

I was thankful for my good fortune in having so many Western friends, as when they appeared on the scene, it often made a difference to the way I was treated by nurses and *amahs* alike during all my hospital stays.

Due to my condition, some members of the ward staff would lose patience with me, scold me, or act unkindly or indifferently towards me. With a succession of Westerners regularly appearing at my bedside and the realisation that I could converse in English with them and the foreign doctors, the staff would think again.

Appearing to them now as more than just a simple, unfortunate "boat girl," their attitude towards me would perceptibly change for the better. Perhaps they feared I would mention their conduct to those in authority, or that my foreign friends would complain. Whatever the reason, I was glad of their change of heart.

Finally, the day I had been anxiously awaiting dawned. It turned out to be July 29. That morning, I became very concerned when I learned that my wound, though now healthy inside, was deeper than I had realised — five inches! This shocking revelation induced me to worry that the operation would not be successful and I would have to undergo further surgery.

The surgical team had drawn up a plan and had assured me everything would be all right. Nevertheless, I remained scared. I remember clearly — it was at 1:45 p.m. when the orderly wheeled me into the operating theatre. My heart beat heavily as panic gripped me.

On seeing my nervous state, the theatre staff tried to calm me and joked in a futile effort to divert my fearful thoughts while they transferred me to a long, narrow surgical bed, so narrow that I was forbidden to move. Aiyahh, so rigid was I with fear that I could not have moved anyway!

Above the thud of my heart I could hear clinking sounds as the doctors and nurses busied around me, arranging the instruments needed for the surgery. I was given the anaesthetic and I remembered no more.

Due to the complexity of the wound, the surgical team was forced to change their original plan as they went along. Consequently, the operation took five hours to complete, much longer than expected.

Thankfully, my tummy had been spared. The skin for the graft and flesh to fill the deep hole had been taken from my left thigh.

Immediately after the operation, I was sent to Intensive Care. I could neither feel the twenty-eight stitches in my thigh, nor the surgery to my sore because of my paralysis. Somehow, my upper back and left arm had been severely bruised during the surgery and this now caused me considerable pain. I cried out to the nurse who did her best to comfort me but I did not have a good sleep that night.

The next morning, Doctor Lau discovered that my wound was swollen and some stitches had given way. I also had a high fever. She diagnosed that the wound had become infected, so I was sent back to Queen Mary Hospital for antibiotic injections and a blood transfusion. After two weeks, I was back in the Tung Wah Hospital again where Doctor Lau instructed the nurses to give me antiseptic baths twice a day along with strong antibiotic injections. Gradually, I began to feel better and within two months, my wound, which had been the size of my palm, had completely healed.

During these last two months, while my body healed, I witnessed events that greatly disturbed me.

At first, except for a few surgical cases staying briefly, there was only me in the ward. Soon, several brain-damaged or comatose patients began to fill the beds. They were fed by tube and they could not move or talk. Day by day, these poor souls were dying around me. I felt so sad and lonely. One day I was drowned in gloom when three patients died within a few hours of each other.

As if my life in this ward was not dismal enough, relatives of the departed often wailed, screamed, ranted and raved in their grief. I could understand their feelings but I felt there was no need to put on such a dramatic display.

It was hard for me to cope with this atmosphere of death, let alone these disturbing lamentations. So when a group of mourners put on an alarming display of grief one day and then accused the nurses of not giving enough oxygen to their loved one to keep her alive, I had had enough. In the strongest tone I could muster, I scolded the mourners for upsetting everyone and scaring me beyond bearing.

My outburst shocked them into embarrassed silence. Then, to the relief of both patients and staff, they slunk out of the ward.

That night, the trauma of the day and the recurring memory of the thud of the bodies being dropped into temporary metal coffins by the mortuary attendants and the clunk of the lid haunted me and I could not sleep.

The worst days were when I heard the plaintive cries of children calling for their mothers who had just passed away. "*Amah! Amah!*" would echo through the ward. Their grief and bewilderment were genuine; they did not know how to put on an act of remorse. I felt so sorry for these children — they had to face the rest of their childhood with no mother to care for them.

One morning my neighbour died of cancer. The nurse bathed and dressed her, drew the curtains around the bed and then left the body awaiting removal by the mortuary attendants. By coincidence, the curtains around my bed were drawn that morning because I was giving myself a bed bath.

I was totally absorbed in my struggle to bathe and did not pay much attention to the rattling sound approaching. Then suddenly, I was panic-stricken. It was the mortuary trolley! Aiyahh, what if the men make a mistake and come through my curtains? They would find me naked!

Instantly, I cried out as loudly as I could: "Don't come in here. Don't come in here. I'm not dead. I'm not dead!"

My panic succeeded in amusing a fellow patient who burst into loud laughter. Frantically, I fumbled around for something to cover my body and then froze in my bed till I heard a nurse direct the men to the correct bed.

Wah, what a relief, I thought. I had been saved from what could have been the most embarrassing moment of my life.

Life became brighter for me towards the end of my stay in this ward. In the evenings, I would wheel myself midway along the ward to watch television. My bed was very high, so I always needed someone to help me into and from my wheelchair. Most of the nurses would help willingly, but I will never forget one evening when I made the mistake of asking the wrong one: "You can do it on your own," she snapped. "There is no need to bother me."

I could not contain my anger. "Can't you see that the bed is too high for me," I exploded. "If I could move myself, I would not bother you."

She must have been embarrassed by my chiding her, because then, reluctantly, she asked an *amah* to help her lift me down into my wheelchair. I wondered why someone so petulant and so unfeeling had ever joined the nursing profession.

Despite all these events I tried to count my blessings. I'm sure it was God's will that I had the good fortune to be treated by Doctor Lau who tried her utmost to cure me. She was a very conscientious surgeon and often checked on me to make sure all was going well. We were both very pleased with the outcome of the operation and I will be forever grateful to her for her patience and skill.

On returning home in October, I continued to teach my two students and I began to learn French with a new teacher. Before leaving Hong Kong, Marlene had asked a friend to find someone to teach me French and by December, a German lady had volunteered. Her name was Michaela Collins.

Michaela's proficiency in languages impressed me. She could speak French, English, Mandarin and a little Cantonese. Once a week she came to my flat determined to teach me French. She dictated in French, so that I could write it down in Braille and then she translated the text into English, which I also wrote down. I listened to tapes and learned the dialogue by heart, striving to pronounce the words correctly but having had no foundation of the language at school, I found French very difficult. Nevertheless, I persevered. Teaching me was a painfully slow process and I appreciated Michaela's unfailing patience with me.

Rocking the Boat

Being back with my family in Ap Lei Chau was not all rosy of course; there were still the upsets caused by my father who was just as incorrigible as ever. He continued to avoid responsibility for family affairs and left the expenses and the organisation of important events, such as family celebrations, to my mother.

It seemed to my sister, my mother and I that his outside interests were more important than anything relating to his home life. Ironically, most of his friends considered him to be a great guy and this praise made him very proud of himself.

Now that he had three women at home to contend with, he was more obstinate than ever. He was also very careless. Irene, who did most of the housework, and I constantly reminded him to be neat and tidy, a necessity with four adults sharing such cramped living conditions. Our criticism infuriated him and his temper would flare. This friction between us was hard for poor mother to bear.

On many an occasion, he staggered through the door in a drunken stupor. He would curse and blaspheme and accuse us of making his life a misery, or he would regale us with his grandiose, idealistic aspirations in a thundering voice. These outbursts reverberated throughout our building, often disturbing our neighbours. We three women would try to calm him down but for our efforts we were showered with even louder abuse.

Despite all this, he was not without virtues. He was neither a sly nor greedy man and he often gave help to others without hesitation, financially or otherwise. He dreamt of becoming a millionaire, so every week he bet on horses and bought lottery tickets. One day he announced, "If I ever win a pot of gold, I will donate some money to the Duchess of Kent Hospital and the Tung Wah Hospital for all they have done for you."

He was very fond of children and some of his earnings were spent on buying snacks and toys for them. He especially spoiled my eldest brother's four children and also a toddler who used to peer through the iron grill in the doorway of the flat opposite. If he had no gifts for her, then he would give her money.

Unfortunately, his immediate family rarely benefited from his big-heartedness. Even during our direst need, he would hesitate to help us and he would often complain that we children had neglected to recompense him, mainly moneywise, for all that he had done for us.

He seemed to have inherited the same character and behaviour as his father, for they both liked to help others but seldom paid much attention to their own families. "Town saint and house sinner," I believe is the Western expression — an appropriate description of them both.

Being the eldest grandson, my father was spoilt by his grandparents as a child and was considered an important person by his brothers and male cousins. His education began at the age of twelve when he attended a poor village school on the coast of Guangdong Province together with four of his "brothers." Their grandfathers were brothers and it is the Chinese custom to call the members of the same clan brothers or sisters.

There was only one teacher. He endeavoured to teach his small class mathematics, history and to read and write Chinese.

Each morning, the boys rose early and were given money to buy their breakfast on the way to school. My father always received more money than the others because his grandmother secretly gave him a few extra coins. However, he liked to gain favour with his brothers, so he shared his extra money with them.

The boys resented having to attend school for the whole day, so to relieve their boredom the youngsters often played pranks on the teacher, driving him to distraction.

On one occasion, they altered the hands on the school clock to a later hour so the teacher thought it was time for them to go home. Another time they pretended to have severe stomach pains and ran out of the school. Instead of going home, the boys spent hours playing hide and seek and climbing trees. Finally, they decided to return to school. Definitely expecting to be chastised, they entered the room only to find their teacher fast asleep.

Education was not taken seriously and nothing was learned. So this first attempt at educating my father was not a success.

When my grandfather found that his fishing business was prospering, he announced that he would send my father to a boarding school in Guangzhou where he would surely receive a sound education.

His son was enthusiastically welcomed by everyone in the school, including the staff who never punished nor scolded him for his constant bad behaviour. This preferential treatment was due to the abundant supply of seafood he brought for the teachers after his regular visits home. The teachers knew they would lose this treat if they ever upset him. Not surprisingly, father did not do well at his studies. At the age of eighteen, he left the school with no qualifications and joined his father in his fishing business.

Father continued to be very popular and acquired a host of mostly idle friends.

Two of those happened to be government officials keeping watch for pirates and smugglers in the harbours of Guangdong Province.

One day, my father did these friends a favour by finding a source of suitably equipped boats that they could use for their surveillance. In return, they presented him with a new boat as his commission.

It was the acquisition of this boat that enabled my parents to leave grandfather's boat and start their own business transporting cargo along the coast of southern China before I was born.

Although my father was irresponsible in many ways, he did help with the crisis my grandparents were faced with when two of their sons wanted to get married.

It is the Chinese custom for the groom's parents to finance weddings and give a dowry to the bride's family to compensate them for losing their daughter to the groom's. My grandfather was beside himself with worry because he could not find the money to pay for their wedding ceremonies. So my father came up with another of his bright ideas — smuggling!

He sought the help of some friends in acquiring a cargo of grain and salt. He then hired a crew to ferry it to Hong Kong, a very dangerous venture, because not only pirates had to be avoided but also the patrolling Customs officials.

The smugglers escaped detection and they made many more of their clandestine trips, which turned out to be very profitable. The money my father made he contributed to the expenses of his third and sixth brothers' weddings. Number one brother had come to the rescue.

My father demonstrated his big-heartedness again when my second and fourth aunts' husbands were entangled with the law.

These aunts were a burden on the family. They always returned to the family boat when they were in trouble. Time after time, they took advantage of the family's generosity and gave nothing in return. This caused a great deal of unpleasantness and bickering among the brothers and sisters.

My mother always maintained that these women were partly responsible for causing the family to sink into poverty. My father could not deny that his sisters were troublemakers but he would not chastise them; he would only complain about them behind their backs when he was drunk. Despite the amount of unpleasantness his sisters had caused, number one brother came to the rescue again and paid their husbands' fines.

Although father's methods of obtaining money were, to say the least, a little suspect, he felt very proud that he could assist his family in their time of need. Even now, when he has had a few drinks, he boasts that if it were not for him the rest of the family would have perished. He believes the family should show him more respect and appreciation. Unfortunately for him, the family no longer listens to him.

In 1986, a few members of our family on my father's side suggested that he retire from his part-time job as a caretaker of a block of flats because of his advancing years. He insisted that although he was in his late seventies, he felt very fit and as long as he could maintain his good health, he should go on working to compensate for his idle youth!

At no time did he ever compensate his wife and children. As far as we were concerned, he earned money only for himself, though sometimes, when he was in a good mood, he would buy us food from a cooked-food stall. Usually, he would buy so much that we could not eat it all, and we would complain that he had wasted his money. He would rather be extravagant in this way than give my mother money towards the household expenses, or even buy his personal daily needs. We could not understand why. What a ridiculous joke!

Let Them Swim

My sister Irene is a petite, very slim, young-looking woman, now approaching her late thirties. Her complexion is rather pale and her mid-brown hair is usually worn short and permed. She is cheerful, friendly and generally has no lack of energy and enthusiasm.

She was thirty years old when I returned to live at home in 1985 and she proved to be very supportive towards my mother and I. Besides working long hours at a factory she cleaned the flat, ran errands and generally helped as much as she was able.

Even when she was only about six years old, in the days when I was in the boarding school, she was responsible enough to shop in the market, wash her clothes and tidy the boat while my mother was out at work. I remember my mother being surprised when she went home for lunch one day to find that little Irene had cooked the meal.

Yet when I lived at home during my younger years, Irene and I did not get on well together. We always seemed to quarrel. This was usually over sharing household duties, but I wondered if the cause was more related to her being ashamed of me because I was handicapped.

One job we shared on the boat was cleaning the ancestral altar. I remember being very dismayed one day when Irene showed disrespect to our ancestors. She happened to be in a very bad mood and threw their effigies into the harbour. "Let them swim," she snapped. Her irreverence shocked me and I feared we would incur the wrath of our ancestors. Maybe they forgave us because Irene was so young.

There was no water source on our houseboat and though this was the time when my father's friends lodged with us, they were of no help. So the heavy task of water collection was left to Irene and me, or my mother after she had finished work. Most days, Irene and I walked a long way to queue at the public water tap. Then we struggled home with sleeves and trousers rolled up; Irene carried buckets on each end of a pole across her shoulders and I carried one in each hand, as my back was not the right shape to carry the buckets on my shoulders.

During drought water restriction periods, we were permitted to collect water only every four days. We used to take as many containers as we could manage and wait three or four hours in the strong sun for our turn at the standpipe. The boat-dwellers often jostled and fought each other for position in the queue. This frightened us and we would be relieved when the police arrived to keep order.

We also helped mother assemble plastic goods handed out by factory owners. We thought we were lucky to earn just two dollars each.

Later on, mother taught us how to attach plastic handles to nets. This time we earned three dollars for ten dozen. With our pocket money, sometimes we would walk down to Aberdeen Pier to buy congee and noodles served from a sampan.

I was at boarding school when Ah Kong, our lodger, gave up cooking for a while and found work in the gambling centre in Aberdeen. He collected bets and distributed winnings and Irene, then in her teens, earned pocket money by helping him when she had no school.

He was very fond of Irene and during a spell when his bets were operating in his favour he bought her a gold ring. He gave me one, too, but I believed at the time that the gift was only to ward off envy on my part rather than because he liked me.

The gift affair was not on my mind for long. Ah Kong's reign as a *loong* did not last; a run of bad luck had reduced him to a *chung* again. Poor Ah Kong! Irene and I felt so sorry for him that we returned the rings.

Irene had started school when she was seven but she had no interest in learning and after reaching primary six she refused to go on with her studies. She felt working was easier and more enjoyable than studying. My parents voiced no opinion on the matter; only my second brother tried to explain to her the disadvantages of giving up so soon. She took no heed of his advice and found herself a job in a local factory.

About two years went by before she complained that work was hard and she wanted to go back to school again but it was too late, she was too old to apply. So she continued working and took up five or six subjects at night school.

Soon she found so many subjects too burdensome and decided to concentrate only on English. Even this she could not handle. After a couple of years, she abandoned her studies altogether — it seemed she had no aptitude for learning.

When I arrived home in 1985, she had been working for more than fifteen years but had been unable to find a satisfying job. I felt that if she could speak reasonable English her prospects of finding a better job would increase, so I tried to teach her.

Unfortunately, she absorbed very little. I tried my best to encourage her but when I reminded her to revise she made me feel I was forcing her to learn.

She used to dictate to me sometimes, which I thought would help improve her English, but she soon gave up because we would end up quarrelling. There was no enthusiasm in her voice and her reading was as laboured as pulling a cow up a tree. I used to become so exasperated with her stumbling.

In her favour, besides being a cheerful, friendly girl, Irene is innocent, dutiful and caring. When Ah Kong died of bronchitis in 1977, it was Irene who arranged his funeral and saw that his ashes were sent to his daughter in China. Irene had been putting a little money aside for Ah Kong and it was just enough to give him a simple ceremony. It was a sad, quiet affair because he had no family in Hong Kong and few friends. His *kai* son did not appear on the scene either, so Irene made sure the proper rites were performed. She also represented the women of our family who would remember Ah Kong with great fondness, always.

Irene managed to hold down a variety of jobs: a domestic worker in a hotel apartment complex, a messenger in the Queen Mary Hospital and she progressed to being a laboratory technician in the same hospital. Her English improved gradually because the friendships she formed with my foreign friends gave her the incentive to learn.

9

Bridging the Ocean

A lady who became a regular visitor to my home was an American — Nancy Willis. She was lively, attractive, and I would guess in her mid-thirties. The colour of her hair intrigued me, I could see it was fair but sometimes it was almost blonde!

I had met many Americans before, but Nancy's strong accent was new to me. She explained that being from Kentucky she had a southern drawl. I first met Nancy at a Bible study meeting at a Baptist Church member's home. During a chat, she said she would like to visit me at home. A week later, she arrived at our door.

While I was showing her the photographs of my Lourdes pilgrimage; she said one day she would love to take me to America! This took me by surprise. Throughout my life, generally my compatriots had demonstrated frustration and annoyance with my handicaps. So, it seemed strange to me that here was a foreigner disregarding my disabilities and offering to take me to her homeland.

A few months later, when I was admitted to the Duchess of Kent and Queen Mary hospitals with a pressure sore, Nancy continued to visit me once a week, often bringing toiletries and other things I required. When I was very poorly, she washed my hair and occasionally trimmed it to keep it tidy.

In no time she had endeared herself to my neighbours in the ward. They could not speak English, but with her open, friendly manner Nancy managed to communicate. Her husband Harvey also came to visit and despite being a very busy man, he took over Nancy's role when she went to the United States to study for six months.

Harvey once brought his pastor to see me at the Tung Wah Hospital. They gave me half a watermelon. After they left, since there was nowhere to keep it and my fellow patients declined to share it with me, I ate the whole lot.

I did not realise that, when in poor health, one should not eat an abundance of watermelon. I was plagued with vomiting and diarrhoea for the next two weeks! Now I realised why my wiser wardmates had refused a share.

Soon, because Harvey, a very handsome man, paid me so many visits during Nancy's absence, the nurses spread the rumour that he was my beau. When I heard this, I could only laugh.

During my hospital stay my doctor gave me permission for one day's leave so Nancy could take me to her apartment. She wanted me to try out a new wheelchair that had been bought with funds provided by the Baptist Church members. A chair had been delivered to me previously, but it had been too large, so I was to meet the wheelchair manufacturer's representative at Nancy's to make sure the second one was the right size.

Once inside her apartment, Nancy said: "Make yourself at home Mary. Wash your hair if you like. You can stay here, too, if you wish; I don't want to take you back to the hospital."

Her words touched my heart; I had feared that I was causing her a great deal of bother. I thanked God for friends such as Nancy.

Among my foreign friends, Nancy and Harvey were the most attached to my family members. Some Sundays we gathered at my home, and on special occasions they would visit and shower us with gifts. They were especially close to my niece, Cathy, and nephew, Carl, who looked upon them as their second mum and dad.

Ah So was particularly impressed by the generosity and care the couple showed towards her children. This helped change her attitude towards me, which hitherto had not been so warm. Moreover, the unconditional love and joy these Americans had brought to our home had encouraged the relationships between all our family members to become closer. The couple had set an example to us all of how kindness and concern should be bestowed on all regardless of differences.

Indeed, Nancy and Harvey had opened up a whole new world to me through their friendship. They were dismayed at the lack of facilities for the disabled in Hong Kong, and they realised how difficult it was for me to go out and about, even locally.

Often they took me to the Baptist Church Sunday services and introduced me to many of the congregation. This gave me the opportunity to meet people from all over the world and to become accustomed to a variety of accents.

After one of the services, we went to a Peking restaurant with family groups from the congregation. This was very much like the Chinese tradition of family gatherings at restaurants on Sundays for *yum cha,* meaning "drink tea." Once the meal was served, I was intrigued whether these *gweilos* would be able to cope with their chopsticks, but I soon found that they coped very well.

On another occasion, two former patients of the Duchess of Kent Hospital, who had become friendly with Nancy and Harvey during my last stay there, invited us to a *dim sum* lunch in the United Centre, Queensway.

When Nancy and Harvey called at my flat to pick me up, Cathy and Carl happened to be there. Being fond of the children, Harvey insisted that they should come with us.

My friends were thrilled to entertain the American couple. But at first, because they had difficulty communicating in English, they were rather tongue-tied and embarrassed. They soon felt at ease when Nancy and Harvey, against a background of the usual Chinese restaurant cacophony, made hilarious attempts to speak Cantonese.

Amid their giggles, the young ladies did their best to order the most delectable items from the passing *dim sum* trolleys. As a result, we guests, aside from Cathy and Carl, who were more interested in joking and playing with Harvey than eating, especially enjoyed the meal.

In great humour, we thanked the young ladies for entertaining us when the time came to leave and invited them to accompany us on a walk around the shops in the area. I enjoyed this spree immensely as shopping was a rare event for me.

About a year after our acquaintance, Nancy and Harvey adopted a twenty-month-old Chinese girl. They called her Amy. She would shriek with glee when she came to my home and found Cathy and Carl there to play with. Her parents were especially keen for her to learn Cantonese, and gain an insight into the Chinese way of life before Harvey's Hong Kong work contract ended.

On the day of the Moon Festival in 1988, Nancy invited three of my hospital friends, together with my students Cammie and Kitty, my sister Irene, Cathy and Carl and their mother Ah So to a party at her home in Repulse Bay. We were all very excited, especially Cathy and Carl who were always anxious to play with Amy.

Once inside the apartment, we presented Nancy and Harvey with a box of mooncakes, a basket of traditional Moon Festival fruits — persimmon, pomelo and taro — and an electric Chinese lantern that Harvey promptly hung from the ceiling. Then we were introduced to Nancy's American neighbours who bravely practised their Cantonese with us while we munched potato balls, hot dogs, salad and mango pudding.

When we finished eating, Harvey showed us around the apartment. It was luxurious, and we were astounded at the size. Being accustomed to living in minute units with just the basic essentials, we were enthralled. "Wahhhh, a Jacuzzi bath!" we exclaimed. That really impressed us. We wished we could be rich like them one day, but we could only dream.

Uncharted Waters

Cammie and Kitty had been very patient and considerate with me using them as guinea pigs while I struggled to become a proficient teacher of English. I will be forever grateful to them for being instrumental in starting me off on a career, which, even without my handicaps, a girl with my background would never have considered.

Cammie wanted to work in an office. To do this she needed to improve her English and pass the public examination, which she had failed at school. With my assistance, she tried to cram the examination syllabus within a year.

I was content with her improvement in spoken English and her pronunciation was good. But her written work, especially her essay writing, was weak. I felt she should not have been in such a hurry but I did not have the courage to suggest that she learned with me longer. I did not want her to think I wanted her money.

Eventually, without any comment from me she realised her weakness. But this did not deter her from taking the examination at the end of the year's tuition. Much to the amazement of Carolyn and myself, she just scraped through.

Kitty had also failed the public examination in English at school and wanted to try again. She was very keen and continued to take lessons with me while I was in hospital, though only when my health permitted. I was amazed at her keenness.

She had great confidence in my teaching methods and felt she did not need to attend evening classes as well. This increased the pressure on me to help her succeed, which was worrying because I did not yet have confidence in myself as a teacher.

Kitty was an obedient student and revised her lessons diligently. I supplied her with as many books as I could get hold of to give her extensive reading practise. Her reading was soon fluent and her pronunciation clear, but her comprehension remained poor. In her essays, she could not put the bones together or expand the subject. I used to pass her essays to Carolyn who marked them and wrote comments to encourage her to do better.

On the whole, Kitty's work was not satisfactory and when the examination approached, I doubted if she was up to the required standard. I decided the best thing to do was to support her all the way. But when the time came, she failed the examination.

It was a nerve-racking and upsetting experience for both of us. The poor girl had tried her utmost to learn, but with coping with a full-time job and having only one lesson a week with an inexperienced teacher, she could not succeed.

After this experience, I realised I must improve my understanding of how to teach and try to assess the standard and ability of my students accurately.

All was not in vain, however. Despite Kitty not achieving her ambition and Cammie just scraping through, they both, along with Carolyn and myself, recognised that their English had improved significantly since I had been their teacher. This gave me encouragement to try again and an opportunity soon presented itself.

Since my homecoming in 1985, a young lady member of the Catholic Church had been bringing me Holy Communion every week. Now, in July 1988, she was leaving Hong Kong to study abroad and a neighbour of ours, Mrs Chan, took over her duty.

I asked Mrs Chan if she would put a card on the local supermarket's notice board for me. When she saw that I was offering English tuition, she expressed surprise and wanted to know more. To my surprise, she asked if I would teach her son Louis, a Form 1 student. Of course, I agreed.

Within a few weeks, Louis' younger brother Kevin started lessons. Then their friends, Charlie and Michael, followed suit. The four were students at St. Peter's Roman Catholic School in Aberdeen.

Gradually, I took on even more students and by the beginning of 1989 my workload had increased significantly.

I sometimes had difficulty in arranging times for the students to come as most wanted their lessons out of school or working hours. And when some altered their times because of other commitments or illness, it often meant I had to teach more than one at a time. When this happened, I used to panic.

It happened that some days, five or six students would come and I would be extremely busy. But other days, when only two or three turned up, I found time to make Braille notes and tapes for teaching, or write my own essays for Carolyn or Nancy to correct.

The four boys continued and would come for extra lessons when their examinations approached. I was very pleased with their progress.

There is a Chinese saying: "A million things begin with many difficulties." This was certainly true in my experience, especially when I began to instruct students whose English was very poor.

I had to be very patient, and repeat words over and over with them until they could say them correctly. Fortunately, in compensation for my blindness, I am blessed with acute hearing and rarely miss a word badly pronounced.

Some days I grew weary of constantly repeating words and instructions, my voice becoming more hoarse as each lesson passed. And I wondered sometimes if some of my students were afflicted with defective hearing.

Nevertheless, I struggled on, urging these young people to concentrate and absorb my tuition. I sympathised with them because I realised that they had fallen by the wayside in their English studies at school and had had no chance to catch up. It was doubtful whether any other private teacher would have taken them on, or even if their parents could have afforded the fee.

To improve these youngsters' poor English was a great challenge for me and I did not intend to give up on them. There was also a selfish motive — I did not want their parents or anyone else to think I was a useless teacher because I was handicapped.

I admit that I was always relieved when a new student happened to be attending a reputable school, as then my workload would not be too exhausting. But at this time, many of my students were from boat families and they usually did not attend these schools. Some, who had left school, were taking commercial courses in adult learning centres, and others were still at school but feared they would not pass the public examination.

Many boat families were established in homes on the land by now, though some still fished for a living. If both parents go out to the fishing grounds, their children are often left to their own devices at home. Sometimes they get up to more than just mischief and their studies are liable to be neglected or not taken seriously.

In most families, only the father goes fishing and the children are left under the firm control of their mother. This has contributed to many boat children being a great credit to their parents and I hoped this would be the case with my students.

About five boat girls came to learn with me at this early stage of my teaching career. I fully understood, being one myself, how they did not want to fail. So with the help of my friends Carolyn and Nancy, who were always on call, I set about bringing these young girls' English up to standard. But aiyahh — pulling a cow up a tree would have been much less exhausting.

My students' success at school meant a great deal to me and I was elated when their marks in English improved. Conversely, I became very depressed when they did not do well for I could not help but blame myself.

I would say that most of my students were diligent and attentive, but there were some who just came to have fun and would not take their lessons seriously. They were noisy and disruptive to the other students, and I had to scold them soundly. Some even tested my eyesight! But I would either guess what they were up to, or other students present would tell me of their pranks. Usually, I would laugh and explain that it was they who were losing out by using up their lesson with silliness, not me.

So as time went on, my students and I would gain a better understanding of each other. If I scolded them, they knew it was for their own good and did not sulk. And when they were in low spirits over their studies, I explained that if they just put in a little more effort they would do well.

During lessons we worked hard and I was firm with them. But afterwards, if we had a few spare minutes we would share snacks while they regaled me with gossip or told me their problems. I had become a regular "agony aunt" to many of them.

A steady stream of students, mingled with visits from my foreign friends, kept me fully occupied. If my friends happened to come when I was teaching, they would converse with the students, read their essays and assess their progress. Cathy and Carl would come over for lessons most days, too. On occasions, students, friends and my family would gather for barbecues or celebrations, usually held out in the corridor or on the staircase landing where there was more space.

At first, it was difficult for my parents as they hardly ever had the place to themselves to relax or watch television. Conveniently, my father used to disappear in the afternoons when most of my students came. He was a caretaker of a block of flats in Happy Valley and he worked most afternoons and nights. Irene worked full-time as a housemaid in the Repulse Bay Hotel Apartments. She loved to join in and help organise social events with the students and my foreign friends when she could.

Amid all this hectic activity my mother would position herself on her low stool just outside our sleeping cubicle. And, while trying to catch a hint of breeze wafting through the window, she would sit in silent contentment, observing the life she had been drawn into since my homecoming.

From time to time, attempting to make myself heard over the noise from the construction site outside, I would shout at her: *"Hoi moon-a. Hoi moon-a,"* meaning open the door. She was quite deaf, so rather than having to startle her with my shouts, I was always glad when students were present to open the door.

Other than that, mother would rouse herself only if a foreign friend had arrived. She would hoist herself up from her stool, then toddle into the kitchen to pour a cup of tea from our flask, making sure she used only the best china cup. Later, around four-thirty, she would prepare the ingredients for our evening meal.

Heung Jiu, observing my mother on her little stool one day, remarked that she sat with an air of dignity about her. She could imagine her as the mistress on the prow of a sailing junk as it sailed before the wind.

I had never dreamt my life could be so full and satisfying. My family shared my joy, too. And though no word was uttered, I suspected they were a little proud of me.

EBB and Flow

In March 1989, my German friend Michaela Collins and her Irish husband Kevin left Hong Kong to settle in Switzerland. Michaela had taught me French regularly on Wednesday mornings for more than a year. Regrettably, as I became busier with my students and had less time to practise my French, teaching me must have been more like dragging a herd rather than just a cow up a tree.

A new teacher came for a few months before she found she could not continue the lessons. Then a young French seminarian replaced her. His efforts soon fizzled out and I was left with no teacher at all.

In was in early June of this year that I received the phone call that really raised my spirits.

"Mary?" a voice enquired.

Without hesitation I exclaimed: "Heung Jiu, you're back!"

A month before, Heung Jiu's husband, Derek, had returned to Hong Kong to work after working fifteen months in Taiwan and almost three years in Greece. She had told him not to telephone me because she had wanted her arrival, a month later, to be a surprise. We had corresponded and she had phoned me several times during those years away but our international phone calls were always brief. Now, we could talk for hours — local calls being free of charge.

Within a couple of days she came over to see me and a few students who had gathered to meet her. She was impressed by the progress I had made in my teaching and promised to visit every week to assist me by conversing with the students.

I was overjoyed at her return and thereafter I rang her everyday without fail for a chat and an English lesson. Now, she had plenty of time on her hands because she had returned to Hong Kong without her children. Her youngest daughter was at London University and her son and eldest daughter Christina were now working and living in London.

On a subsequent visit, while we were chatting after the students had gone, Heung Jiu suddenly exclaimed in horror: "Mary, you've got a hole in your ankle!"

"Don't worry. It's dry and it's healing," I assured her.

"How on earth did that happen?" she asked as she inspected the wound.

Then she noticed the metal footrest of my wheelchair had no cushion. "Your ankle bone has been rubbing on the metal," she concluded. "You need some protection." (Over the years since I had become a paraplegic, my foot had gradually turned inwards and now my outer ankle bone rested on the footrest).

"What about the rest of your body? Do you have any more sores?" she inquired.

"Not that I have noticed. But from time to time my knees and elbows get sore."

At hearing this, she was very concerned.

"Let me see what you are sleeping on."

I pulled back the curtain of my sleeping cubicle and she was aghast to see that all I was sleeping on was a stiff raffia mat on a hard board.

"No wonder you have problems. That arrangement would certainly give me sores."

"But it's cool," I protested.

"I don't care if it is cool. You need something else," she replied firmly.

She went home and immediately set about making me a cushion for my footrest. Within a week my feet were protected, and I had a two-inch-thick foam mattress with a pretty cover to sleep on, too.

About a couple of months after Heung Jiu's return, there was an important matter looming. Within the next few weeks I needed to get a new Hong Kong Identity Card. Heung Jiu had helped me obtain an ID card years before, so I mentioned the matter to her.

"Oh, not again, Mary!" she exclaimed in dismay. "Can you remember the performance last time?"

Of course I could remember, that was why I was worried.

It had been towards the end of 1984 and my long stay in the Duchess of Kent Hospital that the time came for me to renew my ID card. As usual, when any official business cropped up, I panicked. I desperately needed someone to help me so I plucked up courage and mentioned my problem to the social worker at the hospital. She told me that if I could find a friend to accompany me, we could be taken to the Immigration Department in the hospital bus. Heung Jiu gladly agreed to come with me.

At nine-thirty on the appointed day the friendly bus driver loaded me onto the bus with the wheelchair lift, and Heung Jiu sat herself down beside me. Then off we went to Wan Chai.

Once inside the building, we were astounded to find there was no lift to the basement where the identity card office was located. So Heung Jiu went to enquire whether she could renew it for me. But the staff insisted I go down in person, and their answer to my access problem . . . stop the escalator!

Our driver positioned himself and my wheelchair at the top of the escalator. But as he wheeled me on, he suddenly realised that the escalator had not been stopped. Instead, it was going upwards. The driver shouted, Heung Jiu screamed and my heart turned somersaults.

The poor driver! I did not realise that my wheelchair wheels had bruised his feet as he avoided a catastrophe.

With the staff shouting apologies in the background, I heard our driver assure me that the escalator was now at a standstill and he proceeded to bump me down the escalator backwards. I muttered under my breath as I tried to gain my composure.

I do not know whether it was because I was disabled, or whether it was because I was accompanied by a foreigner, but I did not have to wait in the long queue for submitting the forms or for my photograph to be taken. I was treated like an important person for a change and attended to immediately.

I did not feel very important, however, when I was photographed. I felt like a fool as I wobbled on the stool. There was no support for my back, so Heung Jiu had to crouch below me out of camera range and hold on to my floppy lower half to ensure I did not topple over.

The whole affair was an experience neither of us wanted to repeat, so I could fully understand Heung Jiu's dismay when I mentioned I needed to renew my card again.

"It's disgraceful that a public building is not designed to accommodate the disabled," Heung Jiu said in a disgusted tone of voice.

"I'll ring the Immigration Department — maybe they have installed a lift by now," she said as she left my flat. The next day she rang to say that no lift had been installed, but we could go over to the office in Kowloon, which did have a lift.

So the next Saturday morning, her husband Derek drove us over to the Kowloon office. Once again I was treated like a VIP, and all went smoothly until I had to balance on a similar stool as before for my photograph to be taken. I had put on a lot of weight since I had been discharged from hospital, making it difficult for poor Heung Jiu to hold my heavy, wobbly torso on the stool from her crouching position below. "If you fall on me, you'll flatten me!" she cried.

So one good friend had returned that summer, but now, two months later, another good friend was about to leave. Nancy's husband was being transferred to England in August.

The first time Heung Jiu met Nancy and her little daughter Amy, which was at my flat, Nancy told her that they were going to live in England at the end of the month.

"Will you be going to London?" asked Heung Jiu.

"Not exactly," replied Nancy, "Guildford in Surrey."

"I don't believe it," cried Heung Jiu, "whereabouts?"

"We will be renting a house in Burpham."

"What a coincidence! exclaimed Heung Jiu. "My house is only a five minute drive from there."

Then Nancy continued: "Harvey and I are hoping Mary will be able to visit us next summer."

"That would be lovely. Then she could visit my family, too," enthused Heung Jiu.

I expressed my keenness to go, of course, but I reminded them that my physical condition had to be taken into account and that the trip would cost a great deal of money.

"Never mind the money, Mary," said Heung Jiu. "It will come from somewhere."

Before my favourite American couple left for England, Harvey arrived at my door with a brand new computerised typewriter — a farewell gift for me. A few days later, my friends were gone.

I missed them terribly, as did my family, especially Cathy and Carl. Ever since I had met Nancy and Harvey in 1986, they were always on hand to give me their support in any problems that arose with my health, or any other matters. I would not forget their goodness and their kindness and the friendship they offered my family and my friends.

Logging My Course

In 1988, Carolyn suggested, as had Father Edward previously, that I try to write my story. So I began to write essays about my life, though not in an organised way or with very much detail. Secretly, I hoped that one day my essays could be expanded and made into a book, but who would help me? I wondered. Months later, when discussing my essays with Frances, I told her of my ambition to write my life story. She thought this was a good idea and, as the essays were rather a mess with corrections, she offered to take them home and retype them for me. This is a beginning, I thought.

Heung Jiu was a friend of Frances's, and since she had returned to Hong Kong, on a few mornings a week, she had joined her in taking toy trolleys around the wards of the Duchess of Kent Children's Hospital. As they left the hospital one day, Frances mentioned that she was retyping my essays. "I wish I could find someone with a word processor who would edit them and then put them into book-form for Mary," she said.

"I wouldn't be able to do it, even if I had a computer," Heung Jiu remembers saying. "Not only would I be scared stiff of the machine, but I haven't typed for more than twenty years." They laughed and then forgot about the idea until nearly two months later.

Heung Jiu's husband came home from work one day and announced that he was going to buy a computer to do office work at home. And when it arrived, Heung Jiu remembered what Frances had said about my essays. So she asked him if he would show her how to use the word processor. He did not understand much about the machine himself, but with the help of a manual he began to show his wife how to use the word processing programme.

The next time Heung Jiu went to the hospital, Frances gave her some of my essays and wished her good luck. Then day after day Heung Jiu persevered with putting them onto the computer and would ring her husband at the office when she got into difficulties.

One morning as she typed away, she was just thinking that maybe my essays could be used as a basis for an autobiography, when the telephone rang.

It was her friend who lived in the same complex. "Gill," she said, "there's a lady in the next block advertising plants for sale — here's the telephone number."

Heung Jiu thanked her friend, replaced the phone, then immediately dialled the number. The lady gave her the address of her flat and Heung Jiu promised to go over within a few minutes.

On returning to her study to switch off the computer, Heung Jiu suddenly realised that she did not need any plants. She had inherited quite a number on moving into her flat a few months before and had bought a few more since. However, having promised the lady, she thought she had better turn up.

"I'm sorry about the mess," the lady said as she let Heung Jiu into her flat. "I'm moving to the UK and amidst the chaos of packing, I'm frantically trying to finish a book."

Heung Jiu could hardly believe her ears. She then proceeded to tell the lady what she had been doing and thinking about when the phone rang. The lady was very interested and was keen to hear more about me and my essays.

Heung Jiu was even more astonished when the lady announced: "I work for a publisher. I can help you if you ever consider publishing."

She wrote down a list of publishers and also the name of a gentleman who she was sure would be willing to help and advise us — Anthony Lawrence, a former BBC foreign correspondent and now a writer and broadcaster, resident in Hong Kong.

The lady warned Heung Jiu that the essays would have to be in good English, otherwise a publisher would not be interested no matter how good the story.

Heung Jiu had not thought about attempting to get my story published and considered it strange that the lady had automatically assumed that she would.

So when she rang me with her news, she suggested that instead of giving me the usual English lessons everyday on the phone, we should concentrate on putting my muddled "Chinglish" essays into good English. It would be a more interesting English lesson for us both, she maintained. I agreed.

Thereafter, day after day she read my essays to me on the phone, then edited them and read them back to me, teaching me new adjectives, phrases and idioms she had inserted along the way. The following day, she would quiz me to see if I had remembered them all.

Constantly, I wracked my memory when we tried to fill in the gaps in my story. Sometimes we added more than fifty per cent to an original essay.

When I was not teaching, I worked away on my new typewriter bringing my story up to date. I also added everything I could drag out of my mother about my early childhood and my family's past. This information was sparse and I had to explain to Heung Jiu that we Tanka people differ from Westerners in that we hesitate to give details of our past or family history — we are very private people.

Unfortunately, it took me a long time to come to grips with my new computerised typewriter. Sometimes I got into terrible tangles and would fume with frustration. If Heung Jiu could not put me right, I used to be held up for days until her husband had time to come over and sort me out.

After about six months, Heung Jiu rang Anthony Lawrence. The lady had already told him about my essays and he had been waiting for a call from us. There were now about one hundred pages to show him and he was more than willing to read them.

Heung Jiu delivered the pages to him the following Saturday. Exactly a week later, he rang to say that he was riveted by the story. "You must persevere," he said. "There is a lot of work to be done and a lot more of Mary's family's background should be added just in case you ever think about approaching a publisher."

We were thrilled. "But it's going to take us years!" exclaimed Heung Jiu. Only now did she confess that her English was not really good enough to help me write a book. "I can't remember ever learning grammar at school," she told me. "Never mind Mary, you are good at grammar, so let's have a go."

So undaunted, we continued our daily lessons, and at least once a week she came to my flat to help out with my teaching and discuss the details of my memoirs between lessons.

Sunny Forecast

The Chinese New Year of 1990 found Irene and I almost bursting with excitement. This was the result of Nancy's and Harvey's visit from England a few weeks before when we had discussed Irene and me going to stay with them in England the following July.

While Amy played with Cathy and Carl in my flat one afternoon, my two friends and I planned the details of our epic journey, not only to England, but also to France and Switzerland. Irene and I would leave Hong Kong on July 16 and return on August 12.

The first week we would spend with Nancy in Guildford and then Harvey would drive us all to Paris for a few days. After returning to Guildford for a week, Nancy and Harvey would put us on a plane for Switzerland. Here we would stay a week in Basle with Michaela and Kevin Collins, and then return to Guildford for the remainder of our holiday.

Fortunately, my health was good and there was enough money in my mother's and Irene's joint bank account to cover our fares to England. My friends told me not to worry about the other fares and expenses.

As soon as possible after the Lunar New Year holiday, Heung Jiu booked direct flights to London for Irene and me with British Airways. The airline required a doctor to fill in a form stating my ableness to fly. I acquired this from a doctor at the Sai Ying Pun clinic after she had given me a medical check-up. With this submitted, Heung Jiu then spent weeks running around town obtaining our visas. Nancy and Michaela had sent letters stating the dates they had invited us to stay with them for Heung Jiu to submit with our visa application forms.

First we applied for the UK visas. Mine was straightforward, but there was a hitch with Irene's. The staff at the British Immigration told Heung Jiu there had been an unauthorised alteration in Irene's Certificate of Identity. So Irene, upset by all the fuss, had to apply for a new one.

My sister had wanted nothing to add to her worry that she might lose her job at the Repulse Bay Apartments through taking a four-week holiday. She was only entitled to one week's paid leave at that time but she was prepared to take the rest unpaid. Heung Jiu had helped her compose a letter to the manager requesting the four weeks in order to accompany her disabled sister to Europe and we were anxiously awaiting a reply.

During the two months preceding our trip, while Heung Jiu was enthusiastically organising the paperwork, Irene was becoming more and more tiresome. Not only did she moan about getting a new CI, but going shopping for presents for our hosts in Europe proved to be too much of a chore for her. I told her not to let the preparations for our holiday get on top of her. After all, there was plenty of time. I suggested that when she wandered around the shops in her leisure time looking for new clothes to wear on the trip, she would no doubt come across something suitable for our friends.

She knew by now that her request for unpaid leave from her job had been refused. But the holiday would go ahead she decided; it was important to her and I could not manage without her. She would just hope the job was there for her when she returned.

I knew she was very worried about how she was going to cope with me on such a long journey. So to quell her anxiety, I related my experiences during my first trip to Europe in 1985. I assured her that I did not wish to be a burden on her. At home I could do most things for myself and it would be the same on holiday, I told her.

Irene realised that to fulfil her dream she had to keep on good terms with me, for it was my friends who had invited us. So after our talk, she did not argue and complain anymore. I thanked God for her change of heart for I needed her as much as she needed me.

In the Clouds

While waiting patiently for the day of departure, my normal routine was enlivened by yet another exciting event. I received an invitation to a luncheon from Lady Ford. Her husband Sir David was the Chief Secretary of the Hong Kong government and the event was to be held at their residence.

Lady Ford was on the committee of the Duchess of Kent Hospital and she also helped out in the Fund Raising Office. In gratitude to the ladies who assisted in raising funds or worked with the patients, she hosted this occasion. In a small way, I had also assisted in raising money for the hospital when my knitting was sold at the annual bazaars.

Being good friends of the hospital for years, Helen Spinks and Heung Jiu had also received invitations. Just after twelve on the afternoon of May 16, they arrived at my flat to take me to Victoria House.

They remarked how smart I looked in my red outfit and red and white necklace as they wheeled me down to the car park. As requested by Heung Jiu, the driver drove the car very carefully, making sure not to swerve around the bends along the winding roads that climbed the Peak, just in case I became carsick.

Victoria Peak offers magnificent views of Hong Kong both day and night, and scattered across its upper slopes are the homes of the rich and high-ranking government officials. It was at the entrance of one of these stately mansions that we found Lady Ford waiting to greet us.

The driver and the servants helped me out of the car and into the entrance hall. I remember feeling very embarrassed at all the attention I received.

I was pushed into a huge, bright room where about twenty women had gathered. Many were old hands at the hospital and came up to greet me.

We all had so much to talk about. Everyone was delighted to hear about my teaching, my impending trip to Europe and also the effort to write my memoirs.

There was a buffet laid out in a large room adjoining a vast light and airy conservatory. Helen, Heung Jiu and I were honoured with a place at Lady Ford's table.

A petite lady in her late forties, Lady Ford seemed younger than her age. Despite her husband's elevated position in the government, we chatted at ease with her. She had not changed one iota. She was still the same "Sai Sai Jiu" — meaning "Little Jill" to distinguish her from "Dai Dai Jiu" meaning "Big Jill" the nickname for Heung Jiu at the hospital — we had known in the days before she had become a "Lady." Whenever I, or friends had come across her, no matter what the occasion, official or otherwise, she had always spared a few minutes to chat with us.

After a very impressive lunch, we went out into the garden from where there was a panoramic view of the harbour. It had been a dull, damp day, but the rain held off while we posed for photographs and chatted till Heung Jiu's car arrived at 3:30.

This had been an occasion to remember; I had never been invited to such a grand house before.

I thanked Lady Ford as she made sure that I was comfortably loaded into the front passenger seat. Then we waved goodbye.

Though the car wove its way down towards my home very slowly, on the return journey I was not so lucky — I began to feel queasy. My practice — nibbling ginger to ward of motion sickness — was not effective.

But knowing me well, Heung Jiu and Helen had prepared for such an eventuality — plastic bags and tissues were in their handbags. This was not all they were prepared for, knowing that my outings were rarely plain sailing. On arrival at my block, when we found that the lift to my floor was not operating, they summoned all their strength and carried me up the stairs.

Fishwives and Feuds

Heung Jiu's weekly visits were becoming more and more stressful and exhausting for her. Construction work was going on immediately next to our block and the noise was tremendous. Living as we Hong Kong Chinese do, in an overcrowded environment, we seem to have developed an immunity to noise. But Heung Jiu was a Westerner and happened to live in a quiet location near the Duchess of Kent Hospital. Though I had become accustomed to making myself heard over the din by now, she found trying to converse exhausting. At times the noise became so unbearable for her that she just had to leave.

I will never forget her visit when she found there was more than the usual construction noise to put up with. Sitting on our sofa when she arrived one afternoon were three loquacious elderly matrons. "This is my second grandmother and my fourth and fifth aunts on my father's side," I explained to her.

She greeted them and then we sat at the table for our usual English lesson. However, the chatter between the old ladies and my father was so loud that even the construction noise was drowned. Agitated, Heung Jiu suggested: "For heaven's sake, let's go into the balcony area. Perhaps there we can hear ourselves speak!"

My home was very small, so despite the move we were still disturbed by the volume of their chatter.

"What are they quarrelling about?" asked Heung Jiu.

"They aren't quarrelling," I said. "My third uncle died of cancer recently and they are discussing his death."

"Well, I could hear them shouting way along the corridor and it sounded like a fight to me," she said. "What on earth could arouse such excitement and disturb the whole block?"

"They are saying that their brother was killed by his doctors because he should not have died so young."

"Why shouldn't he have died so young?" she asked.

"Because he had long ears," I replied.

At this, Heung Jiu laughed. "What's that got to do with the length of one's life?"

"Well, some Chinese believe that the length of one's ears determines the length of one's life. Apparently, third uncle's ears were very long, so he should have lived well into his nineties."

"My ears are quite large," said Heung Jiu. "Maybe I'll live to a ripe, old age."

With the bellowing still bombarding our ears, I advised Heung Jiu: "We had better abandon our lesson. My fifth aunt is sure to have enough breath, and my fourth aunt enough gossip to shout non-stop for the next three or four hours!"

She agreed with my suggestion and we began to talk about the old ladies.

Heung Jiu remarked that my second grandmother looked very smart and much younger than my father and his sisters, which, of course, she was.

I related the story of how she became my grandfather's second wife, explaining that she had joined us from Macau in the 1950s. She had one daughter from a previous marriage and three daughters by my grandfather. Though they were settled then, her three youngest daughters who came with her to Hong Kong did not attend school, but learned to read a little with the help of a religious organisation that gave lessons on Sundays. When they became teenagers, they worked in local factories earning only a meagre wage.

Second grandmother now lived in a public housing estate in Tin Wan, Aberdeen. By now, all four daughters had married and she had sixteen grandchildren. Her eldest daughter by her first husband and eight of her grandchildren lived in Guangzhou. Sadly, she seldom saw this family because it was a long way for her to travel, and the family had never been able to visit her.

Two of her daughters and their families lived in their own homes in Hong Kong, but her second eldest daughter and her husband still lived with grandmother in her small apartment. Unfortunately, there were many quarrels between them. We attributed this to the fact that grandmother had thoroughly spoilt her second daughter because she was the weakest child of the family, having been born with a heart defect.

Though times were hard and her living conditions very poor while she was married to my grandfather, second grandmother persevered. She was grateful to him, for without his help, particularly when she was a starving, young widow and mother accused of a serious crime, she would not have survived. Even to this day, she has remained loyal to his memory and my family has never heard her say a word against him.

She came to see us regularly and her three daughters came on the second day of each Chinese New Year to pay their respects to my father as their eldest brother. On the other hand, the four daughters of my first grandmother — two of whom were visiting today — seldom came to visit us, even though they lived nearby.

Heung Jiu said that I closely resembled my aunts. "You are like three peas in a pod," she laughed.

"I hope I don't resemble them in character; they are the aunts who have given our family so many problems."

"Are they the sisters-in-law that gave your mother a hard time when she lived on the family boat before you were born?"

"Yes," I replied. "Especially my fourth aunt."

I explained to Heung Jiu that decades ago, my first grandmother had found a wallet in the street. It contained American dollars. Not realising what the strange money was, she gave it to my fourth aunt. No one knew how much money there had been in the wallet but the amount was discussed and mused about until the story was that it had been in the thousands.

My third uncle was very disgruntled about the matter. His jealousy grew as the rumoured size of the windfall multiplied. "Instead of giving it to a daughter, mother should have given it to a son," he grumbled. My father and my sixth uncle said nothing.

Gossip began buzzing again when fourth aunt purchased two small flats in Kowloon. Because she only kept a small fish stall in a market, suspicion was aroused that she must have used the windfall from the wallet.

Jealousy and rage festered within my third uncle until one day it came to the fore. It happened at a banquet to celebrate my second grandmother's birthday at a restaurant in Aberdeen. Aunt and uncle had come face to face and soon they began to quarrel.

To the amazement and embarrassment of the rest of the party, my aunt, who by now was slightly drunk, found the courage to castigate her brother. In a thundering voice she accused him of spreading false rumours about the source of the money she had used to buy her properties. She thumped the table so hard that crockery rattled and cups overturned.

Astonished by such behaviour, diners stared and waiters rushed to the table, but they could not subdue my aunt. My father wanted to intervene, but thankfully, a cousin advised him not to get involved. He would have certainly made matters worse; he would have taken the side of his brother, being not overly fond of his sister.

My grandmother was shocked and upset by the confrontation of course — a disruption at a birthday banquet would certainly bring bad luck. "She's just a mad woman," she told the waiters. "She will calm down when she's had her say."

The fracas ended with fourth aunt declaring vehemently that she had worked hard for the money to buy the flats. No one believed her. And to this day there is still speculation on how much money the wallet contained.

10

Western Shores

On the morning of Monday, July 16, 1990, the day of our departure for our European holiday, Irene and I arranged to treat our family to lunch at a rather posh restaurant in celebration of our father's birthday. My family and my second brother's family shared two taxis to the restaurant where we joined my second grandmother who had already arrived.

I did not enjoy the celebration. My enthusiasm palled when my brother had complained about my clumsiness when he helped me from the taxi.

Cathy's behaviour had further dampened my spirit. A cold had made her miserable and she fussed over her food. She persistently asked for a cold drink, which her mother refused to order because she believed it would aggravate Cathy's cold. Cathy became even more fretful. She moaned and whined till eventually she began to scream. Cringing with embarrassment at her behaviour, we tried our best to make her happy, but that morning little Cathy was not at her best and no one could placate her.

After the lunch we took taxis home where I planned to take a nap. I lay on my bed but could not relax. Our departure was drawing near and I knew there were still things I had to do before 7:45 p.m. when Heung Jiu and Derek were to call to take us to the airport. I took a bath at about 4 p.m. and then packed my last-minute things into my hand luggage. Irene returned at about 4:30 p.m. and though quite exhausted and rather agitated by the excitement of the day, she immediately followed suit.

Satisfied that our packing was done and our travel documents and money checked and secure, we ate a light meal all the while chatting to my brother and his family who had come over to accompany us to the airport.

Our excitement soared as we heard footsteps coming along the corridor. Cathy and Carl rushed outside. "It's Auntie Gill and Uncle Derek!" they exclaimed. "Wah, they've arrived!"

All of us, including my mother, bundled out into the corridor and in procession made for the lift. The trundling of the wheels on our suitcases and the giggles of Cathy and Carl attracted the attention of some of our neighbours who came out so see what was going on.

When one of them asked where we were going, I sensed that my mother gloried in her reply. "Oh, my daughters are going on a month's holiday to England, France and Switzerland. Ma-lai has many very dear *gweilo* friends in Europe and she and Choi Ha will be staying with them."

It was unlike my mother to boast or be proud, but to her it was a great honour to have foreign friends because working-class Chinese, such as us, rarely had a chance to associate or even pass the time of day with them. Moreover, some of these neighbours had often poured scorn on our family because of me, so it seemed that my mother grasped this opportunity to let them know that having a handicapped daughter at home was not a curse.

On our arrival at the British Airways check-in desk, we were delighted to find Father Edward awaiting us. I knew he was a very busy man and I had not expected to see him there. After all the years he had carried a concern for me, I should have guessed; here he was with his gentle greeting and his warm-hearted best wishes. He was a little sad that he was unable to stay to see us through to Immigration because he had to leave to catch the 10 p.m. ferry back to his home on Cheung Chau Island, but he could spare time to join our happy group for photographs. Before he bade us sisters farewell, he handed me an envelope containing a card and some money to spend on our holiday.

My wheelchair had been checked in with our luggage and I was now using a clumsy airline chair, which was far too big for me. The airline staff that transferred me into it at the check-in counter had obviously not been trained to deal with the disabled. They flustered me and made me cross.

I am always uneasy without my own chair, but I tried to put my feelings aside as Heung Jiu pushed me around the airport shops followed by our entourage. Cathy and Carl could not contain their excitement. Being at an airport was a new experience for them. They jumped along boisterously till it was time for Irene and me to pass through Immigration.

Our farewells filled me with a pang of sadness. I wished my loved ones could experience the great adventure we two Tanka girls were about to embark upon.

Irene and I proceeded smoothly through the necessary departure formalities. We sat patiently in the departure lounge until an airline attendant came to assist us on board the aircraft. To our consternation we were put into what seemed to be a cargo truck. "Aiyahh, what's happening?" I asked an attendant in dismay. "Where are you taking us?"

"Don't worry," he laughed. "The plane is a fair distance from the departure lounge and this is the easiest way to get you there."

When the truck came to a halt, dismay overcame me again when I was lifted from the airline wheelchair by two attendants and stuffed into a tiny metal chair. It was only just wide enough for my small crumpled body to squeeze into. "Larger chairs can't be carried along the aisles," the attendant claimed. "Even big fat fellows have to fit into these small chairs."

"Wah!" I exclaimed. "What a ridiculous joke!"

The attendants carried me up the stairs into the plane and then along the aisle to our seats near the toilets. It was rather a bumpy ride, but I appreciated that the lack of space prevented them from carrying me smoothly.

When we reached our row, I remember feeling extremely embarrassed at the trouble I caused the airline staff. They had to expend a great deal of strength to extricate me from the little chair and then place me in my seat. Irene sat beside me and proceeded to make me as comfortable as possible making sure that everything I would need was within my reach.

A few years before, Irene had been for a short holiday to Japan, so this was not the first flight for either of us. Nonetheless, we were very excited and could hardly wait for takeoff.

Soon the stewardess in charge of our section made herself known to us. "My name is Miss Kam and I am responsible for taking care of you," she informed us. "If you need any help, please press the call button and I will be glad to offer you my assistance. Don't worry about going to the toilet. I will help your sister take you there."

Irene was relieved to hear this, but I was determined not to let anyone take me to the toilet. I understood the cubicles were very small, so there would be no way I could manage to attend to myself properly in such a confined space. Therefore, at intervals during the flight, Irene covered me with a blanket to hide me changing my nappies. Then she hurried to the toilet to dispose of them.

Irene couldn't sleep but I managed to doze for a few hours between the meals. After breakfast, Irene gave me some damp tissues so I could freshen up, then we waited anxiously for the landing.

Irene gasped; through the window she had caught sight of lights twinkling on the landscape of England, which was swathed in the dim light of early morning. I thanked God for being so good to us — our dream had come true.

This time I was transferred from chair to chair smoothly as we were escorted from the aircraft, through Immigration and into the customs hall. Airport staff helped us retrieve our luggage and my wheelchair, then led us into the greetings hall where we found Nancy and Amy anxiously waiting for us.

Nancy, Irene and I were overjoyed at seeing each other again but Amy was a little subdued. She recognised us but there was no smile. Perhaps she did not appreciate having to be at the airport at such an early hour.

The attendant wheeled our luggage to the car park and then helped Nancy transfer me from the airline wheelchair into her car. The Heathrow staff could not have been more helpful.

As Nancy drove us on the half-hour journey to her home in Burpham, a suburb of Guildford in the county of Surrey, we chatted non-stop in our excitement while poor Amy vied in vain for her mother's attention.

As we sped along through the countryside Irene was enthralled, "Such space!" she exclaimed.

When Nancy stopped her car outside her house, the first thing that struck us sisters was the silence. The air was fresh and clean and all was tranquil.

Nancy explained that Harvey was renting the large detached house from English friends. It was one of six of similar design in a cul-de-sac on a modern, private housing estate. Each house had an unfenced front garden and a walled garden at the rear. Irene and I were very impressed.

Once inside, we gazed at the beautiful furnishings while Nancy made me comfortable on the sofa. No sooner had we come down to earth that Irene began to unpack our luggage.

Nancy was delighted with our gifts and Amy was so thrilled with the Chinese pyjamas we gave her that she struggled impatiently to put them on and then danced around the room with glee.

With the excitement over, Irene and I bathed and took a nap till lunchtime. Then early in the afternoon Nancy drove us to see the sights of Guildford, a historic town situated on the River Wey.

First, we went to Guildford Cathedral, a modern, red brick building crowning the summit of a hill overlooking the town. As we approached it along a steep driveway, it appeared to stand out against the sky. We paused before the entrance and then within its shadow I gazed upwards at the soaring silhouette.

Its vast interior was stark in contrast to the ancient churches I had seen on my previous trip to Europe. Nevertheless, an air of holiness and mystery pervaded. The silence was broken only by our hushed voices and the echo of footsteps as Nancy wheeled me around the aisles and told us all she knew about the cathedral.

Later in the afternoon, after exploring the "olde worlde" sights and modern shops of Guildford's town centre, Nancy drove us through the tranquil beauty of the Surrey countryside to the picturesque and ancient village of Shere. I will never forget the delightful scenes we found along its meandering pathways.

We strolled along the bank of the small river flowing through the village. The only sound was the rippling of cool water and the melody of birdsong. Intermittently, the chuckling of Amy would intrigue me — perhaps she had spotted some ducks.

Suddenly, sounds of immense glee filled the air. It was Amy who had attracted our attention once again. We had come to a ford where she could paddle and splash in the shallow water. After Amy had had her fun, we dallied on the narrow wooden pedestrian bridge nearby and posed for photographs. Then it was time to make our way home to await Harvey's return from work.

He greeted us fondly and Amy rushed to give him his present from Hong Kong. It was a Chinese-style dressing gown that we all agreed suited him admirably.

With the help of Harvey's strong arms to carry me upstairs, Irene and I were shown around the house. We were fascinated. As one stepped through the front door into the hallway, there was a large sitting room. It was furnished with two long sofas, occasional tables, a television and an electronic organ. Dotted around were various, mostly oriental, ornaments. Overhead, chandeliers sparkled.

A French door led from the sitting room into the dining room. The size of the dining suite amazed us and I recall the crimson of the curtains and the glistening of another chandelier catching my eye.

At the rear of the house facing the walled garden was the spacious kitchen fitted with very modern units and appliances. Wah, there was enough space for a table and four chairs.

Upstairs were five bedrooms and two bathrooms. One bathroom adjoined the master bedroom and on being shown inside, Irene and I were highly amused when Nancy explained what the bidet was used for. "Wah, fancy having a little bath just for bottoms!" we giggled.

The bedroom Irene and I shared was lovely. Adequately furnished with very comfortable twin beds and an array of cupboards, it was spacious enough for me to move around easily.

Amy's bedroom next door was so cluttered with toys that it would have been impossible for her to play with them all, my sister and I concluded.

The whole house was carpeted but it did not take much more effort for me to wheel my wheelchair on the pile. I remember thinking the house could not have been more convenient if it had been especially designed for me.

The next morning we drove around to Heung Jiu's house, a short distance away, to pick up her eldest daughter Christina. We found she was an attractive young lady with long, blonde hair in her mid-twenties. Though she and I knew all about each other, we had only met briefly in Hong Kong many years before. Today, she was accompanying us to Hampton Court Palace where, to our astonishment, she had never been before. Nancy had already visited most of the popular tourist spots in the short time she had been in England — far more than Christina who had lived there for years.

Hampton Court Palace on the banks of the River Thames had been the palace of Cardinal Wolsey during the reign of Henry VIII. It was huge. Christina, experienced in handling the handicapped, deftly pushed me around the interior of the palace while Nancy, taking my blindness into account, described the decor and recounted the history of the palace in detail. Irene and I spent the whole afternoon amazed at its size and magnificence. We posed for photographs in the splendour of the formal gardens before we made our way to the restaurant to sample the novelty of an English afternoon tea.

On Friday, we four girls took the half-hour train journey from Guildford to London to go sightseeing until we met Harvey from work.

We first toured Westminster Abbey, spending an hour admiring the architecture and imagining the royal ceremonies that had taken place there for almost one thousand years. We passed by Big Ben and then crossed Westminster Bridge, which spanned the River Thames.

By now, it was late afternoon and we were feeling a little weary. So we fortified ourselves with a snack before venturing off to meet Harvey at Charing Cross. From there we trundled in convoy to Chinatown. Exploring Covent Garden in the same vicinity, we window-shopped, listened to Chinese musicians and then finally, dined at a Chinese restaurant.

After our meal, we strolled to Trafalgar Square where we were greeted by a flurry of pigeons. While Amy chased them, I tried to entice them to my hand but they were not interested in my gestures; perhaps it was because I had no tasty morsels to offer them.

On leaving the Square, we walked to New Scotland Yard and then back over Westminster Bridge to Waterloo Station to catch the train home. Aiyahh! It had been an exhausting day for us all but thanks to our wonderful hosts, my sister and I saw many of the famous sights of London we had only dreamt about before.

Irene and I were bound for Basle in Switzerland the next morning to stay a week with my ex-Hong Kong friends, Michaela and Kevin Collins. Nancy drove us to the airport for our 9:30 a.m. flight.

The flight was uneventful until the aircraft turned for landing and Irene sighted the Alps. "Wah, what a magical sight!" she exclaimed, and she helped me peer through the window to catch a glimpse of the dazzling white snow cloaking the mountain range.

It was about 1:30 p.m. when Michaela and Kevin met us in the arrivals hall. It seemed to take only a few minutes for Kevin to drive us to their flat in Basle. We took the lift to their floor where on stepping out I was surprised to find that we were already in the hallway of their flat.

Apparently, the owner of the premises had chosen to build the block of flats to accommodate wheelchair-bound tenants and a couple of flats were presently occupied by such people.

In fact, Michaela reminded me that I had jokingly asked her to find a flat accessible by elevator when I knew she was returning to Switzerland, since I might visit. She said she never forgot this request but was doubtful she could find such a place. Most buildings in Europe are low rise and few have the need for lifts. Upon arrival in Basle, a friend had found this flat for them and it had a lift although the friend had not known that Michaela might want a flat accessible by lift. Michaela said she did not believe this was just coincidence — "There is guidance," she said, "in all that happens to us!"

After unpacking our luggage and distributing our presents, we chatted about old times and had a snack on the roof terrace. In the evening we attended Mass at Birsfelden, a village on the outskirts of Basle. On the way back, we stopped to view St. Alban's Church and the nearby ancient water-driven paper mill. We also took a look at part of the mediaeval city wall.

On our return to the flat, tired but still on cloud nine, we enjoyed a dinner cooked by our hosts. It was an unusual combination of bacon, beans, pears and potatoes. We finished with a dessert of fresh cherries.

When Michaela and Kevin had asked me before our trip what we sisters would like to experience in Switzerland, I had given a quick and simple answer: "Real snow!" This was one thing we would never see in Hong Kong, but now, on our arrival, Kevin and Michaela were in trouble. Where could they show us snow in the middle of summer? There was a solution, though.

The next day, we rose bright and early at 5:30 a.m. for Kevin and Michaela to take us to Engelberg, near Lucerne in central Switzerland, one thousand metres above sea level. From this green Alpine resort, we ascended, taking three cable car journeys, another three thousand metres up Mt. Titlis.

It was a relief when I found that this journey was an occasion when I would not be troublesome to my hosts. There was a special cable car cabin for wheelchairs, which the staff quickly placed in between the row of four-seater cabins for one companion and myself. Surprisingly, despite the special cabin, the tickets were free of charge for the disabled. The Swiss have the right idea, I thought.

It was a sunny day but the air grew noticeably cooler as we made our steep and perilous ascent. To prevent altitude sickness, Michaela and Kevin suggested we stop for breakfast in a restaurant halfway up.

The final ascent was immensely exciting. Our tiny cable car precariously swung over the mountainside and then over glaciers as we approached the summit. I heard cries of dismay but fear did not bother me. I was too enraptured by the experience to be scared.

We alighted into brilliant sunlight. I marvelled at the limitless, gleaming white blanket spread before me. I could not believe I was at the top of a snow-capped mountain. Strangely, I did not feel cold.

I leaned from my chair and gingerly sunk my fingers into the snow. What a strange texture! I thought. It was much different to the ice in a refrigerator. I grasped a few handfuls and made a snowball. Then I threw it as far as I could.

I heard Chinese voices . . . must be a tour group from Hong Kong.

Now my wheelchair was stuck in the snow — worhh, how exciting!

Next, we trundled towards an ice grotto. Kevin wheeled me through the entrance and then carefully along a wooden plank which spanned a huge puddle. "Worhh, ice walls!" I exclaimed. The experience was breathtaking — we were inside a veritable glacier!

The descent from Mt. Titlis was as thrilling as the wonderland at the summit. As the cable cars slowly swung their way down, I listened to Irene exclaiming in delight. At the first intermediate stop we alighted and then sat outside on a sun terrace to enjoy a snack in the bright sunshine and clear mountain air. Irene and I were enthralled by the wonder of it all. Without a doubt, our outing that day had been a magical experience for both of us, one we would never forget.

Though it was late afternoon, it was still terribly hot when we drove away from the cable-car station and headed towards Basle. Cars in Europe did not seem to have air-conditioning.

Once back in the city we stopped to spend a pleasant hour taking refreshments. Before dusk descended, Kevin drove us around the city to point out sights of interest.

When evening came, Irene cooked fried rice for dinner. She found a wok in the kitchen and surprisingly, a Chinese-style high-powered gas ring. Our hosts had brought it with them when they left Hong Kong. Apparently, every so often Michaela tried her hand at Chinese cooking, so Irene thought it a good idea to teach her the knack of pressing the rice into the wok during stir-frying to flavour it properly.

Not only was this couple interested in Chinese cooking but also we discussed at length on many an evening two subjects that fascinated them — Chinese medicine and *feng shui*. The latter is the ancient Chinese system of studying the local landscape so that buildings, graves and even roads, railways and bridges harmonise with the area's "breath of nature." The words *feng shui* mean "wind and water."

On Monday, it was back to work for our hosts. Kevin, a PhD, held a position as an agricultural engineer with a multinational pharmaceutical company in Basle, the seat of the Swiss pharmaceutical and chemical industries. Michaela, also a PhD, was an economist with a Swiss bank.

After sleeping a little longer than usual that morning, Irene and I ventured out on our own for a change. We strolled around the locality until it was time to meet Michaela for lunch in a small public restaurant, strangely inside a nearby clinic.

We thought it was a good idea to rest in the afternoon and prepare for the next day. Michaela had to work but Kevin planned to take us on a long journey.

In the evening, tortellini was served for dinner. "Wah, just like Chinese wonton!" I exclaimed.

After the table was cleared, the next day's expedition was discussed at length and checks were made to make sure we were adequately prepared.

The next day with Kevin was memorable. We made an excursion by train to Lucerne and took a cruise on Lake Lucerne in the heartland of Switzerland.

The language spoken in central Switzerland is German and Kevin, whose mother is of German origin, feeling at home in the language, made an excellent tour guide. A cheerful Irishman of robust build with a smile framed by a reddish-brown beard, his enthusiasm in showing us everything amazed us. His endurance in lifting me and pushing me around rivalled even Nancy's and Harvey's incredible efforts. We were so lucky to have such good friends.

On the journey to Lucerne, Irene marvelled at the scenery passing our window, describing it to me all the while. Bright sunshine and crystal-clean air clarified the green, mountainous terrain that soared way up to rocky heights. Here and there a cluster of chalets nestled. Entranced and fascinated, never before had she seen such dramatic scenery.

On arrival at the lakeside, we had time to spare before we boarded the boat. But there was not enough time to explore the famous tourist spots of the mediaeval town, save but a few near the Lake: the famous 14th century wooden bridge called Kapellbrücke, a colourful market and a 17th century church dedicated to St. Francis Xavier which Kevin told us had been built by the Jesuits. Pausing for a few moments in the sunlit nave of this holy place, I prayed, remembering as always, my three special petitions.

It was easy for me to board the boat, a dazzling white-paddle steamer, as the kindly staff helped us aboard before the crowds. I was delighted to find that there was a special toilet for the handicapped on the vessel, but the pedestal was too high for me and I emerged hot and very ruffled.

The lake was vast and for Irene and me, the six-hour cruise passed in contentment.

Even I, with my limited sight, could appreciate the picturesque scenes of green mountains reflected in the shimmering waters of the blue lake, the swift darting of birds overhead and at intervals, passengers attempting to feed some swans. The sun shone and the mild breeze caressed us. Later, though, when the sun went down, I was rummaging for my jacket.

We disembarked in the early evening. With an abundance of photographs taken of our memorable afternoon, we took the train back to Basle.

Later that evening, Michaela cooked us a special treat: Eggs Benedictine — poached eggs on toast topped with a sauce laced with Benedictine liqueur. Oddly, I had no appetite. Later in the evening, I realised why — a fever had begun to stalk me.

The next day, Wednesday, Kevin took the day off again and took us to Basle. He was a great help in advising us on the best souvenirs to buy and converting the prices into Hong Kong dollars. Our shopping completed, we had lunch in a Thai restaurant.

The food had been very spicy and later, while Kevin was pushing me around the streets, my fever began to rise and I vomited. Luckily, I had snatched a plastic bag from my handbag just in time to prevent an embarrassing incident in the street.

I began to feel a little better, so we continued our jaunt. We strolled into the tree-lined Minster Square and then into the Muenster, a Gothic-style cathedral built from local red sandstone.

Michaela cooked a sea trout for dinner, but I was beginning to feel feverish again and could not eat.

The next day, both Michaela and Kevin went to work. So Irene and I spent a leisurely morning at home till lunchtime when we ventured out to find the restaurant we had visited some days before. This time, we had problems communicating with the proprietress who could not speak English. In a trice, a Swiss gentleman came to our rescue and translated our order for us.

While we were patiently awaiting our meal, a Swiss lady came over to our table and greeted us in a friendly manner. She was holding a cute, chubby baby girl who I could detect had no hair.

Irene and I made a big fuss of the child while her mother attempted to converse with us in Mandarin. Neither Irene nor I could understand the language, but gathered the lady had learnt it when she lived in Taiwan. I thought it a shame we could not converse with her.

By the evening, my fever had worsened and Irene was not feeling well, either — she had an upset stomach. Kevin gave us some medication that improved Irene's condition rapidly but only temporarily quelled my fever.

On Friday morning, Michaela's helper, Mrs Klein, came to clean and iron. She brought flowers and vegetables from her farm across the border in the French Alsace and also a loaf of home-baked, savoury bread, which we promptly devoured for breakfast.

A plump lady with a florid complexion and cheerful disposition, Mrs Klein gave me the impression that she was a hardworking, strong and healthy lady with a big heart. Irene and I warmed to her immediately.

I soon realised that she spoke French. When I tried to speak to her in my halting few words of the language, she was very impressed. In a flurry of unintelligible exclamations, she smothered me with kisses and pressed ten Swiss francs into my hand. "Buy some Swiss chocolates," she insisted. I was deeply touched by the warmth this agreeable stranger had shown us and the memory of her never fails to evoke a smile.

Later in the morning, Michaela drove us to the Swiss border where we waited half an hour for visas to cross into Germany.

In Loerrach, just inside the border, we shopped in the main street for toiletries prior to eating lunch at the Black Forest Lounge. Once again, my fever stifled my appetite, but I was determined not to let my malady spoil our day and we drove on to the small village of Sitzenkirch to visit Michaela's aunt and her family.

On our arrival, strong arms carried me up the steep stairs to Michaela's aunt's flat where we were welcomed by a chorus of friendly voices. Hearty introductions were made all round and while we had tea and biscuits, Michaela's uncle picked up his guitar and sang a selection of delightful folk songs in the local dialect, some of which he had written himself. I especially enjoyed one song of a traveller crossing the world, including a visit to Hong Kong, and of his great appreciation for his village on his return.

The charm of this gathering was overshadowed by my fever, now rising rapidly. So later, after returning to Basle, Michaela took me to see a doctor. He diagnosed that I had an infection of the urinary tract and prescribed a course of antibiotics.

On returning home, I took some of the medicine, wearily bathed and then rolled onto the bed. I dozed for a short while and when I awoke, my temperature was almost normal.

The next morning I felt much better and could face a breakfast of noodles before beginning my packing for our departure for London.

Aiyahh, it happened that we took our time far too leisurely. Michaela and Irene had been out to do some last minute shopping and time had passed quickly, unnoticed by all.

Suddenly, to everyone's dismay, we realised that we would have to hurry to catch the flight. So in a panic, our hosts bundled us into their car with our luggage and drove post haste to the airport. Flustered and our minds in a whirl, Irene and I were the last passengers to board the plane.

Unfortunately, our farewell was brief and we could not thank Michaela and Kevin adequately for the marvellous time they had given us.

As our plane soared to the heavens, leaving our kind friends and magical Switzerland behind, I prayed that God would bless Michaela and Kevin and grant them the child I knew they yearned for.

Back in Guildford, buoyant and elated after our wonderful Swiss holiday, there were two weeks remaining for Irene and I to spend with Nancy, Amy and Harvey before our return to Hong Kong.

On the Sunday morning after our return, we joined the congregation of the local Baptist Church in praising God and listening to His holy scriptures. This brought joy to my heart — I had so much to praise and thank Him for.

After the service and exchanging pleasantries with a few of the parishioners outside the church, Harvey drove us home for a quick change and then on to London. Here we had *dim sum* for lunch in Chinatown before driving to Hyde Park.

We started our stroll at Speaker's Corner. I was fascinated and strained my ears to catch a hint of what the speakers were saying above the crowd's heckling. When we reached the Serpentine Lake, we were very surprised to see Chinese dragon boats being raced. "Just like Hong Kong!" I exclaimed.

With Harvey joking and jauntily pushing me along and Nancy, Irene and Amy trailing behind, we arrived at Buckingham Palace.

We peered through the railings at the vast, honey-coloured building in a vain hope of catching a glimpse of the royal family and then we stared at the motionless guards. When we were satisfied we had taken enough photographs, we continued through a tree-lined avenue in Green Park to the seclusion of St. James' Park, jollity bubbling over along the way.

When we returned to the car Harvey drove us to the domed St. Paul's Cathedral, the Tower of London and then across the famous Tower Bridge before he took the route out of London towards home.

The next morning, Harvey went to work and we girls had an easy morning. When afternoon came, rested and ready to face another trip, we found ourselves at Windsor at the Royalty and Empire Wax Museum where I gazed entranced at the wax figures, colourful and glistening in their finery. The talking wax figures were even more enchanting. We enjoyed the visit, but left a little disappointed there was not more to see.

Nancy was determined that Irene and I should sightsee everyday. So on Tuesday, in the searing heat, we went off in her car to the Weald and Downland Open Air Museum, located about an hour's drive away in Singleton, in the adjoining county of West Sussex. The museum spanned forty acres and was dotted with thirty or more buildings preserved from different periods in history — a mediaeval farmstead and a sixteenth century market hall among them.

Before we explored the exhibits, we stopped for a picnic on the grass. Nancy had brought noodles in hot soup and fruit for dessert, a familiar meal that we sisters really appreciated. With our hunger satisfied, Nancy pushed me along a sandy path to view the ancient buildings. The ones large enough for my wheelchair to enter had high doorsteps, so poor Nancy, determined that I should not miss out on anything, used all her strength to hoist my chair inside. "I don't suppose they used wheelchairs in the olden days," I surmised.

We enjoyed the day immensely, but the very hot weather took its toll and we returned home exhausted.

The next day we prepared for our trip to Paris. Nancy took her car to be serviced while Amy played with the neighbourhood children. Irene and I were left to pack our suitcases — we were experienced at this by now.

At 6 p.m., we left to attend a Royal Marine School of Music outdoor concert. We had been invited by Tim and Alison, Nancy's friends whom she had introduced me to in Hong Kong some years before. Irene and I especially enjoyed the fireworks display at the end of the concert; it was the first time we had seen a live display. We had only watched Hong Kong's annual Chinese New Year fireworks on the television.

On Thursday, the five of us rose early and drove through the hopfields and apple orchards of the county of Kent to Dover to catch the 10 a.m. Sealink Ferry to France.

As the ferry departed, Harvey wheeled me onto the lower deck. Then Nancy stayed with me while Harvey, Amy and Irene went to the upper deck to feed the seagulls crumbs from our breakfast in the ferry restaurant.

It was a blissful day. Alternately, I was warmed by the sun and cooled by the gentle breeze. I looked around. The great expanse of sea spread before me, only distinguishable from the sky by dancing shimmers of light. As we sped along, the only sound I could hear above the drone of the engine was of the waves slapping against the hull.

It was a scorching hot day and close to 34° Celsius when we arrived in France. Fortune was on our side — the car was air-conditioned! This was unusual for a car bought in England I was informed. So our three-hour journey to Paris, stopping only for lunch, proved to be very comfortable.

After we had checked into our hotel, dismay overcame us when we found that my wheelchair would not fit into the lift. "Don't worry," said Harvey. "Our rooms are only on the second floor." He duly carried me up the stairs with Nancy and Irene following just behind, carrying my wheelchair. Inside my room, my face fell when I found there was hardly room for me. Only when Harvey pushed the bed aside could I wheel into the bathroom.

Anxious to explore the famous and romantic landmarks of the French capital, we quickly set down our baggage and made for the Eiffel Tower, which was within walking distance from our hotel.

We took the tower's lift as high as it would go, then Harvey carried me up to the next stage to show me a bird's-eye view of Paris. I was thrilled with what I could see but I could not appreciate the vista fully because I was concerned that Harvey should have to carry me. "Don't worry, Mary. I need to lose a few pounds," he assured me as he carried me back down to the lift.

From the tower we drove across a bridge, which spanned the River Seine, to park on the Right Bank opposite. Here, we roamed for a while and posed for photographs against a backdrop of beautiful fountains. By now it was late afternoon, so we stopped for dinner and then made our way through tree-lined boulevards to our hotel. We were tired but no one would have guessed, so exultant were we over the wonderful sights we had seen.

Paris was broiling. The first night I could not sleep well because the bedroom was stifling and there was no fan or air-conditioner to cool it down. Traffic noise kept me awake, too; the room faced onto a busy street and the traffic did not diminish as the hour grew late.

I was loath to complain about the heat, for I considered our merry band of travellers extremely fortunate. I had been warned by my English friends in Hong Kong that the weather in Europe could be wet, cold and miserable. This worried me because going out in my wheelchair in such weather is usually out of the question. Not only is it very uncomfortable, but rain further hampers my sight. It is also very difficult for me or my helpers to manoeuvre my chair on slippery or sodden ground. Thankfully, we were blessed till now; our travels had not been restricted or spoiled by the weather in any way — everyday had been dry, warm and sunny.

Friday's Paris breakfast has stayed vivid in my mind — crisp, crusty bread with creamy butter. It was delicious. It was a novelty because the high humidity of Hong Kong destroys the crispness of food unless one eats in the luxury of air-conditioning.

On leaving the breakfast room my sister and I struck up a conversation with a Chinese family of five. They had been living in England near Guildford for a long time, the mother said. She was puzzled at the relationship between the *gweilos* and us three orientals. "Why are the American couple so kind and friendly towards you?" she asked me. "Is it because they adopted your little daughter?"

"They are my good friends," I explained, trying to hide my indignation. "They do things for me and my sister out of kindness and want nothing in return. Amy is not my child; she is their little daughter. They adopted her from a Hong Kong orphanage when they lived there." My reply surprised her and it was clear that she found it hard to believe that a couple such as Nancy and Harvey could befriend a couple of Tanka girls like Irene and myself.

When I told Nancy and Harvey about this later, they were rather amused. The next time we encountered the Chinese woman, Nancy, being the friendly and agreeable girl she is, exchanged telephone numbers and suggested they contact each other in England.

Harvey had a business meeting that morning, so we four girls caught a taxi to Notre-Dame Cathedral. I marvelled at Nancy's description of its architecture, paintings and monuments.

We found it incredibly hot when we emerged into the sunlight. So after stopping briefly for refreshments and souvenirs, we took a taxi back to the Dome des Invalides, the burial place of Napoleon and some of his family, where it would be cool inside. We dallied here for a while until it was time to return to our hotel to meet Harvey.

Nancy pushed me along with Amy hitching a ride and Irene following behind with our bags. Amy was tired and she wanted Nancy to carry her. Poor Nancy, she had to cope with the two of us. The kerbs of the pavements were high and it was hard work for her to push us both in the unrelenting heat. To make matters worse, we lost our way. Nancy kept smiling, though, and eventually found the way, having us back at the hotel about 4:30 p.m., hot and thirsty and in need of a rest.

We tried to relax but the hotel rooms were like ovens. Harvey suggested the best place to be was in our air-conditioned car, and we all agreed. So as swiftly as we could in our weariness, we piled into the car. Then Harvey proceeded to drive us to Napoleon's Arc de Triomphe, up the hill to the Sacrée Coeur Church — which I could not enter because there were too many steps — then back to the Avenue des Champs-Élysées for dinner in an air-conditioned restaurant. Finally, we drove down to the Seine to take a boat tour in the evening.

I was fascinated. Not only by the illuminated sights and the commentary along the way, but also by the passengers. There were scores of them talking in many languages, flashing their cameras and enjoying as I was, the romantic ninety-minute river-ride through the heart of Paris.

On our last day in the French capital we drove to the Louvre, the principal art museum in France. We entered through the Pyramid, a recent extension designed to facilitate the handicapped — the only one we had encountered on our tour.

Touching the exhibits in the Louvre was prohibited, so I could only appreciate the larger exhibits such as the statue, Venus de Milo and a few of the ancient Egyptian artefacts. In the painting section, we passed by masterpieces by such artists as Renoir, Raphael and Gauguin, but I did not appreciate these as much as coming face to face with the most famous painting of all: the Mona Lisa. It was smaller than I had expected and not being able to see the painting at close hand, I could only see a vague shape. Nevertheless, I was thrilled.

After lunch, we looked around the lobby of the Opera House, disappointed that I could not venture further into the building because there were too many steps and no ramps.

We toured the city for a while before making our way back to the vicinity of our hotel where we snacked at a roadside cafe.

Here, sitting in the balmy night air, I tried to absorb every glimmer, sound and smell. I listened intently to the French chatter going on around me, ruing the fact that my French lessons had discontinued.

The next day, Sunday, August 5, was the day of our departure but first, Nancy and Harvey, keen to show us even more sights of the French capital, took us back to La Grande Arche de la Défense. Here, we took a lift to the top to savour our last panoramic view of Paris.

Later in the afternoon, packed and then bundled into the car, we made our way to the ferry at Calais. We arrived at Dover around 6 p.m. and before disembarking we bought the usual duty-free items and more souvenirs for our friends.

While Harvey drove like lightning through the countryside; one by one we girls dozed off until two and a half hours later when we were roused in Burpham.

What a wonderful time our good friends from Kentucky had given my sister and myself. Their enthusiasm had not diminished for one moment. They had done their utmost to ensure that we did not miss any of the cultural gems and famous landmarks of Paris. How could we ever thank them enough!

Harvey returned to work on the Monday leaving Irene and I to spend another week of daytime sightseeing with Nancy and Amy.

After only a day unwinding from our Parisian experience, we were off to Stonehenge, a prehistoric site in the county of Wiltshire.

Nancy's Chinese neighbour Louisa and her small son Edwin had accompanied us. Once out of the car and strolling along the path to the famous site, Amy and Edwin attracted the attention of a group of tourists. "How cute," they remarked as the little pair skipped along the path hand in hand. We all wondered why the tourists insisted on taking photographs of the "cute little oriental brother and sister"; they were touring an ancient monument in England — not the Orient!

As we approached the stones, which were enormous against the sky on the green, rolling plain, Irene and I were not impressed. We had expected a more beautiful or exhilarating scene. These massive remnants of an ancient religion — even I could see — loomed grey and dull.

"Aiyahh, fancy coming all this way to see some dull, old stones," we remarked rather ungratefully. Sharing the landscape, though, was a flock of sheep grazing. This proved to be more fascinating to us Chinese girls than a lonely heap of gigantic stones.

A more tranquil spot was chosen for the next afternoon's jaunt. After a lunch in the garden, we took a leisurely stroll through Effingham Forest just a short drive from Nancy's home. It was cool in the shade and I remember here and there a gleam of sunlight filtered through the canopy of tall trees.

Soon the shade gave way to vibrant sunlight and a shimmering expanse lay ahead. We had come across a lake. As we stood motionless, swans glided serenely over the water. A mother swan led her offspring in single file away from the lakeside, her cob taking up the rear. "Wah, these swans have this lake all to themselves — what freedom they have!" I remember exclaiming to myself.

Friday was spent mostly in Guildford charging around doing last-minute shopping for souvenirs. Harvey met us in town after work and our day ended with dinner at Guildford's Pizza Hut restaurant, much appreciated by Amy and us sisters, too.

By now, our holiday with our wonderful friends was drawing to a close. What wonderful hosts they had been. Evening after evening, even after long days packed with sightseeing, they had taken us for strolls around their neighbourhood. We would come across folk tending their pretty gardens; they were friendly and always keen to chat. We often encountered children playing along the footpaths. Harvey loved to join in their games, especially when we came upon the local boys racing radio-controlled cars. The memory of those walks in the long, light, balmy, English summer evenings will stay with me forever.

It was church for us on our final morning, followed by a short drive through the countryside to take lunch at our favourite pub in the village of Compton. The weather being hot still, we sat in the shade of an apple tree in the garden. It was idyllic.

Our next stop that glorious afternoon was at a fruit farm to pick berries for Harvey to make his famous Blackberry Cobbler. Nancy, Harvey, Irene and Amy began to pick the berries from rows of bushes in what appeared to be a huge field. I thought I would try to pick some berries but drew my hands away quickly when thorns pricked my fingers. Aiyahh, I could not distinguish the berries from the thorned foliage, so I thought I had better just sit back, gaze, listen and bask in the sunshine.

When a large box of the berries had been gathered, we went home for Harvey to fix his dessert dish for us.

Unfortunately, the dish did not turn out as expected. Harvey had not cooked it thoroughly and the pastry was a soggy mess. Irene and I dared not even sample it. We girls just fell about laughing, but Harvey, a little embarrassed by the disaster, suggested making the dish again. But there was no time; in a few hours we were leaving for the airport.

Now our month-long holiday was sadly over and it was time to say farewell and thank you to our wonderful friends and their lovely little daughter. At the airport, Irene and I were so choked with emotion that we could not find the words to express our gratitude to Nancy and Harvey.

While we hugged goodbye before going through Immigration, Nancy announced that they would see us again in Hong Kong very soon. This was very good news and from then on we anxiously awaited confirmation of the date of their arrival.

At 10:30 p.m., we boarded the plane for the 11:15 p.m. flight — this time with no hassle as we were escorted on board directly from the departure lounge. I had been allocated an aisle seat but a gentleman kindly exchanged his window seat with me, thinking I would be more comfortable. I gladly accepted his offer, as the seat position would mean I could be more discreet in changing my nappies.

The flight went smoothly and Irene and I managed to sleep a great deal of the way. Being a direct flight and having slept for hours, we were taken by surprise when it was announced that we were about to land at Kai Tak Airport. We landed at 8:15 p.m. local time.

Two hours later, frustrated by a long wait for my wheelchair, I followed Irene as she pushed our luggage trolley down the incline to the greetings hall where Heung Jiu and Derek were waiting for us.

Anxious to tell them about our trip, we related as much as we could during the half-hour car journey to Ap Lei Chau. They were especially pleased to hear that we had been on an outing with their daughter Christina.

During this second trip to Europe I had learned a great deal about the Western way of life, giving me a greater understanding of the *gweilos* in my life. I believe it was God, working within His mysterious plan for me, who had guided these "kind hearts" from foreign lands to step into my life. They had arrived at the right time, to help me, bring me joy and leave me with countless happy memories.

Nancy and Harvey's strong confidence in God and the way they put everything in His hands; Kevin and Michaela's strong faith and touching interest in my culture and the altruism of both couples, left me amazed and full of admiration.

Our trip had changed Irene, too. Now she had to admit that having me as a sister definitely had its benefits and perhaps I was not a liability after all. For, if not for my relationship with my foreign friends, she would have never gained an insight into their way of life or have seen the spectacular sights in such genial and enthusiastic company. For her, it was an experience to treasure, something good that cannot be measured.

Prior to our journey, Irene had little experience coping with me and little understanding of my needs. At the outset she was rather thoughtless and lost. Witnessing the consideration and concern my foreign friends showered upon me during the month, her heart was touched.

The realisation that she had lacked a compassionate attitude towards people like me had gradually dawned on her. As a result, she became more broadminded and understanding, not only towards me but also to others of similar plight. I thanked God that I would not be such an embarrassment and burden to her anymore.

Sea of Troubles

Back in the family fold, it took Irene and I quite a few days to recover from our travels. Having distributed our presents and tirelessly recounted our holiday details to everyone, our exuberance finally subsided. I settled down to teaching and recording my trip for Heung Jiu. Irene, having lost her job at the hotel, set about finding a new one.

Everything was going well until August 22, eleven days after our return from Europe. On that day my adopted brother, Chan Sum, was killed in an accident at work. He was crushed by falling machinery. We were all stunned. It was a great tragedy for Chan Sum's wife and four children and our family, especially for my parents, as he had been their first son.

My second brother, his wife and Irene rushed over to the New Territories to console the family.

Chan Sum's wife, Li Ho, who had often shocked us by taking other people's misfortunes lightly, was totally distraught and inconsolable. The children, now adults, were so shocked they could only shake their heads in disbelief.

Since Chan Sum had died suddenly, his wife insisted he be buried rather than cremated. Some Chinese share this belief but I have yet to know the reason. My parents, Irene, Chan Lai Yan and Ah So went to the funeral. I did not attend, as it would have been too troublesome to take me in my wheelchair.

Chan Sum's employer paid for the casket and the ceremony at the funeral parlour, other expenses would be covered by donations from the mourners.

In Chinese culture there are a variety of ceremonies for the repose of the departed. In my family's case, a mixture of Buddhist and ancestral worship rituals were performed.

The evening before Chan Sum's burial, my family, dressed in the traditional white mourning garments, assembled at the funeral parlour to receive his friends and relatives who came to pay their respects and condolences. As the guests entered they handed a representative of the family some special white envelopes, traditionally containing an uneven amount of money. An even amount is considered unlucky. Then the parlour attendant, in a loud voice, called for them to bow three times before the photograph of my brother, which was posted at the front of the parlour. In turn, the bereaved bowed to the guests.

That evening at the funeral parlour, my family lit candles, burned incense and paper replicas of the comforts Chan Sum would need in his afterlife. Since he was considered to have led a hard mortal life, the burning of "hell money" followed. This would enable him to buy the luxuries he had been denied on earth. Six monks, hired by our family, beat drums, chanted

Buddhist scriptures and begged Kwan Yin, Goddess of Mercy, to save my brother from suffering in the underworld.

It is deemed that a child is not worthy of his parents' respect at his funeral ceremony. This custom stems from the belief that it is inconsiderate for a child to die before his parents because he will not be there to take care of them during their old age. My parents did not adhere to the custom and went to the funeral to show their special love for their adopted son. They did not, however, go with the mourners to his burial. This simple ceremony took place at the family gravesite in Wor Hap Shek in the New Territories where my grandparents are buried.

After the burial, we hoped Li Ho would perform the proper rites at home to comfort my brother's spirit. If these were not fully observed his soul might become a "hungry ghost" and we definitely did not want any more of those to harass our family.

It is believed that the ghost of the departed returns to its family about a week after the funeral. A monk predicts the precise day at the funeral ceremony. In the meantime, a lantern is hung at the door, incense burned, and rice, chopsticks and fruit displayed before the deceased's photograph, usually placed between two lighted candles on a table. It is important that the rice container is full to the brim so that the ghost will be able to see the rice inside.

On the day of the ghost's return, the family is often scared, but, as a special welcome, the deceased's favourite food is prepared and placed on the table. This is shared with friendly spirits, who not only guide the ghost home from the spirit world but have also checked on the family and made sure that everything is in good order for the ghost's return.

We Tanka burn incense and make offerings of food three times a day for twenty-one days after a burial. After this, the mourning is over. Finally, the family celebrates the ceremony in which the deceased's image is placed in the ancestral altar to be worshipped and to perpetuate his memory.

However . . . if the food has not been disturbed, it means that the ghost has not returned. In this disastrous event, an old woman with a good reputation as a medium is hired to evoke the spirit of the deceased relative. When it enters the medium's body it speaks with the voice of the departed and answers the family's questions.

Whether or not Chan Sum's ghost came back to his family, I do not know, but one night following his funeral, I was alarmed when I was awakened by what sounded like an opening door. "The wind," I assured myself.

Then, as I settled down, I heard my mother's voice. It sounded as though she was speaking to someone. I sat up and gazed around our sleeping cubicle but could distinguish no human shapes. I had often heard her shouting in her sleep and usually she was scolding someone but this time her voice was soft and gentle and I could not hear what she was saying.

My puzzlement soon turned to fear. The back of my neck tingled and clamminess crept over my body as the thought struck me: "Aiyahh! She's talking to Chan Sum's ghost! Perhaps he has come back to apologise for not being a filial son."

The next morning, my mother assured me that Chan Sum had not visited her during the night — not as far as she could remember.

I had not been close to Chan Sum. He had been about sixteen years older than me and when he was seventeen, he left the family to work on a relative's fishing boat. When he happened to spend time on our houseboat, he treated me well. I cannot remember him ever hurting my feelings or thinking that I was a nuisance to him in any way. Despite this, I recall only two occasions when he came to see me during my long years in hospital: once in 1979, when I formed the impression that the only reason he came was to gain favour with my mother because he wanted her to lend him money; the other time was in 1981.

Chan Sum's dream had been to own and be master of a fishing vessel. After he married, he spent three months studying for his Master's Certificate at the Marine Department. He worked hard and qualified but he could not raise the money to buy his own boat. Disappointed, he and Li Ho moved to Cheung Sha Wan in the New Territories. He had found a job as a labourer, which was more profitable than working on someone else's boat.

His wife gave birth to two children while living on their sampan in Cheung Sha Wan Harbour before they moved to a small flat in a resettlement estate in Kwai Chung.

After the birth of Li Ho's third child, my mother was forever at her beck and call. My sister and I dreaded the occasions when mother struggled over to Kwai Chung to help Li Ho and left us to fend for ourselves. My sister was still quite young at the time and I was blind — we needed the care of our mother.

When their children were young, Chan Sum and his wife used to visit our family often. They came without fail at Chinese New Year and other important festivals. One of their visits was memorable — they gave my sister and I a pair of new shoes each! We were thrilled.

In turn, our family was very generous to them and year after year the children spent their summer holidays with us. So we could not understand why there were times, at family banquets and the like, when my sister-in-law ignored my mother and even hinted to other relatives that my parents had not done enough for her family.

As the children grew older our families grew further apart until the children no longer came to see my parents. We assumed that they were old enough to earn their own money now and were afraid my parents would expect some support from them. Nevertheless, the two eldest children found the goodness in their hearts to visit me a few times during my ten years in hospital.

Once during those ten long years I was told that I could be discharged if my mother could find somewhere for me to live. My second brother and my sister said it would be awkward, if not impossible with a wheelchair, to live in the tiny family flat and there was no lift to the floor level, either. So Li Ho suggested that I live with her if my parents paid the expenses for her and her family to move to a larger flat, which proved to be impossible.

I was really looking forward to leaving hospital but all I could do was bury my disappointment and agree with my mother that it would be far better for me to stay in hospital.

More friction occurred when Li Ho maintained that because Chan Sum was an adopted son, he had no responsibility to support or care for his parents. Ironically, after the death of her husband, she needed the compassion and support of our family. She also sought my second brother's advice regarding claiming compensation from Chan Sum's employer.

Li Ho's attitude upset us. We had also incurred her anger when we would not comply with her plans for celebrating my father's sixtieth birthday.

When a Chinese person reaches the age of sixty or more, he or she may decide to celebrate their *dai sau,* meaning "great age," with a banquet, usually organised by their children.

Li Ho had decided that she should organise an impressive banquet for my father but . . . aiyahh, she wanted my mother and my sister to pay the bulk of the cost!

Apparently, Li Ho had heard that my sister had just received some redundancy money after losing her job. She thought Irene should contribute towards the celebration costs and the remaining expenses would be paid from the birthday money presented by the guests.

Disregarding the cost, my mother and sister would not have agreed to Li Ho's suggestion anyway. They and I felt that my father had not been a good enough husband and father to warrant such a show of respect and gratitude. He had helped only others out of their difficulties and paid no regard to his own family's problems. We also resented that he had been giving money to Chan Sum regularly when there were times we had desperately needed his support. My father revealed these handouts to us during one of his less-than-sober tirades.

My father had been fond of Chan Sum and his family, and from time to time he would stay with them. They used to buy him cigarettes, wine and daily *yum cha* at a local restaurant. After a while, he would outstay his welcome and they would ask him to leave. Keeping him happy cost them money.

When my father heard of Li Ho's plans for his birthday, he also said that it would not be a good idea. He knew deep down what the family really felt about him and that it would be hypocritical for us to honour him in such a way. Li Ho was very disgruntled at our rejection of her proposal and now there was an even wider rift between us.

Just after the funeral, some of our relatives blamed my sister for my brother's untimely death. Apparently, Li Ho had told them that during an argument on the phone over his neglect of our parents, Irene had cursed him. We were very angry at this accusation. "How dare this woman spread such a rumour and who was she to complain anyway?" we grumbled. Many were the times that she had blasphemed my parents and cursed our family.

It was true that Irene had sworn at Chan Sum. She had taken the call when he rang to say that he had in his possession a wedding invitation card for my parents. My third uncle's daughter was getting married and he had thought Chan Sum would deliver the card. When Irene asked him to bring it over, his reluctance to do so caused her to lose her temper. She admonished him strongly for not visiting us for more than five years and accused him of being a coward for not having the courage to face his parents.

A few weeks later, my mother rang Chan Sum to explain Irene's sentiments and to express our family's sorrow at the animosity between us. Shortly afterwards, he came over. He was pleasant enough and we chatted amicably.

To my surprise, not only did he give my parents some money but he gave me some, too. He paid special attention to my mother and on hearing her complaining of pains in her ankles and various other joints, he was concerned. He advised her to see an herbalist in Kowloon and a short while later she went to stay with him for two weeks to seek treatment. He was very kind to her during that time and he paid for her herbal medication. She returned home satisfied that the rift had been mended.

Much later, the first time Li Ho and her youngest son came to visit us at our present home, which we moved to early in 1992, they came across my fourth aunt who was selling dumplings below our block. Li Ho asked her to come up to our flat with them. We welcomed them fondly and the exchanges were friendly until Irene commented on the amount of money Li Ho had just handed my parents. Li Ho was upset and sparks began to fly between them, with my busybody aunt chipping in with her opinion when she could. My parents said nothing, and I sat shocked and silent in my chair listening to the furore, remembering a time when my father would have defended Li Ho — but now, he would not dare.

"You cursed my husband dead," spat Li Ho. "Now you are happy."

This accusation so rankled Irene that, in a fury, she vehemently told Li Ho to leave at once.

Incensed, Li Ho made for the door followed by her son, my aunt and my parents. They were going to meet my second grandmother at a nearby restaurant. Li Ho's son was to treat them all to *yum cha*. Irene and I were not invited.

11

Another Shore

Over the years we had become increasingly dissatisfied with our Ap Lei
Chau flat. It was far too small for four adults and there were safety problems
— such as the metal security grille at the entrance to our flat being
impossible for me to open. This made my life very difficult.

The estate was old and provided scant facilities and the whole area was
run down and rather an eyesore. So, besides longing to live in a more
comfortable flat, we yearned for a better environment and amenities.

A place that could provide all this for us was the new Wah Kwai
government housing estate on Hong Kong Island, just north of the mouth
of the Aberdeen Channel. We had heard good reports about the
development and this, coupled with the fact that it adjoined the older Wah
Fu Estate, which was renowned for its good *feng shui*, caught our interest
and we were very keen to live there. The news that the estate was nearly
finished and the fear that all the flats would soon be allocated, prompted me
to write, on November 7, 1990, to Father Edward's older brother, Father
John, a former teacher who lives in the Wah Yan College, Kowloon. Also a
Jesuit priest, he has worked in Hong Kong for more than fifty years and has
long been a campaigner for the rights of the handicapped. He is one of the
founders of the Hong Kong Society for Rehabilitation, the founder and
organiser of the Joint Council for the Physically and Mentally Disabled, a
member of the government appointed Access and Transport Committee
and he is also involved in the running of the REHABUS service.

Like his younger brother, Father John is fluent in Cantonese and has a
keen sense of humour. Disregarding his fearsome, large, bushy eyebrows

and that he is a little shorter and stockier than Father Edward, the brothers are the spitting image of each other.

I became acquainted with Father John in 1985 when I was in the Duchess of Kent Hospital, and gradually we became friends.

Years later, when I was living at home in Ap Lei Chau, knowing he was experienced in contacting government departments on behalf of the disabled, I thought I would ask him to assist me to solve a problem.

I had applied about a year before, with the help of a social worker from the Duchess of Kent Hospital, for ramps to be constructed at the flat, but the estate manager would not co-operate.

Father John listened sympathetically to this unhappy story and agreed to help. He talked to the management and as I had anticipated, the job was carried out without delay. The new ramps meant a lot to me and I was so grateful to Father John.

Within a month of submitting my letter to Father John, a group of officials from the Housing Authority came to look around our flat. They agreed that it had problems and was especially not suitable for me. One of them remarked that he was confident we would be offered a new flat. He was right.

In December 1990, we were offered an apartment in Wah Kwai. We were thrilled but my mother and Ah So were very disappointed after they saw it. They found it was located immediately next to the garbage collection point and the electricity room. My mother and I would be flat-bound most of the time and would have to bear the smell from the refuse and also the noise of the generator. Taking this into account, my mother refused to accept it.

We waited more than six months before another flat in Wah Kwai was offered. This time the location was fine and my mother's acceptance of it sent us all into a frenzy of joy.

Then the estate management told us that the alterations to the flat to facilitate my condition could not be carried out because they had not received instructions from the Housing Authority. Beside myself with worry, I telephoned Father John and Heung Jiu.

The next day Heung Jiu and her husband Derek came over to take my mother and I to meet Father John at the Wah Kwai management office to sort out the problem.

Unfortunately, Father John did not come because he was not well. So the four of us, accompanied by a lady staff member of the management office, went to survey the flat.

Between us we decided what needed to be altered and the management lady agreed the work should be carried out, as I was a special case.

Father John arranged for a government architect attached to the Kowloon Rehabilitation Centre to survey the flat the following week. My mother and I, Irene, Heung Jiu and three people from the management office joined him there to discuss the alterations I required.

Finally, after about two hours of discussion, it was decided that the kitchen sink and all the light switches would have to be lowered and ramps constructed in the kitchen and bathroom doorways. The major alteration would be to the bathroom and this took up most of the discussion.

Owing to the position of the bath, I could not get to the toilet bowl, so all agreed it would have to be removed. "But to have a bath was one of the main reasons you wanted to move!" exclaimed one of the officials, remembering the content of my letter.

I could not deny this but when my mother saw the bath initially, she had exclaimed: "Wah, if I ever get in there — I'll never get out." The same would apply to me. So between us we decided it would be better to have a shower instead of the bath, making sure it did not drench the whole room, especially the toilet bowl. We explained this to the official and he did not raise the point again.

We understood from the architect that he would send a letter to the estate management office and to the Housing Authority, detailing the plans for the alterations. He reminded us that the alterations would not be carried out until the funds were approved by the Welfare Department.

The officials left, and now all was quiet.

"What's your mother doing?" Heung Jiu asked in a puzzled tone.

Heung Jiu watched fascinated as my mother muttered prayers and burned joss sticks in each corner of the flat. Then I heard Heung Jiu chuckle. She had realised that the joss sticks were stuck in turnip halves.

Finally, mother burned special paper money to bribe the spirits not to disturb us after we made the place our home.

Almost four months went by and the work had still not started. All this time my parents were paying rent for the new apartment as well as for the old. This could not go on indefinitely.

On enquiring about the matter, we were told by the Housing Authority that they had not received the relevant letter from the architect. My mother had received a letter from him some time before and we had assumed it was a copy of the one sent to the Housing Authority. Now we learned that this was the letter that should have been submitted and it was up to us to forward it to the Authority. On realising this, we sent it off without delay.

Two days before Christmas 1991, the news that the alterations had been completed set off a flurry of activity.

My brother, very disappointed that he had not also been allocated a new flat in Wah Kwai as he had hoped, was nevertheless overjoyed for us, and he and Irene immediately instructed contractors to decorate and equip our new home. It needed painting, cupboards and shelves installed, wooden interior walls constructed to divide the flat into rooms and the floor tiled.

As soon as the work was finished, we chose the day we would move into our new home. It was to be January 8, 1992, exactly one year and two months after I had sent my letter to Father John.

Irene and my brother spent many days shopping. The major items they purchased were a large dining table and four dining chairs, six stools, a sofa-bed, a washing machine, a gas heater, a vacuum cleaner, a cooker-hood, two televisions, a video recorder, two telephones and two bunk beds.

We had longed for the day when we could replace our drab old furnishings and appliances for new and we all clubbed together to buy them, not minding in the least spending our last dollar in making our spacious new flat as luxurious as possible.

Over the Christmas holiday my mother was not feeling well, so Irene did most of the packing. She worked hard and when the big day dawned, twenty-four large boxes were ready to go.

At 11 a.m. a group of youths arrived to carry the boxes downstairs to the lorry we had hired. They were members of a Christian organisation. A group of brethren had been visiting me fortnightly for the past six months and they had offered to send strong hands to help with our removal.

While the lads loaded the lorry, Jennifer Ashworth, a friend from the Baptist Church, drove my parents and me to our new home.

The boys did a fine job. We were amazed at their swiftness; it seemed they were experts at this kind of thing. They declined our offer of payment but accepted just enough money to buy their lunch.

Later that day, the telephone rang. It was Father Edward. He had gone to our old flat and was surprised to find it empty. A neighbour told him we had just moved and gave him our telephone number. I explained to him that a few days before I had tried to locate him to tell him our removal date. "Never mind," he said. "Give me your address and I'll come over now."

About twenty minutes later, he arrived. As he walked through the door he was clearly astounded at the contrast between this new flat and the old. He looked around and noticing our new furniture, modern fittings and appliances, he was concerned that we had plunged ourselves into debt. I assured him that we had paid for everything ourselves; we had been quietly saving for just such a day and had borrowed not even a dollar. Relieved, he wished us all the best in our new home.

Chan Lai Yan, Ah So and Irene worked hard unpacking, filling cupboards and arranging the new furniture, which had been delivered just prior to our moving in and within a couple of days our flat was ship-shape and very comfortable.

I was extremely pleased there were ample shelves, drawers and cupboards built into the sitting room wall. I commandeered most of this storage for my teaching books.

I had always kept them graded in plastic carrier bags in the old flat, which prompted Heung Jiu to call me the "Bag Lady." She could not fathom how I could possibly find the bag I needed for each student among the tightly wedged jumble of bags.

When she arrived at our new home on her return from her Christmas holiday in England, she was amazed when she stepped over our threshold. "Mary, the flat's beautiful!" she exclaimed in delight. "It looks so big! I can't believe it's the same concrete shell."

We were now living on the sixteenth floor of a thirty-five-storey block in a large coastal development of nine blocks. Each floor was served by two spacious lifts. The area of the flat, 410 square feet, had been divided into a living room, large bedroom, bathroom and kitchen. The main door led directly from the corridor into the living/dining area. Across the living room, a window looked out at Pok Fu Lam Road and a green mountain beyond.

The bedroom was furnished with two bunk beds and between them a desk directly under the window. The desk supported a new speaker telephone and a new television. My mother could now watch her soap operas and use the telephone without hindrance from the daily stream of students and visitors.

Amid the tower blocks of the estate spread landscaped gardens, splendidly adorned with colonnades and fountains. Residents could chat with their neighbours while their children played in the playgrounds. The estate had its own large shopping complex, restaurants, wet market, clinic, kindergarten, playgrounds, basketball courts, taxi rank and a bus station — everything required for comfortable, modern-day living.

When Easter came we decided it was time to have a house-warming dinner. We invited Father Edward, his brother Father John and my three friends: Carolyn, Heung Jiu and Jennifer, along with their husbands. My brother and his family came, too.

Ah So cooked an excellent meal, assisted by Irene. Coming from a family of fisherfolk, Ah So excelled at cooking seafood. Our guests marvelled at the dishes she presented. "Far tastier than any restaurant could offer," they commented.

In October, we invited the same group of friends to a special dinner at our favourite local restaurant in celebration of my mother's eightieth birthday.

It was a proud occasion for my mother, not only because her dear family and our foreign friends were gathered to enjoy a dinner in her honour but also because we could afford to celebrate in such lavish style. She was gratified that we could now begin to show our appreciation for the help and kindness our friends had shown us over the years.

After the dinner, as Irene and my brother carried me down the stairs from the restaurant, my friends remarked on the excellence of the food. "Yes, the food here is very good," I admitted. "But this is not a famous restaurant. One day, we will take you to a restaurant especially renowned for its food."

Nancy, Amy and Harvey came for a short visit from the United States, where they were now living, in December. The couple had been informed by a Hong Kong adoption agency that a little girl was available for them to adopt. She was fourteen months old and they named her Sophie. Naturally, Nancy, Harvey and Amy were very excited and we, of course, shared in their excitement and were very pleased for them.

A few days later, we held a party at home for the happy couple and their two little Chinese daughters. More than thirty people attended, among them Carolyn, her husband and her mother, my blind friend Joanna, her husband and two children, my brother and his family, of course, and many of my students.

At first my students were shy but with a little encouragement they began to converse with my foreign friends. Now, with my students at ease and the little ones providing a great deal of amusement, a merry time was had by all.

Steady As She Goes

When I moved flats I worried that I might lose some of my students but this was not the case. They still came, though for some, it meant having further to travel.

Soon, as word spread locally about my teaching, other young people from Wah Kwai and Wah Fu Estates began to add to their numbers.

Heung Jiu came every week to help out, thankful that I was living only ten minutes drive away from her home now and if Carolyn could not visit her assistance was just a phone call away.

Cathy and Carl came to visit regularly. I would instruct them in English and if my English-speaking friends happened to be there they would converse with the youngsters and hear them read.

Encouraged by myself and Father Edward, Carl, at twelve years of age, had qualified for entry to the prestigious Wah Yan College, which was run by the Jesuits. He was a bright boy with a quick mind but his academic performance during his first year at his new school did not please us. He did not do at all well in his exams due to his impatience and careless application.

When he came for English tuition he would listen when I cautioned him to be patient and not rush through his exercises, but as soon as he left he would forget my advice and charge through his studies like a bull.

Tall for his age, he was a big lad — due to his penchant for eating Western junk food, we believed. He would invariably arrive at our flat after school, hot, bothered and puffing. Wiping the perspiration from his scarlet, chubby face, he would make straight for the fridge to find a cold drink.

When he had cooled down a little, he would sit across the table in front of his books and proceed to delay our lesson by regaling me with stories and anecdotes, exaggerated beyond belief. Highly amused, I would listen intently, and after a while, I would reluctantly remind him to get down to his studies.

Despite his impetuous nature, Carl always had time for me. He was more than willing to run errands and would oblige if I needed something read to me. I usually rewarded him with a little pocket money. This made him very happy.

A week after we moved in, I made the acquaintance of Mary Ho, a kind, unaffected lady in her mid-thirties. My parish priest had asked her to deliver Holy Communion to me every week and soon we became friends. She worked as a receptionist at the Caritas Centre in Aberdeen but still found time to take me out from time to time. Applying facials was her special skill and she gave Irene and I the treatment occasionally, free of charge.

The group from the Christian organisation, which helped with our removal, continued their visits every other Tuesday evening. About eight of the brethren came to a party at our flat not long after we moved in.

I discovered that most of these young people had been drug addicts. Firmly believing that the power of God had helped rid them of the craving for drugs, they had been willing converts to Christianity.

Each time they came, usually in groups of three or four, they would lay their hands on my head and beseech God to bestow his mercy on me and cure me of my afflictions. Then, after each prayer, they would ask me if I had heard God speaking to me or if I felt any different physically. I desperately wanted to believe their prayers would be answered, but sadly each time I had to reply: "No. I didn't hear anything and I don't feel any different, either."

After one of the sessions I thought I could feel a little sensation in my legs but it turned out to be only imaginary after all. Though I viewed the young Christians' healing attempts with a degree of scepticism after this, deep down, I lived in hope.

Conversely, my mother developed great faith in these young Christians. Four times a day they had her praying to Jesus! I would hear her muttering and when I asked what she was saying one day, she answered: "I'm praying. I'm asking Jesus to let you live till you are a hundred." Aiyahh! I could not believe my ears!

"But I don't want to live till I'm a hundred! Not with my afflictions!" I exclaimed emphatically. "What a ridiculous joke!"

The young Christians' visits became less frequent as time went by and then ceased altogether. I am still left wondering why.

Now I not only had a new home, but I also had a new wheelchair. It had been ordered from a manufacturer in England in the April of the previous year and did not arrive till the December before we moved.

Earlier in the year, Matron at the Duchess of Kent Hospital, had informed Heung Jiu that she was sending me some money. It was the unused money left in the account that the Hospital Committee had opened to accept the donations for my pilgrimage in 1985. I had grown too large for the chair I was using and it was rusty and rickety, so it seemed fitting to use the donated money to buy a new chair rather than to spend it on something frivolous.

One day in February, Heung Jiu took me to the Rehabilitation Centre in Kowloon to ask the advice of an occupational therapist on choosing a suitable model for me. The task was very difficult.

There were rows and rows to choose from but most were too high and too clumsy for me. After sitting in about three or four of the smallest ones and listening to the advice of the therapist, we decided to consider only one.

It was British made and its lowest seat height was only an inch higher than my present one. We studied the brochure and the specifications of the chair at home during the next few weeks and Heung Jiu discussed at length all aspects of the machine with the manufacturer's agent in Hong Kong. When we were satisfied it could be ordered equipped with the extra features I wanted, Heung Jiu double-checked the measurements and then sent the carefully completed order form to the agent.

When the wheelchair arrived eight months later, we were dismayed. My feet could not reach the footrests even with my cushion. The leg-rest was too long and the footrests were not adjustable to suit the length of the leg as we had imagined. "Adjustable footrests" in the brochure was very misleading. It meant they could be folded upwards to be no hindrance when folding the chair, not adjusted to the position required along the leg-rest.

When I had tried the wheelchair for size at the Rehabilitation Centre, the length of the leg-rest and the position of the footrest had seemed to be fine. For a long while we were very puzzled until we remembered that when I had tried the chair at the Centre, I was wearing my thick sheepskin bootees that Felicity Wilkes had sent me from Australia. I always wore them on outings but at home I wore only socks in winter and nothing at all on my feet in the summer.

There were other problems, too. The higher seat and the lower footrests left a large gap, which I would be liable to fall through when transferring to and from my chair. Furthermore, the wheelchair was also supposed to have adjustable armrests but they could only be adjusted to a higher level and I required them to be lower.

Heung Jiu was really upset. "For two weeks we carefully considered all aspects of the chair — how could we have made such an error," she lamented. "Why on earth can't wheelchairs be designed and manufactured in Hong Kong to suit the stature and needs of its disabled. It's ludicrous that chairs have to be ordered from Europe; they seemed to be designed for larger people."

We despaired at having to return the chair to the agent, for where would we find another one to fit me?

In the end, after much deliberation, we found a way of solving the problems. The agent happened to have an armrest that suited me: a desk-type which was lower and Heung Jiu made a cushion to put at my back which pushed me forward a little and an extra-thick cushion for my footrest. Now, my feet rested comfortably. She also put some extra straps across my leg-rest to stop me from falling through.

Heung Jiu had no problem making the cushions but the straps to stop me falling through the gap between the seat and the footrests of my chair were a different matter. I required them to be waterproof and to dry quickly because I would use the chair in the shower. To make them out of the synthetic material leg-rest straps were usually made from would be out of the question; it did not dry quickly and therefore would rub sores on the back of my legs.

In the end, Heung Jiu sought the help of Terence, a bright, young occupational therapist at the Duchess of Kent Children's Hospital. We went to see him for his assessment of what I needed and in no time he had designed some straps that were very suitable — he had them made for me, too.

So by the end of March 1992, I was using my shiny, new wheelchair. At first it had felt strange but after a while, much to Heung Jiu's relief, I adjusted to its innovations and larger size and I was happy.

Flying Colours

At the conclusion of a farewell lunch given by Heung Jiu and her husband, Derek, before their departure to live in Malaysia in March 1993, Heung Jiu presented me with a package. With my family looking on, I carefully opened it. "It's a framed photograph!" I exclaimed.

"No, it's not. It's your Certificate of Merit — I've had it framed."

To a chorus of "Wahs" from the Chan clan, I held the certificate in front of me and posed for Derek to take photographs. I felt very proud.

Six months before, I had taken an English oral examination — something I had always wanted to do.

For a long time, Heung Jiu had been making enquiries, both in Hong Kong and in England, regarding an examination that would be suitable for me to sit. In the end, we decided that the most hassle-free exam for me to take would be the Proficiency in English Language Speaking Skills held by the Hong Kong Examination Authority.

We were given a date in October 1992 for me to take the examination and assured that special arrangements would be made to facilitate me.

Late in the afternoon of the examination day, Derek drove Heung Jiu and I to the Southorn Centre in Wan Chai.

"I'm nervous, Heung Jiu," I confessed.

"There's no need to worry, Mary. Just talk to the examiner as you talk to me and you'll get top marks."

The examination took the form of an interview. Two English ladies asked me questions, mostly about Chinese culture and festivals. I was slow to respond at first because of nervousness, but I soon felt at ease and chatted away as though I was talking to my foreign friends. Two months later, I learned I had been awarded a Credit — the highest award.

By the end of June 1993, I had been presented with yet another certificate to hang on my wall. On the 20th of that month, I had been awarded a Merit Certificate in the fourth Outstanding Disabled Person's Award Ceremony, which was held at the Royal Hong Kong Jockey Club. The award was sponsored by Rotary International District 3450 and hosted by the Joint Council for the Physically and Mentally Handicapped and the Rotary Club of Admiralty.

Months before, Father John had proposed that I submit an entry form for the award, even though the deadline for entries had passed. His brother, Father Edward, would be my nominator. Fortunately, the committee was very obliging and accepted my late entry.

I received the news that I had been chosen for an award by telephone at the beginning of June. A letter enclosing an invitation card to the award presentation ceremony to be held at the Royal Hong Kong Jockey Club followed soon after.

Nine individuals had won awards for "transcending the limitations of their disability to demonstrate remarkable ability in their personal endeavour and their commitment to the community as an individual" and two groups had won awards for "the dedication and contribution to their members as well as the community as a rehabilitation self-help group." There had been thirty-four entries and the committee had awarded a certificate and a cash prize to eight winners and a merit certificate only to one person and that was me.

On the presentation day, Irene and Father Edward, who was my sponsor, accompanied me to the press conference scheduled for 4 p.m. I was delighted when Anthony Lawrence, who had kindly given me advice on writing my book, arrived. He was able to meet Father Edward for the first time.

Afterwards, there was a cocktail party where we were introduced to the judges. This was followed by a dinner at 7 p.m.

Besides my sister Irene, I was permitted to invite three other guests to the dinner. So I invited my friends Mary Ho, Suit Mui and Father John.

The dinner was a tremendous treat. It was Western and the crockery gleamed and the cutlery sparkled. "Wah! This is posh," I remember thinking. The vast room was posh, too — the glistening crystal lights attracted my eye and my wheels sank into the carpet.

Father Edward sat next to me at the table and guest after guest mistook him for his brother Father John, founder and organiser of the Joint Council for the Physically and Mentally Handicapped, which was hosting the event. This caused a great deal of merriment throughout the evening. Only when the brothers stood side by side could the difference between them be seen.

When it was all over, our taxi dropped Father Edward in Aberdeen where he was now living and Irene and I arrived home at around 11:30 p.m. Our parents were very excited. "Wah!" they exclaimed. "We have seen you being interviewed on the television news."

I went to bed that night exhausted by the day's excitement, which I had enjoyed enormously.

12

Guiding Light

In 1992, my oldest friend, Father Edward, retired after more than forty years ministering to the Hong Kong community. Since then he has been resident chaplain of the St. Mary's Home for the Aged in Aberdeen, only a stone's throw from the Seminary where he lived when we first became acquainted.

Being in his seventies now, he is not as nimble as he was and at times his memory lets him down. Nevertheless, his mind remains very active and he is still ready to help his fellow man in any way he is able. Apart from taking medication to control his high blood pressure and having the odd dizzy spell, I am pleased to say he keeps well.

Coming from an Irish Catholic family of seven children: two girls and five boys, he was one of the three brothers who entered the priesthood. Two were assigned to minister in Hong Kong — himself and his brother John.

Father Edward, the younger of the two, arrived in Hong Kong by ship in August 1949 to join the South China Regional Seminary in Aberdeen. He taught there until 1959 when he went to Rome to study for his Doctorate in Theology.

After returning to Hong Kong in 1963, he set up the Catholic Marriage Advisory Council, a group of lay counsellors. He worked within this organisation until he went to Vietnam in January 1971. Being able to speak French, he was assigned to teach in a seminary there for three years.

He returned to Hong Kong at Christmas 1973 and resumed his work with the Marriage Advisory Council, taking up residence in a flat in Robinson Road in the Mid-Levels district of Hong Kong Island. In 1978, he moved to the Jesuit Wah Yan College in Kowloon.

In 1986, he moved to the Xavier Retreat house on Cheung Chau Island where he helped Christians perform the "Spiritual Exercises of St. Ignatius," until he retired.

Soon after we became acquainted in the mid-1950s, he tried his best to change my dull and hopeless childhood. In seeking help for me — a poor, sick, crumpled waif — from medical specialists, he had brought hope to my distraught mother. Indeed, by stepping into my life at that critical time with his care, concern and desire to do all he could to improve my unfortunate circumstances, he changed my fate.

Only after this gentle, humble, compassionate priest stepped onto the deck of our houseboat all those years ago did I begin to experience joy and foster hope. The abundance of relief and happiness that I have known through him cannot be measured. I am blessed to have known him and will think of him with gratitude always.

My father joined Father Edward in the St. Mary's Home for the Aged in July 1993. He had had a succession of health problems since we moved to Wah Kwai early in 1992 and we could no longer cope with him at home.

He had kept a low profile when we were in the process of moving to Wah Kwai and he did not express any opinion on the matter. Perhaps he knew we three women would not have paid any attention to his opinion anyway. To his credit, he did contribute five-thousand dollars to our furnishing fund that was greatly appreciated.

When we had settled in, he enjoyed his new home and was very proud when friends and relatives came to admire it. He was especially keen to roam the estate garden that led to the banks of the channel he had often navigated in his fishing days.

Sometimes he would come across his sprightly second mother, Ah Mei, also a new resident on the estate who still lived with her son-in-law and daughter.

Just before we had vacated our old home, my father retired from his part-time job as a caretaker. He had been feeling unwell for some time. After we moved to Wah Kwai, he had several strokes. Each time he was hospitalised and each time he recovered the use of his limbs, but each attack really unnerved him and left him weaker and more confused.

His lifestyle was now restricted by his health and this caused frustration to grow within him. He drove everyone at home to distraction with his short temper. He could not look after himself properly, either. My mother and I were not able to manage him with Irene working full time.

Daily, the situation at home was becoming intolerable. Irene and my father were always at loggerheads with each other. She continually scolded him and he continually lambasted her. The day came when his behaviour drove us to make a decision: I asked Father Edward to send me an application form for the St. Mary's Home.

I had visited the Home when I had been to see Father Edward with Carolyn and Nancy and Harvey when they came in the previous December, so I had some idea of what the place offered and was sure it would be suitable for my father.

In the end, my father reluctantly completed the form and, with some persuasion from Father Edward, the Superior of the Home agreed to admit him.

He did not want to go, of course, but we three women would not give in. We continually reminded him that after his second stroke a paramedic had recommended that he should apply for entry into a home for the elderly as soon as possible.

Eventually, after a great deal of argument, we convinced him he would be much better looked after and would be much happier in the Home. We also convinced him he would not be lonely in his twilight years there. After all, the Home was adjacent to his old haunts and he would more than likely find some of his old cronies residing there.

So it was a Thursday morning at the end of July that my mother, Irene, Ah So, our friend Mary Ho and I accompanied him to the Home in a convoy of taxis.

We were shown around the Home by a tall, slim, young nun. The Home was pleasant enough and finally we left for home confident that my father would be happy and well cared for there, especially as our good friend Father Edward was around to keep an eye on him.

At first, he felt very lonely and missed his family, but after a few weeks when we asked him if he liked living there, he replied: "Well, it's better than living at home, I suppose. The *amahs* do everything for me. They bathe me and clean my room. My bed is soft and it's wide, too, so I can't fall out. I have several good meals a day and the nuns are kind to me. Father Edward comes to see me everyday as well, so I am happy. So don't miss me, just continue to take good care of your mother."

I must admit, initially, I felt the occasional pang of sadness over my father no longer living at home with us. In fact, we all missed him. But very quickly we three women began to appreciate a home life without friction; there was peace and quiet at last.

Our family has endeavoured to visit him every Sunday. If we happen to take him out to a restaurant, we invited our good friend Father Edward along, too.

Father Edward has become my father's very best friend in the Home. Who would have thought that they would end up spending their declining years together!

Even more incredible: who would have ever imagined that the banishment of my father to a home for the aged would have been instrumental in bringing about his spiritual awakening!

Apparently, he looks upon Father Edward as his saviour and rises very early every morning to attend Mass. Amazingly, he is prepared to sit very patiently through the hour-long ritual in the hope of redeeming his soul and is taking instruction to become a member of the Catholic Church.

The rascal has never prayed in his life as far as I know and has never expressed even an inkling of religious sentiment. We were all astounded to see him embrace the faith as suddenly as he did. The irony of it amuses me — what a ridiculous joke!

Dark as Night

I had just sent my final essay to Heung Jiu, gratified that my memoirs had ended on a high note, when a devastating loss occurred.

Exactly three weeks before Chinese New Year Day 1994, on Friday, January 21, at about 11 a.m., the telephone rang. I was teaching at the time, so I excused myself from my students and picked up the receiver. It was my sister-in-law, Ah So, struggling to speak. My heart began to palpitate as I wondered what could have happened.

"Your brother has jumped to his death. What should we do?" she said, her voice trembling.

"I don't know what to do, Ah So. I don't know what to do," I choked helplessly.

"Please, please, phone Father Edward and Mary Ho," she pleaded. "Maybe they can help us."

Then I heard a man's voice. A policeman had taken the phone.

"Please come to keep your sister-in-law company — she could faint at any moment."

"But I can't come," I cried. "I am blind and paralysed!"

"Aiyahh!" said the policeman, sounding rather taken aback, "then I'll have to find someone else to take care of her."

Immediately, fighting to restrain my sobs, I rang Father Edward and Mary Ho. Luckily, they answered. Stunned by the news, both made their way to the Queen Mary Hospital Casualty Department without delay.

On their arrival they were asked to identify my brother's body. He had sustained terrible injuries as he had jumped from the roof of a fifteen-storey block of flats. The doctor certified his death and the body was taken to the Victoria Mortuary.

As soon as my sister Irene received the news of Chan Lai Yan's death from a colleague working with her at the Queen Mary Hospital she rushed to Ah So and later accompanied her to the local police station.

Meanwhile, sad and still shocked, Father Edward and Mary Ho returned to their work places.

Later that afternoon, newspaper reporters turned up at Ah So's flat to interview her. She told them she believed her husband's work pressure had driven him to suicide.

He had worked for the Urban Services Department as a driver of garbage collection and street-cleaning lorries. For about six months before his death, he had been extremely dissatisfied with his job. His department had modernised and he had complained that the latest lorries were difficult to drive. Moreover, he had been required to drive all over the territory rather than just locally as before. He had had to work with different work-gangs at each location and adapt to a variety of working conditions. Our family sympathised with him because we realised that at his age, about fifty-four, all this change was difficult for him to cope with. Family members and Father Edward had urged him to discuss his grievances with his supervisor but he had failed to find the courage to do so.

Chan Lai Yan had been baptised a Catholic but he had neglected his religious duties for some time. As his depression grew deeper, despite not having a strong faith in God, he sought solace in prayer and the Church, but to no avail. He had consulted a psychiatrist as well, but neither counselling nor medication improved his mental state.

The next morning, Irene, Ah So and her son Carl, together with the eldest son of my deceased adopted brother went to the Victoria Mortuary for a second identification of my brother's body.

Carl was deeply shocked at the sight of his father's corpse. He stood silently, fighting back the tears. When his mother whispered: "Ah Ching, you should greet your father to let him know you are here," he burst into tears and wailed: "Papa, I am here."

But from that moment, until after the mourning period, he hardly uttered a word.

Little Cathy was told of her father's death the day it happened but it did not seem to sink in until two nights later when she woke up very distressed. She screamed that her father was hugging her too tightly.

When the sad news spread, his colleagues came to help Ah So fill in application forms for such things as a pension and funds towards the funeral expenses. They also helped to organise the funeral.

Irene took a week off from work to comfort Ah So and help her with the things she had to organise. Frustrated by being closeted in my home, all I could do in this terrible time of bereavement was sit, answer the phone and worry — mainly over my parents' reaction to their son's suicide. My mother happened to be in hospital at the time and her doctor had thought it best to keep her in hospital until after the funeral. We had to consider carefully the right moment to tell both our parents.

The funeral was to take place on Tuesday, February 1, but at 7 p.m. the evening before we were also required to be present at the funeral parlour in North Point for the mourning ceremony. I went by taxi with Father Edward, Mary Ho and my cousin Ah Ping.

When all the mourners had arrived, prayers were said for my brother, led by a Canossian Sister, Margaret Wong. Afterwards, Father Edward gave the eulogy.

I could not hold back my tears as I looked through the window of a small room at the vague shape of his corpse lying there. It appeared to be swollen, much fatter than he had been. "Poor Chan Lai Yan," I sighed, "why did you do such a stupid thing?"

More than a hundred people attended the mourning ceremony; wreaths covered the walls of the parlour. Adhering to custom, the "grey hairs" of our family did not attend. Even if my parents had known of their son's death, they would not have attended his funeral.

Carl's headmaster, as well as his vice principal and form mistress attended and offered their condolences. Cathy's school was represented by her headmistress and a pupil. Also present were my brother's colleagues and his head of department.

The next morning, a friend, Barbara Simpson, picked up Father Edward in her car, then collected my cousin Ah Ping and I to take us all back to the North Point funeral parlour for the funeral. It was to take place in the big hall there at 10 a.m. with Father Chan, parish priest of St. Peter's Church, Aberdeen, officiating.

The glass-topped coffin was taken from the little room and placed in the middle of the hall for the mourners to pay their last respects. My brother lay peacefully, dressed in new clothes. He was also covered with several blankets, which are traditionally given by his closest relatives to ensure that he sleeps cosily. Father Chan led us in prayer and blessed the coffin, then we all filed out to follow the hearse to Cape Collinson for the cremation.

My brother's colleagues would collect his ashes a few days later and with Ah So take them to the new repository at the Chai Wan Cemetery.

After the funeral, a coach took the mourners to Aberdeen where the "consolation meal" was to be held in a restaurant. Barbara dropped Ah Ping and I near the restaurant, as both she and Father Edward could not stay for the meal.

The worry of the funeral was now over but we still had the great anxiety of telling my parents of their son's demise. I feared my mother especially would not be able to bear the great shock and I prayed for her.

Our family had discussed, over and over, the matter of telling our parents and finally decided to wait until my mother had come out of hospital before either of them was told.

On the morning of Chinese New Year's Day, Irene brought my father and Father Edward from the St. Mary's Home by taxi. My mother gasped with surprise when she saw Father Edward come through the door; she had not expected him to come for the celebrations. The widow of my adopted brother, her eldest son and his wife and my cousin Ah Ping arrived, too, together with Ah So, Cathy and Carl.

We did not know what to say when my parents said they were a little puzzled as to why so many had turned up that morning.

After lunch, Irene knelt down in front of my mother and told her of Chan Lai Yan's suicide. Shock immediately took hold of her and she could not speak or cry for a while. Conversely, my father became confused and kept on asking of my brother's whereabouts. Not until I had explained what had happened very slowly and deliberately from the beginning did he understand.

In an attempt to soften their grief, Father Edward explained to them that death was not final — it was the beginning of everlasting life and we should pray for Chan Lai Yan so that his soul could enter the Kingdom of Heaven.

We had told my parents at last and they had taken the sad news much better than everyone had expected. The relief was tremendous. It had been such a strain for us, trying to carry on as normal and being careful of what we said.

A few days later, my family, including Ah So and the children, held a lunch in our favourite local restaurant, inviting Father Edward and the Simpson family. The widow and four children of my adopted brother Ah Sum came, too.

Sadly, since Ah Sum's death three years before, our families had drifted apart through bitterness on both sides. Now, in coming together at this tragic time a chance had occurred to become reconciled. My brothers' widows and their children became very much closer. Both families had experienced a devastating loss and they could now identify and sympathise with each other.

I felt the Chan family should have been indebted to Ah Ping, the fourth child of my late third uncle. Single and in her mid-forties, she is in poor health and cannot work. Nevertheless, she takes care of her elderly mother and her unemployed middle-aged brother. She is thoughtful and is always at hand to help any member of the Chan clan. I believed it was due to her influence that my adopted brother's widow became more open-minded and less stubborn and this undoubtedly contributed to her wanting to be reconciled with our family at this time.

The fact that we were now united with Chan Sum's family was a great joy to me and helped alleviate the sorrow I felt over the loss of Chan Lai Yan. I hate to be hypocritical and have to admit that I have not suffered the agony the rest of my family has suffered since I never really got on with him.

Though I found the strength to forgive him for the way he treated me, I remain disturbed by the resentment I sometimes feel towards him. Once while crossing the road with him, I was nearly knocked down by a taxi because he was not watching out for me. He was ashamed of his blind and "camel humped" sister and left me behind when he went to visit his *kai ya* with Irene and my mother, saying if I went he would not go at all. Another time he blamed me when the television set broke and I had not touched it. All small things, but they mounted up over the years and they hurt.

I am inclined to think that it was not only the worry over his job that drove my brother to take his life. I felt that perhaps he had a guilty conscience over not being a proper filial son as our parents had gotten older. I know the financial demands made on him were not too great since Irene and I both contributed to the family expenses. If we all went out for a meal together, we did not object or question him if he made an excuse not to contribute.

After Chan Lai Yan died, his family received his pension from his government job and various charitable organisations made monetary donations to the family. I am sad to say that the family's belief that Ah So did not tell us exactly how much she had received caused much upset and things got worse.

Father Edward, Irene and I had given Ah So a great deal of advice on where to raise money for her and her children in their bereavement. When I asked her one day how much newspapers' readers had donated to her family she became very angry and refused to tell me. "Aiyahh — she thinks I am after some of the money!" flashed through my mind. We had always been open among our family about money and her reaction to my question caused me to lose whatever sympathy I felt for her instantly and I scolded her for being so secretive.

Regrettably, this incident sparked more recrimination. In her sorrow, Ah So blamed my parents for her husband's suicide. Because they had lived to an old age and had always recovered from illnesses, and particularly as my mother had recovered so well from her last illness, Ah So believed her husband had to die instead. Irene and I were furious when we heard that both our sisters-in-law had bemoaned the fact that my parents were still alive at their vast age, yet their husbands had died so young.

In turn, my mother voiced her own opinion on the cause of her second son's death. She said she regretted allowing him to marry Ah So, one of six sisters. Gossip had reached her ears that other members of Ah So's family had met premature deaths and mother believed that the ghosts of these members had taken Chan Lai Yan's life. My father believed this, too!

Apparently, years ago, a Taoist clairvoyant predicted that Chan Lai Yan would hang himself or jump to his death. Sadly, this prophecy came true and it has been a great tragedy for all our family. Undoubtedly, it will take a long time for all those close to him to come to terms with him taking his own life; the gap this has created in the lives of Ah So, Cathy and Carl will be hard for them to bear.

When Ah So and the children came to visit after the sad days of casting blame, the atmosphere was very strained. Cathy and Carl, though a little subdued, behaved normally, but their mother would not speak unless spoken to.

Their visits soon ceased altogether. They moved to another housing estate in Ap Lei Chau and did not inform us. We did not hear from Chan Sum's widow, either. Reconciliation, which had so gladdened my heart, proved to be short-lived. I was very disappointed.

As the months went by and there was still no contact with Chan Lai Yan's widow and children, I began to worry that his death had inflicted a permanent scar on our family. I desperately wished the recriminations would die away so that our families would come together again, recognise the good left in our lives and live together in harmony. Only this, I was sure, would enable Chan Lai Yan to rest in peace.

No Resting on My Oars

The forty-three years I have lived have been for the most part stormy, and during the long years that I languished in hospital I often despaired of what would become of my life. After my "journey of hope" in 1985, the black clouds hovering on the horizon gradually developed silver linings, giving way in recent years to almost cloudless skies.

I survived the storms and overcame the difficulties in adapting to a visually impaired, wheelchair-bound existence outside the protective walls of an institution; I thank God for these achievements.

Though I have not yet achieved all my ambitions, I have fulfilled three. I have passed an English examination with a credit, I am making good use of the language and I have a worthwhile occupation.

In teaching English to those who have fallen behind in their grasp of the language and cannot afford to pay the high fees demanded by most other teachers, I feel I am providing a valuable service. I remember how frustrated and depressed I felt in my dark days of struggle at school when I could not afford a private tutor to help me keep up, so I am grateful for the chance to help my fellow man. Teaching is hard work and at times very frustrating, but seeing my students do well in their English examinations gives me immense satisfaction and makes the effort of pulling all those cows up a tree worthwhile.

Luck has been on my side with regard to the number of students that have come my way since I started teaching. There is usually a steady number but if this ever begins to dwindle I confess I resort to a little naughtiness to remedy the situation.

On my visits to my father at the St. Mary's Home I usually pop into the chapel to have a quiet word with God. If I happen to require a few more students at the time, I promise God that if He sends them to me I will put a more generous donation in the chapel collection box the next time I come for a chat. So far He has not turned a deaf ear.

Most of my blind friends are telephone operators and I applaud them for landing such suitable employment. During the years I was not able to work, I would envy them and imagine they looked down on me in my uselessness.

In retrospect, failing to be accepted on the telephonist course in 1975 was a blessing. For now I feel that I am at least as successful as my telephonist friends and may even have a more meaningful occupation. Moreover, teaching has proved to be more stable than working for the telephone company. Sadly, many blind telephone operators today are losing their jobs due to the automation of the service.

I thank God for inspiring me to persevere with my teaching and also for giving me the opportunity to expand my knowledge through travelling and the tutoring I receive from my foreign friends. One reason for striving to improve my English is because one day I would like to train to be an interpreter. I would appreciate having the regular income and benefits this career could provide, and the pressure, I would imagine, would not be as great as in teaching. Some parents expect miraculous improvements in their children's school exams and this responsibility is hard to carry.

Before Carolyn left Hong Kong in May 1993, she, Barbara and Father John accompanied me to a demonstration of a special computer for the blind. A speech synthesiser gave it the ability to read aloud.

Surprised and very impressed that a computer could do such a thing, I decided I would love to learn to operate one. I thought it would help me greatly with my teaching, writing and even help me prepare for the written English examinations I still want to do.

When we were told the purchase price, we gasped in dismay. The machine was incredibly expensive, way beyond my means, but the gentleman who demonstrated it, Mr Ng, an old acquaintance of mine, was very helpful. He informed us that the Hong Kong Society for Rehabilitation had set up a fund for the handicapped who were in need of special equipment to help them in their work.

This sounded encouraging but on returning home, thinking I would never qualify for a grant from the fund, I pushed the idea of buying a computer to the back of my mind.

When I happened to come across Sister Maria Lange of the Christian Ministry to Students of the Ebenezer School for the Blind, hope began to stir in me. She said she would ask an associate of hers to visit me and discuss a grant for a computer.

Mr Ng handed me the application forms while he was visiting a few months later; he saw that the special computer would help me greatly with my teaching. When Barbara next paid me a visit she helped me fill in the forms and then posted them off. From then on, I prayed.

With or without a computer, I intend to do my very best to accomplish my aim. I am approaching middle age now and I would like to experience working in society as long as I am able to maintain good health and an alert brain.

It has surely been His will that I have come across so many "kind hearts along the way" who have helped me build on the good foundation of the language I had gained in my Blind School days through the fine teaching of Miss Kwok.

I am especially grateful to my two English friends, Heung Jiu and Carolyn Thompson for their constant tuition. Other Western friends, too, have helped improve my understanding of the language: Nancy Willis, Francis Rasmussen, Charlotte Holt and Barbara Simpson, not least among them.

When I think of it, I am blessed that I have been left with a fair degree of intelligence. The assault of countless operations has left my body a sorry maze of hollows and scars, but despite the many mega-doses of anaesthetic administered into my system, as far as I can tell, my brain has come through unscathed and functions well.

On the home front, I am very content. I appreciate the blessings I have: a loving family, a lovely home and firm friendships. This, coupled with my present good health and the ability to help my fellow man, proves that in the most important things in life, I have much to be grateful for.

My most yearned for blessing has still been denied me. I hope it is God's will that one day sensation will reappear in my paralysed limbs and that my sight will be restored.

EPILOGUE

After completing this book, Mary continued to teach English to students at her home. Oxford University Press (China) Ltd., Macmillan Publishers (China) Ltd., and Addison Wesley Longman China Ltd., were persuaded to give Mary complete sets of English books and tapes for teaching. Kind hearts indeed.

Other milestones:

1992 : Kevin and Michaela Collins, Mary's friends from Switzerland, had a son, Liam, followed a few years later by Eamon.

April 1994 : A computer complete with OSCAR (a type of scanner that can read aloud) was given to Mary by Employ Aid and The Hong Kong Society for Rehabilitation. This generous gift meant Mary could type letters and "read" typed letters from friends and books for teaching English. She also honed her typing skills by typing out editorials from the Braille copies of the *South China Morning Post* she received twice a week.

October 1994 : Mary's mother moved into St. Mary's Home for the Aged in Aberdeen, but went home for weekends.

May 30, 1995 : Mary's father was baptised into the Roman Catholic Church by Father Edward at the Chapel in the St. Mary's Home for the Aged. Mary was astounded and suspects God was too.

October 23, 1995 : Mary's father died of lung cancer at St. Mary's Old Age Home in Aberdeen. A Catholic service was held at St. Mary's Home. His grave is in the Chaiwan Catholic Cemetery.

February 1997 : Mary visited Macau with her sister Irene, Loriane McElhinney and Gael Black. Preliminary enquiries about Mary travelling on the Turbocat in her wheelchair resulted in her being told: "She will have to assist herself." As Mary was not well at the time, she suffered a rare sense-of-humour failure and was not at all amused. The search for Little Salted Fish Street, where she was born, was not successful.

April 1997 : Undaunted, Mary returned to Macau with Irene and Gael and met fifth aunt on her father's side and finally found Little Salted Fish Street where she was born. The son of the midwife who delivered

Mary unfortunately had thrown away his mother's book of births when she died. No proof of Mary's birth in Macau remained. Hopes that Mary could get a European Union passport were put to rest.

The Hong Kong visitors were amazed and amused when aunt and uncle, prior to leaving the flat for a *dim sum* lunch, filled two bottles with brandy. Upon arrival at the restaurant, tea was ordered and the visitors from Hong Kong drank tea while aunt and uncle calmly filled their glasses with brandy.

This was an amazing day as another "kind heart," Mr Ao, a taxi driver, cheerfully bundled Mary and her wheelchair in and out of his cab for most of the day.

June 17, 1997: Father John, S.J., died.

July 1997 : Mary and Irene applied for Hong Kong Special Administrative Region, People's Republic of China passports, and these were obtained in November 1997.

November 1997: Passports were collected, and a celebratory lunch of English fish and chips was declared "dry and disappointing." Mary visited Father John's grave in Happy Valley and was surprised at the easy access. Flowers were placed on the tombstone.

February 1998 : Mary and her sister Irene travelled to New Zealand for Chinese New Year and stayed with Hilary Prior at Rotoiti. Mary ventured into thermal hot pools and cold Lake Rotoiti, but found New Zealand "very quiet."

March 1998 : The family applied to buy their flat at Wah Kwai under The Hong Kong Government Home Ownership Scheme and did so by July 1998.

July 1998 : Father Edward conducted a flat-blessing ceremony. This was followed by a family meal cooked by Ah So and attended by Carl, Cathy and Mrs Chan.

August 1998 : The first five chapters of *Egg Woman's Daughter* were published in the summer 1998 edition of *Manoa*, the literary journal of the University of Hawaii. Mary was paid HK$1,157, and could now say she was a writer.

August 1999 : Heung Jiu's newly-married daughter visited Hong Kong on her honeymoon. Carl managed to keep Mary and her wheelchair out of the harbour whilst getting to the Jumbo Floating Restaurant, where a celebratory dinner was held for the newlywed couple.

September 1999: Employ Aid and The Hong Kong Society for Rehabilitation approved Mary's application for a new computer.

October 1999 : Mary had a brief spell in Queen Mary and Tung Wah hospitals with a fever and skin problems.

December 1999 : As Mary's computer had become a dinosaur, Employ Aid and The Hong Kong Society for Rehabilitation supplied her with a new computer complete with a 40-character Power Braille board. This incredible generosity meant Mary could use e-mail and allowed her to be more in touch with the outside world. Mary took computer lessons from Eric Yip, a delightful young man blind since he was two years old but a genius on computers. Eric gave instructions to Mary in Cantonese, Mary translated them into English for Gael Black to write down, then Mary transcribed them into Braille.

February/September 2000 : Mary was back in Tung Wah Hospital with pressure sores. She had a steady stream of visitors, including many *gweilos*, much to the amazement of the nurses on the ward.

September 13, 2000 at 5:30 a.m.: Mary Chan Ma-lai died.

November 4 : Mary's ashes were taken to the Chaiwan Catholic Cemetery, Row 3A. This is the same row as the graves of her father and brother.

For some who attended the simple ceremony to place the ashes, it was not an ending, but a completion. A copy of *Egg Woman's Daughter* will be taken by kind hearts to Mary's grave and, in accordance with traditional Chinese practice, ceremoniously burned.

— Gael Black, March 2001

APPENDIX: The Duchess of Kent Children's Hospital

The Duchess of Kent Children's Hospital is run by the Society for the Relief of Disabled Children. The Society, a voluntary body, was founded in 1953 to bring about free medical and surgical rehabilitation for the disabled and sick children of Hong Kong. At that time, hundreds of children were suffering from poliomyelitis and tuberculosis, diseases that were spreading rapidly through the densely populated squatter areas and the crowded tenements that abounded in the colony. Some general hospitals provided surgery for these children, but after treatment they returned to their crowded homes and unhealthy living conditions. This, of course, was not conducive to the satisfactory recuperation from major surgery. So, in 1956, a 50-bed Convalescent Home was founded at Sandy Bay. In 1962, the Home was expanded to one hundred beds and a Physiotherapy Department was added. Also at this time, Red Cross teachers began providing a school curriculum for the patients.

Due to the shortage of beds in Hong Kong's general hospitals during the sixties, the surgical treatment of many children was being delayed. In 1968, a Children's Orthopaedic Hospital was added to the Home, bringing the total number of beds to 200. It now housed a modern, well-equipped operating theatre, a large outpatient department, a modern X-ray department, a laboratory and a pharmacy. And after the visit by the Duchess of Kent in 1970, the centre was named The Duchess of Kent Children's Orthopaedic Hospital and Convalescent Home.

The hospital was the first of its kind in South East Asia and from its humble beginnings it grew into one of the largest children's orthopaedic hospitals in the world. Since its inception, children from all over the region have sought treatment there, not only for orthopaedic ailments and skeletal deformities, either congenital or caused by diseases such as poliomyelitis or tuberculosis, but also for general paediatric surgical problems. A special surgical unit was set up to deal with these general cases in 1977 and the hospital's name was changed to The Duchess of Kent Children's Hospital at Sandy Bay.

Pioneering work in the correction of spinal deformities, such as scoliosis, dates back to the advent of the hospital. Thousands of disabled children worldwide have indirectly been helped by the pioneer surgeons who have taught their highly specialised, universally acclaimed techniques to orthopaedic surgeons of other nations. Every year, at least two overseas fellows are invited for a six-month period to learn the techniques developed at the hospital.

From the time the hospital was founded in 1968, all treatment, medicine, schooling and food has been provided to patients free of charge. Until 1991,

100 per cent of the annual cost was provided by the Government; the Hospital Authority then took over the management of the hospital, including running costs. The Society still must raise the funds necessary for special projects. Expansion of The Duchess of Kent Children's Hospital at Sandy Bay has been made possible over the years by the many public-spirited organisations and individuals who have supported the hospital in the fund raising for special projects. These special projects have included:

1987: New Child Assessment Centre
1991: Orthopaedic Appliance Department
       Occupational Therapy Department
       Physiotheraphy Department
1996: Centre for Spinal Disorders
1997: Patient Activity Centre

The hospital's capacity remains at around 130 beds for residential patients, but its outpatient appointments have soared to 10,000 per year in recent years. Looking ahead, the hospital is committed to developing into a tertiary referral centre of excellence in the assessment and treatment of patients suffering from paediatric orthopaedic problems, spinal disorders and neuro-muscular disease.

Books From Asia 2000

Non-fiction

Behind the Brushstrokes Appreciating Chinese Calligraphy	*Khoo & Penrose*
Cantonese Culture	*Shirley Ingram & Rebecca Ng*
Concise World Atlas	*Maps International*
Egg Woman's Daughter	*Mary Chan*
Farewell, My Colony	*Todd Crowell*
Getting Along With the Chinese	*Fred Schneiter*
The Great Red Hope	*Jonathan Eley*
Hong Kong, Macau and the Muddy Pearl	*Annabel Jackson*
Hong Kong Pathfinder	*Martin Williams*
Hyundai	*Donald Kirk*
Macau's Gardens and Landscape Art	*Cabral, Jackson & Leung*
Quaille's Chinese Horoscope	
Quaille's Practical Chinese-English Dictionary	
Red Chips and the Globalisation of China's Enterprises	*Charles de Trenck*
The Rise & Decline of the Asian Century	*Christopher Lingle*
Tokyo: City on the Edge	*Todd Crowell & Stephanie Forman Morimura*
Walking to the Mountain	*Wendy Teasdill*

Fiction

Cheung Chau Dog Fanciers' Society	*Alan B Pierce*
Chinese Opera	*Alex Kuo*
Chinese Walls	*Xu Xi*
Daughters of Hui	*Xu Xi*
Getting to Lamma	*Jan Alexander*
The Ghost Locust	*Heather Stroud*
Hong Kong Rose	*Xu Xi*
Last Seen in Shanghai	*Howard Turk*
Riding a Tiger	*Robert Abel*
Temutma	*Rebecca Bradley & Stewart Sloan*

Poetry

An Amorphous Melody	*Kavita*
The Last Beach	*Mani Rao*
New Ends, Old Beginnings	*Louise Ho*
Round Poems and Photographs of Asia	*Madeleine Slavick & Barbara Baker*
Woman to Woman and other poems	*Agnes Lam*

Order from Asia 2000 Ltd
Fifth Floor Tung Yiu Commercial Building, 31A Wyndham St, Central, Hong Kong
tel (852) 2530-1409; fax (852) 2526-1107
email sales@asia2000.com.hk; http://www.asia2000.com.hk/